R.S. THOMAS: CONCEDING AN ABSENCE

R.S. Thomas

Conceding an Absence
Images of God Explored

Elaine Shepherd

First published in Great Britain 1996 by
MACMILLAN PRESS LTD
Houndmills, Basingstoke, Hampshire RG21 6XS
and London
Companies and representatives
throughout the world

A catalogue record for this book is available
from the British Library.

ISBN 0–333–64968–0

First published in the United States of America 1996 by
ST. MARTIN'S PRESS, INC.,
Scholarly and Reference Division,
175 Fifth Avenue,
New York, N.Y. 10010

ISBN 0–312–16098–4

Library of Congress Cataloging-in-Publication Data
Shepherd, Elaine, 1941–
R. S. Thomas : conceding an absence : images of God explored /
Elaine Shepherd.
p.   cm.
Includes bibliographical references and index.
ISBN 0–312–16098–4
1. Thomas, R. S. (Ronald Stuart), 1913–   —Religion.
2. Religious poetry, English—History and criticism.   3. God in
literature.   I. Title.
PR6039.H618Z86   1996
821'.914—dc20   96–15981
                                                          CIP

10   9   8   7   6   5   4   3   2   1
05   04   03   02   01   00   99   98   97   96

Printed in Great Britain by
The Ipswich Book Company Ltd
Ipswich, Suffolk

For Peter and our sons

Contents

List of Plates

Acknowledgements

I would like to acknowledge my indebtedness to my colleagues, particularly Ruth Evans, John Peck, John Freeman, Robin Attfield, Kevin Mills and Medwin Hughes. I am grateful to Robert Willoughby of London Bible College for references, and to Helen Wilcox of Groningen for good advice. Peter Keelan supported my research in the Salisbury Library and Jane Erskine, senior secretary, helped to prepare the text.

I am especially grateful to Roger Ellis, without whose enthusiasm, commitment and editorial skills the project might never have been completed, and to my friend Kay Hughes who painted the cover picture.

I thank my sons, Christopher, Geraint and Daniel, for their support, and my husband Peter for his care and encouragement, without which I would never have begun what seemed so large a task. I dedicate this work to them.

Grateful acknowledgement is made for permission to quote from the following copyright sources: from *Later Poems* and *Experimenting With an Amen* by R.S. Thomas, by permission of Macmillan Press Ltd; material from *Counterpoint* by permission of Bloodaxe Books Ltd. R.S. Thomas gave generously of his time and all remaining texts appear with his kind permission. Parts of Chapter 1 and 2 first appeared in a different form in an article entitled: 'Where Flesh Meets Spirit: R.S. Thomas's Marginal Land', originally published in *Grail: An Ecumenical Journal*, Vol. 10, No. 4 (1994).

Plate 3, Edgar Degas, *Mademoiselle Dihau at the Piano*, is reproduced by permission of the Mansell Collection, London. Plate 7, Edgar Degas, *Woman Combing*, is reproduced by permission of The Louvre, Paris.

God offers to every mind its choice between truth and repose.

Emerson

It's the attempt to define Him – that's when the trouble begins – perhaps we shouldn't attempt to define Him.

R.S. Thomas

1

Introduction

In the year 63 BC the Romans stormed the temple in Jerusalem.[1] They were astonished to find, on entering the Holy of Holies, that it was empty: there was no great idol or object of worship; at the heart of the faith there was a great absence. Images of God are essentially problematical. According to all the great religions God is transcendent, 'Other than' the things he has created, unlike anything we can think or know. The position is stated unequivocally by Nicholas of Cusa:[2]

> How can the intellect grasp thee, who art infinity? The intellect knoweth that it is ignorant of Thee, because it knoweth Thou canst not be known, unless the unknowable could be known, and the invisible beheld, and the inaccessible attained . . .

This is most disconcerting and begs the question, if it is not possible to know God at all, let alone image him, how can Nicholas so confidently address him? We may note that Nicholas refers to God in negative terms; God, he says, is unknowable, invisible and inaccessible. And yet, although he declares that God cannot be known, he still defines him: through those things which, he says, he is not. This is the classic *via negativa* mode, the way of negation. It seeks to maintain intellectual integrity while at the same time providing a means by which we can talk about God. It is a way of describing God which is well known to the mystics. Meister Eckhart expresses the negative way even more radically:[3]

> Thou shalt know him without image, without semblance, and without means. . . . If thou lovest God as God, as spirit, as person, or as image, that must all go. – 'Then how shall I love him?' Love him as he is: a not-God, a not-spirit, a not-Person, a not-image; as sheer, pure, limpid unity, alien from all duality.[3]

How, then, do we image to ourselves the one who is, in the words of Dean Inge, the 'ineffable Absolute of which nothing positive can be predicated'?[4]

A helpful expression of the being of God is found in that enig-matic Name which was revealed to Moses – YHWH – and which is translated 'I AM THAT I AM' (Exodus 3.14). It underwrites God's mode of being while it avoids the use of simplifying images. But we notice that the language cannot avoid at least one qualifying term. The pronoun implies that God is like his creatures in one way at least: the use of the word 'I' presupposes that God is personal. It may be worth returning to the mystics for a moment and compar-ing them with this line of Scripture.

In the passage from Nicholas of Cusa we note the preponderance of the second person, the 'Thee' and 'Thou' of respectful address.[5] There is no doubt here that he is in relationship with a person. And since relationship implies a certain level of knowledge, he seems to know something about God after all. While God cannot be known, he can, it seems, be known about. If we return to Meister Eckhart we find something equally interesting:

> Love him as he is: a not-God, a not-spirit, a not-Person, a not-image; as sheer, pure, limpid unity, alien from all duality.

Here we have not only personal identity in the form of 'him' and 'he', but a form of poetic description which verges on 'image': 'sheer, pure, limpid unity'. The noun, when it comes, is abstract; the language steers us away from form and in its place inscribes an ethereal beauty which is meant to evade the grasp of the imagina-tion. But to describe God as 'sheer, pure, limpid' is surely to say something positive about him, to indicate something of what he is 'like'.

What we have now found in each of these passages, then, is the *via positiva*, the way of affirmation, and this demonstrates the way in which the two *vias* presuppose each other. While each of these passages purport to image or know God only through what he is not like – that is, the *via negativa* – neither can escape the inferences of language, which inscribes into the text its opposite, what he is like – the *via positiva*. In the light of this contradic-tion we must ask whether it is possible to maintain that integrity which we noted earlier as being so important. The challenge has been met from both the Jewish and Christian perspectives. Thus, David Goldberg and John Rayner, writing in *The Jewish People: Their History and Religion*,[6] say:

Maimonides is the outstanding exponent in Judaism of the *via negativa*, which maintains that the only assertions we can validly make about God are negations: we can only say what He is not. And yet the classical sources of Judaism do make many positive statements about Him. Are they, then, to be dismissed? Most Jews would say: no, but they must be understood metaphorically. Such metaphors are not illegitimate as long as we remember what they are: mere pointers to a mystery which must for ever transcend human understanding.

F.C. Happold in *Mysticism*[7] says:

Nevertheless, though the negation may be truer than the affirmation, it is possible and legitimate to make affirmations about the nature of the Divine Being. One must, however, be conscious of their limitations and realize that they can never be more than symbols, images, approximations, always inadequate, always in a sense, untrue. When we speak of God as Goodness, Beauty, Truth, Love, we are not guilty of a 'laughable presumption', provided we realise that what we are actually doing is translating into inadequate word-concepts something which springs from inner experience of Him.

This tension, as it were, between the integrity of the reason and the valid expression of intuition lies at the heart of the problem and reiterates itself in many forms. The religious poet, then, must acknowledge the theology of imaging God, being concerned with Absence and Otherness and also with Presence and likeness. As we explore the religious poetry of R.S. Thomas, we shall note how often Thomas chooses images which both can and cannot function as images of God, and how often the *via negativa* requires the *via positiva* in order to function at all. The language which he chooses to use will result in one or other of these oppositions being foregrounded, but whichever it is, its effectiveness lies in the power and appropriateness of the image. This question of the power and appropriateness of the image raises further questions.

We must be careful not to underestimate the power of the image; it has far-reaching consequences. The image we choose to stand for God not only influences but forms the concepts we hold about the nature of God. The choice of image can expand or limit, enhance or distort our concept of God. It has often been pointed out, for example, that while the image of God as Father is helpful and encouraging to those whose experience of a father has been a positive one, it can, for those whose experience of a father has been a painful and negative one, convey an idea of God quite contrary to that intended. We can demonstrate, too, how society might respond differently to the same image at different times. In our contemporary society we might want to ask whether, given 'Father' as a legitimate image for God, 'Mother' might not function as an equally appropriate image, especially in view of the fact that the alternative image has as long a history.[8] We might question whether mothers, too, do not have any qualities which might usefully be applied as images of God.

It is a problem with which modern theology, for all of its sophistication, has only recently begun to come to terms. We have only to consider the controversy over the ordination of women priests to realise that the problem of imaging God is a contemporary one, for one of the arguments, still current, propounded against the ordination of women is simply that as Christ was a man it is not possible for women to represent him.[9] This in turn raises questions about how God, and the nature of God, is perceived in the modern era, and reveals how unhappy people can be with certain unorthodox images of God.

These are just some of the theological problems inherent in imaging God. But there are other, literary, problems for the religious poet, and it is to these that we turn now:

> The religious poet today cannot rely upon a common fund of religious imagery and religious symbolism, upon liturgical phrases, and great sayings from the Scriptures, to which each of his readers can bring his own private wisdom and experience . . . the modern poet is likely to estrange many of his readers if he employs words and symbols which are connected with beliefs they do not share. A phrase which is full of meaning to him, and to those accustomed to use it or hear it in the same context, may to others seem a mere piece of pious jargon.[10]

In this passage Helen Gardner is noting the difficulty of the enterprise of writing religious poetry in an age of unfaith. Writing in 1949 she was able to see the problem as lying in 'words and symbols which are connected with beliefs they do not share'. For many of our present generation we might say 'words and symbols which they have barely heard, and the significance of which they do not understand'. Helen Gardner proceeds to explain how, in *Four Quartets*, Eliot copes with the problem by using religious references in a particularly discreet and sensitive way. She says:

> The effect is quite different from the effect in *Ash Wednesday*, where the private meditation is transformed into the ageless prayer of the Church. Here it is more as if two worlds suddenly for a moment touch, and we see that what the poet has been speaking of is what Christians speak of in another language.

R.S. Thomas comes to terms with the problem of religious language in a variety of ways. He presents natural images in such a way that the secular reader, innocent of the implicit religious image, will be able to produce a satisfactory reading:

> That man Prytherch, with the torn cap,
> I saw him often, framed in the gap
> Between two hazels with his sharp eyes
> Bright as thorns, watching the sun rise.
>   'The Gap in the Hedge'[11]

The poem makes a satisfactory 'nature' poem, but for the religious reader the intimations of Easter are delicately presented.

Sometimes Thomas uses conventional religious symbols but employs them in a number of unconventional ways. When a poet uses symbols, especially if they are private symbols, we deduce their meaning through the consistency of their application. There is no such guarantee of a consistent meaning in Thomas's symbols. Images recur, but their flexibility is pushed to the limits. Thus the image which finds its origin in the wounded side of Christ is presented in a variety of forms, often located not in the person of Christ but in the person of God. Even then the implications vary. Compare the following extracts, which represent a period of some ten years:

> His are the echoes
> We follow, the footprints he has just
> Left. We put our hands in
> His side hoping to find
> It warm.
>   'Via Negativa'[12]

> There was the sound
> of thunder, the loud, uncontrollable laughter of
> God, and in his side like an incurred stitch, Jesus.
>   'Rough'[13]

> He put his hand in his side
> and drew out the thorn for the letting
> of the ordained blood and touched her with
> it.
>   'The Woman'[14]

The mood of the first extract is one of tentative faith and reminds us most closely of the metaphor's origin in the Resurrection story. The second extract, however, suggests a relationship which is totally alien to the received wisdom: Jesus is the product of pain and the image of God conveyed in these few lines is more appropriate to the Greek pantheon than to Judaeo-Christian thought. The poem is one of Thomas's Creation stories. The last example works similarly, in that it, too, is a Creation story of a sort. Here God is endowing woman with her uniquely female biology; but the complex imagery of the side, the thorn and the blood need even more careful explication. There is no room for complacency, for even the most apparently familiar images are as though written on water, changing even as we read. This brings us to Thomas's approaches to imaging God.

Sometimes God appears in Thomas's poems under metaphoric guise. In these we expect the metaphor to mediate God in some way. Landscape, or Nature, is such a metaphor and some of Thomas's most positive poems are found in this category, but he is well aware of the limitations of metaphor and is not tempted, in Herbert's phrase, to 'rest in nature'. Those poems which explore the tensions of the metaphor are often most rewarding.

The extracts from 'Rough' and 'Woman' would fall into a further category, which I have decided to call the 'mythic' poems. These poems are imaginative recreations of given stories, in this case stories taken from the Judaeo-Christian tradition. Starting from the received text, Thomas elaborates or distorts the familiar story, and so produces unorthodox versions which challenge the readers to define God for themselves. He also applies this method to secular myths and sometimes to stories of his own.

In those poems, which represent what seems to be Thomas's most straightforward approach, God actually appears and is actually addressed, and where the poems follow the mode of the *via positiva* they can indeed be quite straightforward; however, when the poem takes on the mode of the *via negativa* the images are constructed to imply rather than to represent and some readers will find these poems, though often hauntingly beautiful, a little more challenging.

Other poems, while not necessarily presupposing an image of God, use such religious language and imagery as will allow readers to insert God into the text. This category greatly extends the range of poems which might be called religious, taking in many of the song-like poems of the early years, the peasant poems and – particularly interesting in this context – the poems which deal with art.

These are some of the theological and literary problems which affect the religious poet writing in a largely secular age. There is one further problem which should be considered at this point, and that is the question of what constitutes 'religious poetry'. It is particularly fortunate that R.S. Thomas was invited by Penguin Books to edit *The Penguin Book of Religious Verse*,[15] as this necessitates his defining for the reader what he understands by 'religious' poetry. (Interestingly, in true negative mode, he opens with 'I must explain this anthology; first of all what it is not.') The passage is lengthy but certain paragraphs are worth reproducing in full. He says:

> What is the common ground between religion and poetry? Is there such? Do definitions help? If I say that religion is the response of the whole person to reality, but poetry the response of a certain kind of person, I appear to be doing so at the expense of poetry. Perhaps Coleridge can help here. The nearest we approach to God, he appears to say, is as creative beings. The poet, by echoing the primary imagination recreates. Through his work he forces those who read him to do the same, thus bringing them nearer the primary imagination themselves, and so, in a way, nearer to the actual being of God as displayed in action. So Coleridge in the thirteenth chapter of the *Biographia Literaria*. Now the power of the imagination is a unifying power, hence the force of metaphor; and the poet is the supreme manipulator of metaphor. . . . The world needs the unifying power of the imagination. The two things which give it best are poetry and religion. Science destroys as it gives.

This anthology is divided into five sections. Roughly defining religion as embracing an experience of ultimate reality, and poetry as the imaginative presentation of such, I have considered five aspects of that experience: the consciousness of God, of the self, of negation, of the impersonal or un-nameable, and of completion.

The presentation of religious experience in the most inspired language is poetry. This is not a definition of poetry, but a description of how the communication of religious experience best operates. Yet it is some of the poems in this book, which purport to do this, that will arouse the indignation of the religious, more especially of the Christian, reader. Are some of them religious at all? Let me say at once that, by sitting somewhat loosely to orthodoxy, I have attempted to broaden the meaning of the term 'religious' to accommodate twentieth-century sensibility.

Thomas's liberal philosophy roused the indignation of at least one very celebrated Christian reader. Dame Helen Gardner, in *Religion and Literature*,[16] criticises his method thus:

> More serious is the vagueness of the concept 'religious sensibility' as a basis for choice. It is even vaguer than 'religious emotion', and does not provide a sufficiently firm delimitation of the subject-matter of the poems assembled for comparison. We need to establish a criterion of 'likeness' before we can discuss 'unlikeness'.
>
> For the purposes of criticism or scholarship (or the making of anthologies) definitions need to be strict.

While this raises many and complex questions (not the least of which might be how to define 'religious'), the confrontation foregrounds for us the problem of defining the poetry of R.S. Thomas himself. The phrase 'sitting somewhat loosely to orthodoxy' is a revealing one. It defines what seems to me to be the essence of his approach to both religion and poetry. As a theologian he is of the school of the former Bishop of Durham, David Jenkins; as a poet he would not, I think, very readily divide his poetry into the sacred and the secular. It is not possible for the religious poet to set limits to his subject, to define as religious only those things which fall within the conventions of religious observance. While the poet will want to concern himself with man's relationship with God, man does not exist in a vacuum; the poet must also address himself to man's relationship with his fellow man and with the world in which he lives. Consequently, one finds that poems 'about Wales' or 'about Nature' – those for which Thomas first became known – are raising serious religious questions.[17]

I shall consider as religious, then, any poems, however secular they may seem to be, which seem to me to be preoccupied with religious questions, and each chapter will consider a significant image or way of imaging God. This means that sometimes I will focus quite narrowly on single volumes where key images are brought into sharp focus. At other times I will be moving freely across the canon. When art provides the image, I will be concentrating on *Between Here and Now*, though poems from other volumes will also be considered in detail; when the image is that of Nature, I will be concentrating largely, but not exclusively, on 'The Minister'.[18]

Chapters 4 and 5, on myth and science, and the *via negativa*, move freely across the canon. *Counterpoint* is given special treatment and is looked at separately in Chapter 6, because unlike other Thomas collections it is structured around the idea of a Christian reading of history; not an arbitrary collection of poems but a complete work, having its own divisions according to subject matter. While it is treated separately, it will be observed that it tends to reinforce those observations already made on other texts.[19]

I have attempted to use gender-neutral language throughout.[20] I will be working throughout from the premise that R.S. Thomas is a man of faith. There will be those who think it is not necessary to have an opinion about the spiritual position of the writer; they may be right. However, there are readers who, on the premise that one trusts not the teller but the tale, feel they have discerned a falling off of faith in the later work.[21] My own feeling here is that these readers are, perhaps, expecting the wrong thing; that they want faith to be expressed, if not in certainty and stasis, then in smooth, uninterrupted growth. If we come to R. S. Thomas looking for reassurance and comfort, we shall certainly be disappointed. But if we come willing to explore with him what it means to be human, if we are willing to accept all the disorder of life and not insist on imposing order, if we are prepared to 'sit loosely to orthodoxy', then the unorthodoxy of his work, arising as it does from a fearsome integrity, will at least force us to think for ourselves, and at best liberate us for that doubt which makes faith continuously creative.

Thomas's Introduction to *The Penguin Book of Religious Verse* closes with these words: 'Over every poet's door is nailed Keats's saying about negative capability. Poetry is born of the tensions set up by the poet's ability to be "in uncertainties, mysteries, doubts, without any irritable reaching after fact and reason..."' I would suggest that it is with this negative capability in mind that one best approaches the work of R.S. Thomas.

2
Reading the Image

Uncertainties, mysteries and doubts pervade the Thomas text, manifesting themselves initially in his enigmatic titles. His collection of poems on Impressionist paintings, for example, which we might suppose deals with images in their most literal form, has a title as mysterious and enigmatic as any of his more overtly religious texts. Confronted with the title *Between Here and Now*, with its implication of a dimension which should be accessible but is not, we find ourselves, contrary to Keats' maxim, struggling to find fact and reason. The title indicates to us that the relationship between the language of the title and the image in the painting is going to be more complex than we anticipated. Our understanding of how an image functions, and the relationship between image and language, affects our reading of any Thomas text, but has a particular significance when we are making a religious reading. It will be useful, then, to take a little time to consider the complexities of the image.

According to Ezra Pound, an image is 'that which presents an intellectual and emotional complex in an instant of time'. With this in mind J.D. McClatchy muses: 'Only such an image could give us that sense of freedom from time limits and space limits, that sense of sudden growth, which we experience in the greatest works of art.'[1]

The phrase 'freedom from time limits and space limits' is particularly relevant to the title of *Between Here and Now*. The text is divided into two parts, the first of which consists of poems written to accompany a selection of Impressionist paintings chosen from a book by Germain Bazin, *Impressionist Paintings in the Louvre*,[2] and collected under the title *Impressions*. The *Here* and *Now* of the main title correspond to the 'space' and 'time' of the quotation, but the title also juxtaposes two contrasted modes of apprehending and defining reality, and asserts that we operate between these two contrasts. It provides an almost mystical perception of our situation relative to God (and to animals), neither of whom has a 'between', but only a 'here' and 'now' unified. *Impressionist Paintings in the Louvre* contains over 200 pictures of Impressionist paintings. Thomas has chosen to write poems to accompany some 33 of these; the subject matter includes landscape, seascape and portraits of various kinds, but almost half of the paintings which he has selected have women as their subject. Given the interest in the female form demonstrated by Impressionists such as Monet, Degas and Renoir, this is not surprising. More surprisingly, however, where women are not actually central to a particular painting, Thomas has often made them central to the accompanying poem. It would seem that he finds paintings by the Impressionists particularly useful in focusing a response to women. While there are poems about individual women in other collections of Thomas's work, nowhere is womanhood explored so intensively as in the poems which accompany the selection of paintings in *Between Here and Now*. With this in mind we shall make a detailed examination of Thomas's poems on women, and note the similarities and differences which it is possible to produce by utilising those two modes of apprehension noted above.

The women in the Impressionist paintings occupy that space which Thomas sees as being 'between here and now' and represent what Pound meant when he referred to 'an intellectual and emotional complex in an instant of time'. The representational status of woman in these paintings offers simultaneously a distance and an immediacy which other women do not, and which the poet can exploit. (I suggest 'distance' lies in the objectivity which can be applied to a painting but which cannot be applied to a living person, and 'immediacy' to the availability of the painting to the male gaze as owner/viewer.)[3] A dimension which is outside time and space is implied, a condition of being or perceiving which defies both, but which, when applied to an image which is almost iconic in its integrity, reveals both a method and an effect of reading images. The method, I suggest, is twofold, enabling both the poems and the paintings to be read variously as celebratory – that is, celebrating both the myth of woman and the Impressionist style – and also as a questioning of the traditional and mythological images of woman, which Thomas sees inscribed in the paintings and which he expresses in the poems. The effect of this reading will emerge as we proceed. This method and effect is worth exploring further as it might illuminate for us Thomas's approach to imaging God.

The women Thomas has written about exist only in the paintings. Having once existed in time and space in one mode of existence, they now exist as part of an artifact; this allows the poet to 'read' woman in a quite different way from that which he adopts in other collections. It is not difficult to see why these poems on paintings are of particular value to our understanding of Thomas's approach to the image, focusing as they do on a single subject – woman – and making multiple readings of that subject. We will find that many of the problems of reading – or of speaking – woman are also problems when it comes to 'reading' or 'speaking' God. An examination of the various strategies which Thomas adopts in reading images of woman may be expected to alert us to the means he adopts in reading images of God. To that end we will now consider a variety of poems on women, noting those areas of interest which will inform our further reading.

For my exploration of Thomas's approach to reading images I have selected a variety of paintings of women from *Between Here and Now*. The section entitled *Impressions* opens with a poem on a painting by Monet (reproduced as Plate 1): 'Monet: *Lady with a Parasol*'.

The first evidence we find of simultaneous readings of the picture being enacted is in Thomas's choice of title. The language is as suggestive of social or class distinction as the language in a novel by Jane Austen and, like hers, suggests the elegant world of manners. It is adequate for the enjoyment of the picture, but the full catalogue title of the painting is *Lady with a parasol turned towards the right* (1886). It has a companion piece called *Lady with a parasol turned towards the left* (1886).[4] The language of the full title, then, is the technical language of the artist and encourages a different reading of the picture. Where Thomas's abbreviated title offers the layman a romantic picture of a female figure, Monet's original invites considerations of composition and technique.

Of this period of Monet's work, Michael Levey says: 'Light is the screen through which everything is seen, and detail breaks up under its impact.'[5] There is indeed very little detail in this picture. The lines of the gown are implied by a few strokes, and the parasol is so devoid of decoration that, but for the strong effect of sunshine which influences our reading of the picture, it would be indistinguishable from an umbrella. The interior of the parasol creates a deep greenish shade which is cast over the head and breast of the woman. The effect of light is clearly the real subject of this painting, and Thomas's awareness of this fact is made clear in the first stanza:

> Why keep the sun
> from the head when the grass
> is a fire about
> the feet?

However, the appreciative response to Monet's skill is acknowledged obliquely. The effect of intense light is taken as a given, while Thomas, perhaps playfully, interrogates the pose of the woman. But one wonders whether his choice of metaphor is entirely innocent. The manner in which the grass seems to leap like flames at the woman's feet is an interesting feature of this painting. If a comparison is made with the Gothic painting *The Burning Bush* by Nicholas Froment,[6] the similarity in the shaping of the grass as fire is striking. What is significant about this similarity is that in the Froment painting the 'burning bush' is an icon of the Virgin. However, Thomas moves swiftly away from purely artistic considerations.

Line 4 continues: 'She wields her umbrella'. The sentence is broken at the point of maximum impact. The woman becomes the subject, and we note that the register of the language that Thomas chooses to use is now at variance with that of the title. The 'lady' disappears behind the anonymous pronoun 'She'. (We might note that 'the sun', 'the head', 'the grass' and 'the feet' all carry the same degree of objectivity.)[7] The parasol becomes the more functional 'umbrella'. But the term which really changes the status of the woman, and our perspective of her, is 'wields'. Suggestive of strenuous physical activity, it is hardly an appropriate term to use in association with a nineteenth-century 'lady'. The effect is twofold: the imagery develops in terms of warfare, the umbrella becoming a 'shield' against summer's 'missiles'. The reading of woman which Thomas superimposes upon the picture here is, if not quite woman as Amazon, at least a suggestion that she is not as fragile as the values of the time suggest. However, this image is qualified by the pejorative language of the second stanza – it is 'fashion' which explains her use of the 'not too serious' shield against summer's 'unreal' missiles. The image of strength is undercut and a return to nineteenth-century values is effected. A tension is developed, then, between the convention of woman as she appears in the painting, fashionably fragile and etherealised in light, and the woman in the poem, who is solid and has actual physical strength.

In spite of this vacillation Thomas proceeds to demolish the middle-class image of the 'lady', and he does this by drawing on the mores and manners contemporary with the time of painting. We note that at the end of each stanza, an observation is made which undermines the unity of title and subject. So, at the end of the second stanza, we find:

> She
> is brown already . . .

According to the mores of the time, one could not be both 'brown' and a 'lady'. Only women from the leisured classes could afford to keep out of the sun, and consequently only workers and peasants would be 'brown'. (The modern idea of a tan as fashionable and healthy-looking only emerged in 1932, when Coco Chanel bought herself a place in the south of France and allowed her skin to darken. As Angela Holdsworth[8] has it: 'A healthy outdoor look was becoming a sign of affluence, suggesting sunbathing in the Riviera rather than potato picking in Essex.')

Thomas, then, strips away from the picture those elements which have been constructed by the mores of which he is critical, and, as it were, denudes her of what we may take as her 'self-image'. It is interesting to see what remains:

> She
> is brown already. What
>
> she carries is a pretence
> at effeminacy, a borrowing
> from the mystery shadow
> concocts. But that arm . . .

The tension is maintained between the idea of the lady as conveyed by the artist in title and painting, and her actual physical appearance as perceived by the poet. We should be aware that in pushing art to its limits in achieving an external effect of light, the artist has lost any sense of the interiority of his subject. The face is a blur, projecting nothing. In this stanza this interiority is expressed in abstract terms which etherealise the woman, who is held in parenthesis between the physical qualities of her being 'brown' and of 'that arm'. The conjecture made about that interiority is contingent on the external features as observed, not by the artist, but by the poet. The status, perhaps even the value, of the woman is being reconstructed according to a selective reading of her outward appearance.

The woman, or maybe 'Woman', is seen as dissolved in fragments of her person, 'that arm', 'the bust'. We are reminded of Marvell:[9]

> An hundred years should go to praise
> Thine eyes and on thy forehead gaze;
> Two hundred to adore each breast;
> But thirty thousand to the rest . . .

Marvell's construction closes with sexual innuendo – 'thirty thousand to the rest'. Thomas's is less aggressively suggestive, but we should note the line ending 'the bust ample enough'. Thomas is a master at the pregnant line ending; this line begs the question – ample enough for what? The answer comes:

> for a peasant to lay his
> head there, dreaming of harvest.

The implications of 'dreaming of harvest' are not so different from Marvell's 'thirty thousand to the rest'.

So the 'lady' of the title enters her latest incarnation – partner to the peasant. This is not to suggest that there is any intrinsic value in being a 'lady' rather than a 'peasant'. Both terms can be pejorative. The value inheres in the mores of the time which Thomas is utilising. In such a context the peasant is more, shall we say, 'accessible' than the lady. The peasant is thought of as close to the earth, earthy, while the lady is refined, protected. Here, however, she is stripped of refinement, to reveal the basic human being beneath the acquired polish. However, the syntactic puzzlement of the third stanza remains, and we should look at it now.

Thomas's omission of conjunctions and careful placing of line endings force us to read with momentary confusion 'the mystery shadow' and its weighty accompanying 'concocts'. This has the effect of reinforcing the idea of light as knowledge or truth, and shadow as parasitic, even deceitful. Now there is a shift in the site of the tension: it is not now between the construct of the 'lady' and the poet's reading of her, but between the woman's inner self, to which the poet presumes to have access, and her outer self which he chooses to evaluate. Those lines in the centre of the poem which refer to her interior life are couched in pejorative terms, the placement isolating

'What she carries' from the parasol, 'a pretence . . . a borrowing . . . concocts' suggests that the woman has no genuine significance of her own, and denies her selfhood. But if what she carries is a pretence at effeminacy, a borrowing from the mystery shadow concocts, then the implication is being made that 'real' effeminacy has 'real' mystery. By returning to the earlier reference we made to the implicit image of the Virgin, we can produce yet another reading of these ambiguous lines. At the heart of the poem, and perhaps of the woman since this is an extended examination of her person, we find a mystery. The 'borrowing/ from the mystery shadow/ concocts' has heavy overtones of the mystery of Incarnation,[10] and the overshadowing of the Virgin.[11] The more immediate and prosaic reading is obscured by the distinctive syntax. This leads one to suspect that in this male view of woman there is an uncomfortable tension between mystery and materiality. Hence the attempt to come to terms with it by rationalising it. But the rationalisation is also reductive in the extreme. The spiritual has been marginalised in favour of the physical. As in Marvell's 'To His Coy Mistress', the woman has been reduced to less than the sum of her parts – 'that arm', 'the bust'. In the final analysis, she is little more than a pillow for the peasant. The 'lady' is as much an object as the parasol she carries.

What we would seem to have, then, is a whole series of readings of woman which grow out of each other. Beginning with the 'lady' of the title – in both poem and painting – we discern the image of the Virgin informing the first stanza; the suggestion of the Amazon appears and disappears quickly, and the woman herself disappears into abstraction and pretence in the third, only to re-emerge as Virgin again. The fourth stanza confirms her as 'body' and the final image is one linked to procreation and fecundity. The lady with a parasol has many faces, and no face. We are reminded of Simone de Beauvoir's comment:[12]

> Even if a woman dresses in conformity with her status, a game is still being played . . . the least sophisticated woman once she is 'dressed' does not present herself to observation; she is . . . an agent through whom is suggested someone not there – that is the character she represents, but is not.

This concept of the function of the image and Thomas's awareness of the possibility of multiple readings will take on increasing importance as we proceed. The stability of Monet's titles gain a new significance in their, perhaps enviable, ability to be precise: *Lady with a parasol turned towards the right* (1886); *Lady with a parasol turned towards the left* (1886).

A further approach to reading an image is registered when we are confronted with the quite different style of Gauguin and 'Gauguin: *La Belle Angèle*'. This curious painting is a portrait of Angèle Sâtre. According to Bazin, she was frightened by the picture and refused to accept it as a present. It is typical of Gauguin's symbolic style, and we are not surprised by her reaction. The picture is segmented by a semi-circle within which the portrait of Angèle Sâtre is fore-grounded. To the left of the semi-circle the bronze image of a cat is set on a ledge. The background, in both segments of the painting, is the dark blue of a night sky, that segment outside the semi-circle having the added symbolism of moon-washed flowers and foliage. The images are all slightly sinister, but the most disturbing feature about this painting is the relationship which it implies between the woman and the cat. It is suggestive of the occult, of the witch and her familiar, and this is achieved in the painting not only through the juxtaposition of the cat with the woman, but in the catlike spirit which seems to permeate the features of the woman herself. In Monet we saw how Thomas deduced the interior life of the woman from the exterior of her pose and person. He takes a different approach here, reading for us the symbolism which Gauguin has inscribed into the painting.

The first response we make to this poem, which is quite un-like our response to the painting, is to note the paradox in the title. The whole of the poem serves to render the title ironic, for Angèle Sâtre is portrayed as neither beautiful nor angelic.[13] Thus we immediately find a gap between the 'given' of the title and our subjective response.

The universality of the experience of the poem is pressed on the reader in the first line – 'We know someone like this'. The 'We' of the first line is ambiguous, suggesting first the poet and a com-panion, but then insinuating the reader into the relationship. The implication is made that 'we' all know someone who adopts a persona for private reasons. In the picture the circle frames the figure of Madame Sâtre, like an off-centre halo, separating her from the (symbolically primitive) background. In referring to this circle as 'imaginary' Thomas is firmly associating the woman with her setting. It is, he says, only an imaginary circle which separates her from 'the blue of the night, whose flowers are moth-winged'. In reality, he implies, she is a part of, and belongs to, the primitive forces of darkness. His skill in curtailing lines at the most effective point is used to advantage in the opening of the second verse paragraph:

> Beside her
> in bronze is her other

The alter-ego is expressed in terms which suggest not just a second self but the supernatural; for what is beside her is not just her 'other self,' as one might see oneself in a reflection in a mirror, but her 'other' in the form of the primitive bronze. Gauguin has organised the painting to draw attention to the 'spirit of synthetism which he saw in the primitive Bretons'.[14] The images are all slightly sinister – the night, the flowers like moths, the bronze familiar and according to Thomas, the other self the woman is trying not to betray:

> her other
> self, the cat-like image

Thomas explores the oppositions in the picture, noting those features of the woman which are cat-like and mysterious, the narrow eyes, the oddly folded hands, and, in setting them against the Christian symbolism in the painting, expresses in language the spirit which Gauguin conveys here through his brush-strokes: the sense of primitive forces residing beneath a superficially civilised exterior. The woman has a cross about her neck, her hands are at rest as if prepared for prayer and her expression is withdrawn. However, each of these elements is counterpoised by more pagan images. Thomas emphasises the conflict by suggesting the responses she might make to the opposing influences of the cat and the cross:

> the cat-like image
> that causes her to sheath
> her fingers and try looking
> as demure as the small
> cross on her bosom tells
> her she ought to be.

Whereas in 'Monet: *Lady with a Parasol*' he created his own reading of woman, in his response to this painting Thomas endorses the reading of the woman as expressed by the artist. However, Thomas remarks once again a contradiction between the external appearance and the internal reality of the woman in the picture. In each case the woman has two selves – the outer self, adopted for reasons of social acceptability and conformity, and the inner self, less acceptable but, it is implied, more true to the 'real self' of the woman.

In 'Monet: *Lady with a Parasol*', and 'Gauguin: *La Belle Angèle*', Thomas offers two ways of reading the woman's self. In the first he counters the presentation of woman as 'Lady' with a more earthy rendering of her self, and in the second he offers a primitive, pagan 'other' to the woman. Both readings deny a stable centre for the persona. It seems that in these poems the woman is concealing her real self, and this concealment is effected in a number of ways.

Thomas often introduces classical myth as a means of destabilising the reading of the painting. If we look at 'Cassatt: *Young Woman Sewing*' we find that what is concealed is not the actual but the potential self. The picture shows a young woman deep in concentration on a small piece of sewing (Plate 2). She is seated outdoors and her pale blue-white dress, which makes up the larger part of the painting, contrasts with the blobs of the bright red flowers around her. The figure is very still and calm, and Thomas reflects this stillness in his language. The poem opens quietly: 'Sewing'. This leads to quiet reflection and an association of ideas. Two significant points emerge immediately: the allusion to the Fates (Is she one/ of the three fates) and the notion of concealment, or containment, in the figure of the chrysalis. The 'first' of the Fates referred to is Clotho, the spinner of the thread of life. From this reference-point Thomas moves through the various facets of woman as the creator of life, from the mythic 'Goddess of human destiny' (I think it is de Beauvoir who drily adds, 'and thus of men') to woman as potential mother and then to the young woman as holding within herself the potential of her own selfhood. 'She is', says Thomas, 'the chrysalis she inhabits' – an image drawn from the gauzy enveloping fabric of her dress. The motif of the thread is present in all three images. (There is also a nice play on 'knitting' in the association of fingers and brows.) She is the Fate spinning the thread of life; she is a young mother to be, preparing for the birth by sewing; and from the thread she holds she is spinning her own cocoon, from which the butterfly of her real self will emerge. For what we see in the picture is not the essence of the person. That has not yet been formed, but its immanence is suggested by the flowers around her:

> She is
> the chrysalis she
> inhabits, but the blood

The juxtaposition of the chrysalis and the blood suggest two different modes of experiencing life: the one potential, the other achieved. Thomas sets up an association between the white dress (chrysalis) of the girl and the red flowers (blood) in the background:

> in flower about her
> is an indication of the arrival
> of her period to come

The red of the flowers facilitates the pun on 'period' which, together with the concluding metaphor of the butterfly, suggests that her real life begins with her ability to procreate. Although this poem deals in stereotypes of woman, and has similar suggestions of 'two faces' of woman, it differs from those we have considered above, for we find here no suggestion of artfulness in the concealment of the self, and the tone is tender rather than critical.

The problem of articulating woman is complicated further in 'Degas: *Portrait of a Young Woman*', where images from classical mythology merge with those of conventional religion.

Referring to his poems about paintings, Thomas has said:

The poems are attempts to comment and to draw out extended meanings in a way which most of the painters would have found reprehensible, because painting has its own plastic and compositional values.[15]

In this poem he acknowledges this directly. The opening paragraph prepares us for an exposition of the subject which is based on values other than those of light and shade. Thomas chooses his own perspective as he reads the youthful face of the sitter. As the poem proceeds, we are given a conventional appraisal of the portrait; the picture is, after all, that of a modest and unassuming young woman and fully supports the assumptions the poet makes. We note, however, that the language inscribes religious values – innocence, blessings, evil – and becomes slightly archaic in the phrase 'would come forth'. Thus we are quite unprepared for the sudden change of perspective that follows:

> Her young being
> waits to be startled
> by the sweetness in roughness
> of hands that
> with permitted boldness
> will remove her bark
> to show under how smooth a
> tree temptation can shelter

Nowhere is Thomas's use of sliding perspectives used with more devastating effect. He subverts at a stroke the image he has built up in the preceding lines: we discover all those qualifications of womanhood we have previously noted. The element of disguise, of concealment is present, the notion of woman as Ave/Eva, and the equivocation made possible by the introduction of myth. The construction of the second verse paragraph is interesting. It begins with innocence and it ends with temptation. It is not the innocent who is being tempted, however. The innocent is the temptation. In one of his most dense metaphors Thomas achieves some astonishing paradoxes. In four lines he renders woman both Ave and Eva, chaste goddess and subtle temptress, and compromises the innocence with which he endowed the girl in the first place. All of this is accomplished in one labyrinthine sentence.

Thomas's introduction of the tree imagery is entirely arbitrary, but enables him to create some interesting juxtapositions in this reading of woman. The image of the woman as a tree fuses the myths of Daphne and Eve into one. The poem begins by associating woman with innocence, but through subtle use of the tree image ends with an association with temptation. Daphne, of course, was the Greek nymph who, pursued by Apollo, prayed that he might never possess her. She was thereupon transformed into a laurel.[16] (Many of the paintings and sculptures based on this myth choose the moment of transformation, which, of course, begins with the feet, the legs being gradually encased in bark and tendrils leaving the upper half of the female form to be portrayed in the typical, nude, stance.) This is the classic defence of innocence. Any association of woman and tree is certain to create, in the Western mind at least, the image of Eve. Thomas validates this process in the last line of the poem, but not before introducing his own elaboration on the theme, for here Eve *is* the tree. The woman's body is the focus of the temptation. The smoothness under the bark is the body minus the clothes. Under, or within, this bark temptation shelters. The poem calls into question all that we mean by 'innocence'. Thomas, in declaring the young woman to be innocent at the beginning, seems by the end of the poem to be challenging the reader to redefine the word.

The whole suggests the dimension we have been exploring in these poems, the two selves of woman, the acceptable outward self, compliant with social convention and the less acceptable, implied, internal reality. The variation in this poem lies in the fact that the usually hidden, and in this case sexual, self is not here registered as unacceptable or worthy of censure. This woman does not flee from the protagonist as in the Daphne myth, nor is she guilty like Eve. In this reading of myth the tree is to be embraced. There is acknowledged sweetness in the roughness of the 'hands' and they move with 'permitted' boldness; we see that here temptation 'shelters', it does not hide.[17] Occasionally in these poems the response of the male viewer is foregrounded, and this is the case in 'Degas: *Mademoiselle Dihau at the Piano*' (Plate 3). Although the poem uses plural pronouns throughout, it is very much a masculine voice that we hear, and a masculine response which registers. The significance of much that Thomas observes in this painting lies in the expression on the face of the sitter, and it is clear he is working from the colour print, not from the monochrome which is printed in *Impressions*. The colour picture reveals important contours in the face which are flattened out in the monochrome;[18] the mouth is more firmly modelled, the eyes more resistant to the attentions of the viewer; the face holds a strength of character which the monochrome totally fails to capture.

In the picture, Mademoiselle Dihau is seated at a piano with her back to the artist. Her head is turned to look over her shoulder, and, in a manner favoured by the Impressionists, her gaze is directed to a point outside the painting. She appears to be looking at the artist or viewer, and it is the direction of her gaze which prompts the question in the first line – 'Asking us what she shall play?' The question does not hold the poet, however. He moves on immediately to an impression of her character, breaking the line to emphasise the point:

> But she is her own
> music . . .

The strength of character which we noted earlier, the sense of calm dignity and self-possession she displays, dare the audience to remark her personal attraction. It is a challenge Thomas takes up and executes with considerable skill. The poem has an interesting structure. The movement is similar to that in 'Monet: *Lady with a Parasol*'. There we saw how Thomas begins with the figure of the woman, then in the manner of the Impressionist painter, elevates or etherealises her until she almost disappears, before drawing back to the solid, female form at the end. Although Thomas introduces variations, this is a shape he uses again and again. Here, the poet first addresses himself to the figure in the painting. She is then abstracted, elevated, into music and 'We listen to her . . . as the garden listens to the year ripening'. The music blends into and enhances the central image of the autumn garden, where the woman takes on form again; but it is not her own form. She takes on the form of fruit, before she becomes her own person again. We notice that the 'own' of the second line is distantly echoed in the 'owned' of the last, while in between there is a positive crescendo of language:

> Almost
> we could reach out a hand
> for the mellow-fleshed,
> sun-polished fruit
> that she is.

(Here Thomas is following the example of the art critics, who have an unfortunate habit of referring to women in paintings in terms of fruit ready to be plucked.)[19]

We have seen that the expression on the face of Mademoiselle Dihau warns against the temptation to indulge in sexual stereotyping, and Thomas acknowledges this momentarily in the second line where we read 'she is her own' before completing the sentence. The desire in the central image is qualified by 'almost', and throughout the poem we feel the tension between the poet's response to her beauty and his tacit acknowledgment that she is 'her own'. He does not retreat, however, without making at least one foray against her privacy. Multiple readings abound in the lines:

> But her eyes
> are the seeds of a tart
> apple . . .

Once again we note overtones of the medieval Ave/Eva commonplace. We have seen the hand (almost) reaching out for the fruit. Now the image of the apple is presented in terms which encourage equivocation. The double meanings focus on the pun on 'tart'. We are offered the reading that Mademoiselle Dihau has in her eyes the 'seeds of a tart', i.e. the potential capacity for promiscuity, but it is a fleeting suggestion and the swift transition to the next line does not encourage one to linger on it. Next, we are invited to see from the implied rejection in her glance that she is a 'tart' apple, which might suggest equally a judgement of the male voice or of the woman. (A case, rather, of 'sour grapes'?) Again, a tart apple can also be an apple precisely suited to make a dish which is both sweet and desirable.[20] One of the effects of the multiple readings is to blur the distinction between woman as object of desire and woman as symbol of the Fall. Thomas cannot resist offering several readings of the nature of woman; recognising the impossibility of reconciling the tensions, after a possible pun on 'score', he draws this poem to a close by acknowledging the independence of the subject, the

> land so privately owned.

Where women are not central to the painting, Thomas sometimes makes them central to the accompanying poem. 'Degas: *Musicians in the Orchestra*' (Plate 4) is such an occasion. It is a complex and subtle poem: the figures of the men seem at a first reading to dominate the poem as they do the painting, and we may not consider women to be central. There is, however, a powerful sub-text at work, which insistently raises images of women that are both mythological and mysterious. This effect may have been influenced by Thomas's sensitivity to Degas's personal experience, for Bazin informs us:

> It was while painting this scene that Degas . . . crossed the footlights for the first time and discovered the artificial lighting and

the dancers performing their steps above the heads of the musicians in the orchestra. A second recording was thereby super-
imposed on the first, of a quite different universe, made of light,
with dazzling colours and idealised creatures.[21]

Whether this is so or not, the resulting poem has much in common
with Degas's experience. In the painting two-thirds of the surface
are taken up by the members of the orchestra. The rows of players
are seated at right angles to the stage. The dark mass of their formal
dress is intersected by angles created by the white of shirt fronts
and the lines of the instruments. Above the musicians, in the upper
third of the picture, a strong contrast is effected as the footlights
brilliantly illuminate the skirts and the legs of the dancers. All of
the dancers are female, all of the musicians are male. The magical,
mysterious world of the stage is the province of the women; the
substantial, more prosaic world of the orchestra is that of the men.

Thomas recognises this dichotomy, and, like Degas in the quotation above, he too proceeds to superimpose a 'quite different
universe' upon the scene, creating a mythical dimension. The
organisation of the men into rows, the unity of their concentration,
with gaze directed towards the conductor, and their containment
inside the dark parallels of the orchestra pit, invite comparison with
the rowers of a galley:

> Heads together, pulling
> upon music's tide –

The poem opens, then, with one of Thomas's complex metaphors:
concentrating on the men, he suggests first the action of rowers,
and creates an image which, in characteristic manner, he then forces
the reader to adjust in the second line, as he shifts the emphasis to
the music. This pressure for adjustment of perspective continues
throughout the poem, and is only one of many transformations of
various sorts which take place. In the next lines we read:

> it is not their ears
> but their eyes their conductor . . .

The stanza hangs in mid-air, encouraging speculation. With one
image developing into another with even more complex inferences,
the musicians, who are like rowers, have themselves become part of

the mythical world Thomas is creating. It is as if the magic of the stage has spilled over into the real world. The 'quite different universe' exerts its influence on the men. Now the mythological content begins to change the focus of the poem. The phrase 'lest they behold' is held in suspension, and we must resort to the myth for explication. The rowers whose ears were sealed by their 'conductor' were of course the companions of Odysseus, who were in danger of being lured to their death by the music of the sea-nymphs.[22] However, Thomas has already established that the men are creating the 'music's tide' themselves, and it is their eyes, not their ears, that are sealed. For them the danger lies not in what they might hear, but in what they might see. In the Odysseus myth it is the music of the sirens heard over the water that is the source of irresistible temptation. Here, while the men create their own tide of music, the undulating skirts of the women take on the motion of the tide. The province of the women, the stage, now becomes the 'island', the locus of 'irresistible' temptation allied with danger:

> on the stage's shore
> the skirts rising and falling
> that turns men to swine . . .

At this point the Circe myth[23] is incorporated into that of the sirens. Music is still the tide, and the stage the shore, but the skirts of the women now compound the sorcery which 'turns men to swine'. In the Circe myth the men were literally 'turned into swine' by the dangerous, magical goddess. The invisible women at the centre of this poem seem to have the same ability; but by employing a modern, metaphorical, pejorative form for the phrase, Thomas also implies culpability on the part of the men. While this seems inappropriate on the surface given the context (Montmartre nightlife), on a deeper level it may be all too appropriate. Temptation, it seems, is a feature of the very motions of life. I have referred above to the women as 'invisible'. The women as such do not in fact appear in the text. In other poems which we have considered they conceal their real selves beneath their garments, but here they have disappeared altogether and are represented only by their skirts. This creates a tension between the painting and the poem unlike any we have found before. The source of this tension lies between the given situation in the painting and the imaginatively created one in the poem. In the painting we have the gentlemen of the orchestra who are concentrating on their music; but in the poem we have a crew who threaten to lose control by virtue of the disembodied skirts fluttering over their heads. This exaggerated sense of male susceptibility borders on the absurd, and through its inherent humour it introduces a different perspective into the male/female relationship, a perspective which recognises the myth and, in exploring it, disarms it. In making his imaginative reading, Thomas simultaneously creates and subverts his own proposition. The male gaze is turned ironically on the male subjects of the painting, hinting perhaps that men too can be the victims of myth.

The facility with which convention can identify types is registered differently in 'Toulouse Lautrec: *Jane Avril Dancing'*. In this painting (Plate 5) the central figure is Jane Avril,[24] a famous café dancer. She is being watched by two figures, a man and a woman, who are roughly sketched in behind her. Thomas's attack on convention takes a new perspective in this poem. In the colour reproduction which Thomas used, the dancer appears lighter on her feet, more ethereal than in the image conveyed by the monochrome; her dress is more gauzy over her petticoats, bunched up in a manner which suggests that she is swathed in garments which would normally restrict her movement. In this she is like the 'couple in the corner' who are also swathed 'up to the neck'. It is the difference between them, however, which delights us, as the couple, rigidly erect, contained in their own restricted world, look to each other, for – as Thomas interprets it – approval. In his reading of the picture Thomas foregrounds this air of self-approval and what he sees as the hypocrisy of a judgemental response. He imputes to the figures both an enjoyment of the dance and a condemnation of the dancer. Contrasted with the rigidity of these figures, Jane Avril's dance appears to be an act of complete spontaneity, requiring no one's approval, an act of sheer *joie de vivre*.

Thomas employs a variable perspective which shifts between the observers in the picture – the couple in the corner – and the observer outside the picture – the poet or reader/viewer. Thus the opening exclamation 'Such daring!' may be either one of shock as registered by the 'couple in the corner' or of ironic response from the more objective external viewer. The second undercuts the first, and implies a voyeurism on the part of the couple, who are thus being judged by the external viewer. In imputing to them the stereotypical response to women, Thomas allows himself freedom to express an alternative viewpoint. To those who are

> All up to the neck
> in their conventions;

the woman dancing is automatically subject to moral censure, but these onlookers are discredited by the pejorative language Thomas uses to describe them. The external viewer of the dance sees only uninhibited *joie de vivre*, and he challenges the convention that would marginalise the woman. The placing on the page of 'she only' isolates the figure, separates her from her audience. Isolated and enclosed within her dance she finds her own version of heaven, the associative play on prayer and dance focused through the reference to her knees:

> she only
> showing the knees
> by which some would gain entrance to heaven.

But a variety of readings of these lines is possible: 'She is the only one who shows the knees' – in contrast to the conventional couple; 'She is *only* showing the knees' – modesty prevents her from showing more. (Note how depersonalising is 'the' knees.) 'She is *only showing* the knees' and the action is not an invitation to the viewer to anticipate anything of a more promiscuous nature. The choice of response is encoded in the syntax. The prude and the pandar are opposite sides of the coin, as the inner and outer viewers are. In this poem Thomas does not choose to judge the woman. Here we may read the stereotypical response through the background figures, who represent convention in its most stifling and hypocritical form, and it is this response which Thomas judges. These readings, then, may be credited to two sets of viewers: those within the painting, the couple in the corner; and those without, the poet or the reader/viewer. The knees, it is suggested, can be used to kneel in prayer or to seduce. The reading of the text and the reading of the action depend on the reader/viewer. The responsibility does not lie with the dancer.

In 'Monet: *Lady with a Parasol*' we noticed that Thomas challenged those social mores which ordered our reading of the woman, stripping away those elements which constitute 'effeminacy' (Thomas's word) in an effort to expose the authentic 'female'. In 'Jane Avril' he sees an authentic existence; a person who chooses what she will be, indifferent to convention. Of the women painted by Toulouse-Lautrec, Edwin Mullins says:[25]

She may dance for men, whore for men, love men, but her identity is not defined by men. Being beyond the pale has awarded her the right to define herself, to compose her face not as wife/doll/mother/mistress/sinner/heroine but in accordance with her own desires and fears.

It is an interesting fact that in searching for an authentic image of woman the only unequivocal image we have so far discovered should be one of a woman who has been completely marginalised by society.

The final painting in the volume *Between Here and Now* – the only nude from Bazin's collection to appear in the volume – is 'Renoir: *The Bathers*' (Plate 6). Two female figures recline in a primordial landscape. They look into the painting, towards each other, not outwards to the spectator. While the brilliance of the light shows the Impressionist influence, the monumental figures are more in keeping with the classical mode. The combination of the two registers the later style of Renoir. *The Bathers* was painted at a time when, as Rewald says:

> Impressionism lay far behind him; he retained merely the glistening texture of it, yet the shimmering surface of pigment he used now not to render atmospheric effects but to build with brilliant and strong colours an image of life in almost supernatural intensity. The study of nature no longer was his unique goal.[26]

The style of this painting is important: its other-worldliness provides an ideal opportunity for Thomas to draw on all those myths of woman, both religious and classical, which inform so many paintings of the nude. Renoir himself provides grounds for a mythological treatment of his figures:

> What admirable creatures those Greeks were! They lived so happy a life that they imagined the gods came down to earth in order to find their paradise and true love. Yes, the earth was the paradise for the gods . . . and that is what I want to paint.[27]

Bazin, too, invites such an approach:

> . . . these two figures have gone back to a state of pristine innocence . . . in a kind of primordial mud of earth, flowers, grass and

stone. . . . The same glowing fluid circulates in their bodies and in those Eden–like meadows.[28]

But Thomas does not take advantage of either of the possibilities offered here. Throughout this collection he clearly feels free to read the paintings in any way which seems appropriate to himself. He uses them to explore the contradictions of the myth of woman, which figures her as both Ave and Eve; which identifies external beauty but also imputes the potential for sin. The myth of the Fall hovers in the background, while classical myth adds its complications. But in this poem we find that Thomas completely rejects the use of the mythological, both religious and classical; here woman is neither Ave nor Eve; she is *apparently* as devoid of cultural assumptions as she is of clothes.

Confronted with the Impressionist painting, Thomas has had to come to terms with what it represents as woman. He recognises that woman is other than that which the artist has expressed, but he also recognises the validity of that expression. This is what he has in mind when he says of Degas, 'he intended other things/ tonal values'.[29] The surface texture of the subject interested the Impressionists: the effects of light. But in achieving it the subject was lost. Finding a way of replacing the subject is the burden of these poems. But how does one find an authentic way of recognising the body, which does not rely on the myth or stereotype of woman? Just such a dilemma was foregrounded long before Thomas in an essay by Lawrence. He says:

Courbet, Daumier, Degas, they all painted the human body. But Daumier satirized it, Courbet saw it as a toiling thing, Degas saw it as a wonderful instrument. They all of them deny it its finest qualities, its deepest instincts, its purest intuitions. They deny it the best imaginative existence.[30]

Typically, perhaps, Lawrence locates the problem in an innate hatred of the body and a desire to etherealise it out of existence. So he goes on:

And the real grand glamour of modern French art, the real outburst of delight came when the body was at last dissolved of its substance, and made part and parcel of the sunlight and shadow scheme . . . then they made the grand, grand escape into freedom,

into infinity, into light and delight. They escaped from the tyranny of solidity and the menace of mass form . . . they escaped
from the dark procreative body which so haunts a man, they
escaped into the open air. . . . They metamorphosed it into an
assembly of shifting lights and shadows, all coloured. A web of
woven, luminous colour was a man, or a woman – so they painted
her, or him; a web of woven shadows and gleams. Delicious! and
quite true as far as it goes. A purely optical, visual truth: which
is what paint is supposed to be.[31]

But Lawrence also recognised that form must return:

The glorious escape was all an illusion. There was substance still
in the world. . . . There was the body, the great lumpy body. [32]

Renoir had wrestled with this problem too; in his later years he
had attained what Rewald calls 'the balance between observation
and vision'[33] and what Clark refers to as 'The antique balance
between truth and the ideal'.[34]

This has been the problem that Thomas has tried to resolve in
these poems, but for him the real has been perhaps more elusive
than the ideal, and in the majority of the poems we have considered
the vision has been qualified by the observation; usually the vision
of the artist has been qualified by the observation of the poet.

Thomas tries to find in 'Renoir: *The Bathers*' the objective representation of the female form. He treats it with what seems to be
straightforward critical appreciation. After making a gesture towards
an 'imaginative extended meaning' in 'What do they say?', as if
conjecturing what the figures are saying one to another, he shifts
his perspective so that the question becomes 'what do these figures
say to the external observer of Art?'; he retreats to the 'other things'
– the 'tonal values' of the poem we considered earlier – 'Degas:
Portrait of a Young Woman'. This is Art, and here the surface texture
of brush-strokes is given priority. We are reminded of the words
of Professor Alexander: 'If the nude is so treated that it raises in
the spectator ideas or desires appropriate to the material subject,
it is false art, and bad morals.'[35]

At first it appears that Thomas supports this theory, but the
notion is seriously undermined by the sensuous language of the
second paragraph, where we read:

> These bodies,
> smooth as bells
> from art's stroking . . .

The attempted deflection of the sensuous experience compromises
him, and tends, unwittingly perhaps, to support Kenneth Clark's
criticism of Alexander:

> This high-minded theory is contrary to experience. In the mixture
> of memories and sensations aroused by the nudes of Rubens or
> Renoir are many which are 'appropriate to the material subject'.
> . . . it is necessary to labour the obvious and say that no nude,
> however abstract, should fail to arouse in the spectator some
> vestige of erotic feeling, even if only the faintest shadow – and if
> it does not do so, it is bad art and false morals.[36]

Thomas's attempt to escape the implications of the female body is
echoed by William Gaunt, who remarks: 'We cease to think of the
real world; we enter the world of Renoir's mind, the ultimate vision
of timeless beauty.'[37]

This is how Thomas tries to resolve the problem of how to
image women. In the final poem of this collection we note how the
firmness of line appeals to him after the blurred outlines of early
Impressionism:

> These bodies
> . . . keep such firmness
> of line as never,
> under the lapping
> of all this light
> to become blurred or dim.

In the earlier poems and paintings, woman was abstracted through
the application of light and colour, losing form. Now she has form
again, but it is not the form of the 'real world'. Real woman is still
absent; the real superseded by the ideal, the woman by the work
of art. Thomas is right, then, when he refers to values being in
reverse, for these women are external only. Throughout this volume
Thomas has challenged the external appearance as concealing something 'other', whether it is the fashion of the *'Lady with a Parasol'* or
the religion of *'La Belle Angèle'*; the innocence of the *'Young Woman'*

or the challenge in the eye of 'Mademoiselle Dihau'. Now the external is all. Thomas acknowledges the success of Renoir's creation.

Thomas's reading of this painting is deeply informed by his knowledge of its history. For example, the 'firmness of line' which does not become blurred under so much light probably refers to the precautions that Renoir took in his choice of pigment to prevent it from fading over many years. Thomas's choice of metaphor, too, in the second stanza might seem peculiarly arbitrary, unless one is familiar with the comment attributed to Renoir at this period:

I want a red to be sonorous, to sound like a bell; I look at a nude: there are myriads of tiny tints. I must find the ones that will make the flesh on my canvas live and quiver.[38]

> These bodies
> smooth as bells
> from art's stroking, toll
> an unheard music,
> keep such firmness
> of line as never,
> under the lapping
> of all this light
> to become blurred or dim.

This metaphor is Renoir's gift to Thomas. What better image, what richer allusion could he have chosen to describe these figures whom he is determined to keep free of subjective response? Mullins points out how often women in paintings have been likened to fruit and food with all their associations of desire and consumption; in 'Monet: Lady With a Parasol' the peasant lies 'dreaming of harvest'. In 'Degas: Mademoiselle Dihau at the Piano' we read 'Almost/ we could reach out a hand/ for the mellow-fleshed,/ sun-polished fruit/ that she is'. In 'Renoir: The Bathers', although a desire to touch is acknowledged in the sub-text, the inherent sensuousness is deflected by the impersonal 'art's stroking'. The image of the bell also allows Thomas to pursue the theme of art as music, something already hinted at in 'Mademoiselle Dihau'. The 'unheard music' corresponds to Renoir's colours which will make the canvas, in the words attributed to Renoir, 'live and quiver'. The phrase 'toll an unheard music' registers the epiphany of the poem – the moment of heightened awareness for the observer of the painting, when art transcends its subject.[39]

But the most effective means of rendering these figures independent lies in the language of the first stanza, where Thomas establishes his case for an objective attitude to the painting. It is couched in negatives, informing the reader of all those things the figures are not, and indicating the response expected of the viewer. They are 'not to be peeped at'; they are 'no Godivas'; they remain, they do 'not pass'; we look at them, but 'without lust'. We approach the painting, then, by means of a *via negativa*. This pseudo-Dionysian elaboration of all those things the figures are not channels the readers' response into the attitude Thomas requires.

In theological terms the *via negativa* defines God in terms of what he is not, thus leaving him free to be what he knows himself to be. In defining 'woman' in terms of the *via negativa*, Thomas probably makes his most appropriate gesture towards an identification of woman.

In an interview with J.B. Lethbridge,[40] Thomas says of his more controversial religious poems: 'What I am tilting at is not God, but the ideas of God.' In these poems it may be that what Thomas is tilting at is not woman, but ideas of woman.

Here Thomas has set up what Marina Warner calls the 'mighty span'[41] of stereotypical images of women. He has inserted religious implications which suggest what woman is and is not like. Readers must consider the implications of the various readings produced and then decide for themselves. This mode of constructing multiple readings which then demand that the reader arbitrate between them adumbrates Thomas's approach to images of God.

In looking closely at the images of women as they are presented in both paintings and poems, we have been alerted to the difficulty of representation. There is an inescapable opposition between the observation and the vision, or to put it another way, between the truth and the ideal; Thomas tries to come to terms with this by producing multiple readings of woman, within a single text and as a cumulative effect. This fundamental opposition, and the method used to accommodate it, is something which we might expect to see reiterated in Thomas's attempts to represent God. We have so far confined our examination of the image to the female figure as it appears in a secular context. We will enlarge our frame now to take in a variety of subjects and contexts with a view to extending our appreciation of Thomas's technique, beginning with 'The View from

the Window'.[42] We immediately note the interesting and productive inversion of perspective in this poem – 'Like a painting it is set
before one'. We are more used to seeing nature conveyed through
art than art conveyed through nature. The superiority of the natural
landscape to the painted one is foregrounded, and this is achieved
not only through those references to art which suggest its brittle
and static qualities – the landscape, we are told, is 'less brittle' and
'ageless', but also in the way in which the poet intensifies the affinity between the landscape and the human emotions, setting 'cloud
bruises' and 'black moods' against healing sunlight and golden
evenings. Nature effectively ministers to the human heart as its
beauty is converted into images which interact with the pain of
lived experience. No painter can achieve the variations of light on
landscape which the poet sees from the window. The mood-changes
which are indicated by the light are also the stuff of life itself; a
oneing of the human to the landscape which cannot be substan-
tially realised. However, art is not rejected as a conveyer of the
numinous, even though the painterly qualities of the scene might
be referred to in terms of brittleness and stasis. While the limitations of art are recognised, the image of the artist as creator is able
to convey a sense of the creative powers of God:

> All through history
> The great brush has not rested,
> Nor the paint dried; yet what eye,
> Looking coolly, or, as we now,
> Through the tears' lenses, ever saw
> This work and it was not finished?

Whereas the project of the artist, then, has conventionally been
to create an image of nature, here art itself serves as an image, not
just for nature, but for God. God becomes the cosmic artist whose
work, paradoxically, is never completed (the great brush has not
rested) but is always finished. This is what Coleridge would call
the Primary Imagination,[43] here the work of the 'great brush',
which inspires the artist in turn to create, and to approach God as
a creative being. The effect on those who see the painting, or read
the poem, is to 'bring[ing] them nearer the primary imagination
themselves'.[44] In this way the idea of Art can mediate God, can stand
both as an image of nature and of God. We might ask whether art
as it exists in its more 'brittle' or 'static' mode of 'works of art' can

do the same. We might also want to ask whether the subject matter of a painting has any bearing on its ability to mediate a sense of the numinous.

We could explore these ideas by considering a poem on a religious painting which first appears in *Laboratories of the Spirit*:[45] 'The Annunciation by Veneziano'. The poem is not accompanied by the painting in either of the editions in which it appears. Clearly, Thomas believes it can stand alone. It is, however, a fair account of Veneziano's rendering of a traditional and climactic incident in the life of the Virgin. Thomas conveys, in rather general terms, perhaps, the main features of the painting: the winged figure, the Virgin, the space between. He neglects to give the sense of the background which, in the painting, is rather heavy. Instead of the weighty planes of the architecture, his imagery suggests space and distance which creates a peculiar perspective for the reader, suggestive of otherworldliness. The text itself demands the reader's complete attention, controlling the gaze in the manner of a painting rather than a text; the irregular shape on the page, disrupting the reader's expectation, dictates that the reader's eye travels over the surface of the page in an exaggerated manner, paralleling the action of the eye scanning a picture:

> The messenger is winged
> and the girl
> haloed a distance
> between them

This unconventional layout encourages the reader to take a steady, meditative pace through the first four lines: the winged messenger, the haloed girl, the distance between them, are all registered comfortably. Then the sudden density of the next three lines must be negotiated:

> and between them and us
> down the long path the door
> through which he has not

Thomas creates a relationship between readers and painting which is rather like that of the donor to many medieval paintings: the readers, that is, have become a part of the action of the painting. They are invited not only to observe, but to realise to themselves, almost in the manner of affective meditation, the action of the scene.

Thomas suggests that a relationship exists between the reader and the world of the poem. He invites his readers to contemplate 'distance'; not just the distance of 'the long path' between 'them and us', or even the distance in time between the two worlds of painting and reader, but also, perhaps, distance in modes of belief too: 'the door/ through which he has not/ come' indicates how far the modern world has distanced itself from the events symbolised in the painting; the angel, he implies, has not come for us. Further contemplation is invited through echoes of Eliot's 'Burnt Norton' and the passage not taken, the door not opened, into the rose garden.[46]

By using such verbal echoes and not limiting himself to concrete images, Thomas frees himself to construct a further discourse. The ambiguities of the text allow him to describe the painting in a way that reveals, or at least suggests, the theological implications of the incarnation. The mystery of the virgin birth is sustained by the careful phrasing of certain lines which create an ethereal atmosphere, as in

> haloed a distance
> between them . . .

Here the arrangement of the words on the page, and the syntactical ambiguities, reinforce the impression of otherworldliness the poet has created, linking 'haloed' with 'distance' so that the characters and the distance appear to share the halo. This technique, by drawing attention to the 'holy' space between the Virgin and the angel, reinforces the nature of the virgin birth. The absence of human involvement (ironically the angel is normally represented as an adolescent male figure)[47] is assured by the weight given to the line:

> the door
> through which he has not
> come . . .

The image of the door has an emblematic significance, being a type for the Virgin Mary and signifying her perpetual virginity.[48]

A particular relationship is also implied between the Virgin and 'women' when it says:

> On his lips what all women
> desire to hear . . .

Thomas probably has in mind here the words of the angel to Mary: 'Hail, *thou that art* highly favoured, the Lord *is* with thee, blessed *art* thou among women' (Luke 1. 28, a phrase which merits further comment later). We might make the observation that Thomas not only reads but manipulates the symbolism in this painting, making it serve more than one purpose. For example, conventionally we would suppose that the angel is bringing the flowers to the Virgin, the presence of lilies in a painting of this period being a traditional symbol of her purity;[49] by suggesting that the flowers are being taken from her – and by playing on the idea of deflowering as involuntary sexual initiation – Thomas conveys with suitably medieval clarity the implications of the virgin birth.

We might accept, then, that in this poem art can stand as an image of God; that it can convey that sense of the numinous which we require. However, we must reconsider those lines which we looked at briefly above:

> On his lips what all women
> desire to hear

We have already said that Thomas has used verbal echoes to create a further discourse. We cannot ignore the verbal echoes which resonate from these lines. We have assumed that they refer to the words the angel speaks to Mary. However, the words 'what all women desire to hear' beg the question 'What is it that all women desire to hear?', and this sets up tantalising echoes of Chaucer. With a slight shock we realise how close this is to the question which pervades the tale of the Wife of Bath: What is it that all women desire?[50] The answer Thomas seems to offer to this question is that all women desire to hear that they are 'highly favoured'. The assumption is that women want men to favour them, to desire them. The Virgin Mary is the ultimately desired, even though the desire is qualified by the religious context. The sub-text, which reads the Ave as a 'type' of woman, identified closely with the Wife of Bath, suggests that ordinary women as an object of desire are an imperfect image of what the Virgin Mary is. This passage demonstrates clearly that myth which both suggests that woman is an imperfect realisation of the Ave, hence a figure of Eve, whose name was regularly interpreted in the Middle Ages as the inversion of Ave, and points towards the superior realisation of woman in the Virgin.

In our reading of 'The View from the Window' we commented on the distinctive perspective of the poem. But here an even more radical, what we might call a 'sliding', perspective is adopted. With considerable ingenuity, and no little daring, Thomas embraces in one succinct phrase those polar opposites which are inscribed in the mythology of woman and which we have observed in Thomas's reading of Woman; what Marina Warner calls the 'mighty span'.[51]

We are aware, of course, that Veneziano's painting belongs to an age of faith, and so we are not surprised that a reading can be produced which justifies the notion of art as a means of intimating a sense of the numinous. Even so, the use of sliding perspectives which undercut the positive reading is surprising, suggesting that things are not as simple as they seem.

We have already considered some of Thomas's poems about paintings which inhabit a tradition not particularly noted for any overtly religious treatment of its subjects. Those poems, from *Impressions* were anticipated by 'Woman Combing (Degas)' which first appeared, like the Veneziano, without benefit of an accompanying picture, in *Laboratories of the Spirit*.[52] Both poems are capable of standing alone, but the fascinating imagery that Thomas creates in 'Woman Combing (Degas)' produces in the reader an urgent desire to compare the poem to the painting, and it is therefore included here (Plate 7). (The poem is better appreciated, however, if it is read before turning to the painting.) Thomas's imagery totally dominates the actual subject of the painting, submerging the image of the woman combing her hair beneath an image of his own making.

A reader who does not know the painting might at first be incredulous, suspecting an over-imaginative reading on the part of the poet. On turning to the painting, however, we are astonished at the appropriateness of the observation, for the hair the woman is combing is quite extraordinary, flowing almost to the floor, and grasped in two hands in the manner of a cellist playing. The posture of the woman, and the cascade of hair glowing with the warm tones usually associated with the richly polished wood of the cello, fully justify the response of the opening lines:

> So the hair too,
>   can be played?

Thomas responds to the painter appreciatively:

> Painter,
> who with your quick
> brush gave us this silent
> music . . .

With a verbal equivalent of sleight of hand Thomas accomplishes a double transformation – in the hand of the painter the inanimate object which is the brush takes on a creative life of its own. It becomes the 'quick' brush, obviously in the sense that the Impressionist had to work quickly to catch the light; but the barely submerged archaic sense of the word – a sense preserved now only in religious ceremony – points us to the living force that flows through brush and painter and confronts us on the canvas. We barely perceive this religious undertone: the woman, simultaneously abstracted into, or perhaps merged with, the 'silent music', demonstrates Nemerov's thesis that the arts have a 'deep affinity with the sacred'.[53] Now 'The View from the Window', where we saw Thomas responding with both an emotional and an artistic sensitivity to landscape, provides a gloss. If we consider the 'great brush' of that poem and compare it with the 'quick brush' of the Impressionist we can see that Thomas is again demonstrating a Coleridgean view of the Imagination. In this overtly secular poem Thomas sees both himself as poet and Degas as artist as recreating, that is, as 'echoing', the primary imagination. Thus it is the nature of the experience, rather than the elusive religious content, which identifies the response as religious; the existential experience of the caught moment in which art, perhaps, has achieved something of, in Pater's phrase, 'the condition of music'.

The experience, however, is short-lived, for working against this almost mystical impression of the woman producing, or even being, the silent music, is the secular language of the 'abandoned' shift. The poem is held in the tension between the woman who, verging on the mystical, 'combs a sonata' from her hair and is a 'silent music', and the woman whose 'abandoned' shift and 'soft flesh' sound a different note, speak a different language, one which can 'tell us from what score she performs'.

The organisation of the poem is important in engineering this tension. We noted above how the poet began with the painting but moved quickly to an imaginative reading of his own. The poem then moves into abstract terms in which the woman disappears as a distinct and separate figure and reduces to a set of properties; in his interpretation she momentarily disappears, and the moment of heightened perception, is registered in

> this silent
> music, there is nothing . . .

The pregnant phrase holds our attention, and quivers on the brink of the imagination, as 'silent music' and 'nothing' transcend the actual ('at the height of our imagination', says Lawrence, 'we are religious'),[54] before returning sharply to the practical, technical appreciation of the painting; to the colour and light of the Impressionist and the concept of form and solidity in the soft flesh. This sense of solidity is not qualified by the 'light', nor by the language which here attempts to re-enact the style of the Impressionist. Rather, it is reinforced, even emphasised, by the pun on 'score', which grounds the woman firmly in self-consciousness.

This is religious poetry in the wider sense that Thomas himself defined in the Introduction: 'Roughly defining religion as embracing an experience of ultimate reality, and poetry as the imaginative presentation of such.' The moment when the woman has been elevated onto a transcendental plane is the moment of perception, the moment of 'ultimate reality', for the reader/viewer. Although there is a swift descent to the profane, the moment when the numinous was perceived justifies the notion that art can stand as an image for God.

The poems we have considered represent two different kinds of art which have appealed to Thomas, and which produce contrasting modes of interpretation. In the late medieval painting, 'The Annunciation: Veneziano', the painting signifies and creates a set of religious meanings which Thomas exploits; by contrast, the Impressionist mode, represented latterly by 'Woman Combing (Degas)', normally, expressly denies religious meaning in its surface texture. Thomas may read into the painting that religious symbolism which the genre rejects. Two of these poems, again from Between Here and Now, demonstrate the sort of games Thomas will play in creating his 'imaginative extended meanings'.[55] These are 'Monet: Rouen Cathedral, Full Sunshine', and 'Gauguin: The Alyscamps at Arles' (Plate 8). (Monet's Rouen Cathedral, Full Sunshine is not reproduced here.)

As Bazin has observed: 'Light was all that interested Monet.'[56] In order to capture all the possible effects of light on its façade, Monet painted twenty pictures of Rouen Cathedral. The particular picture which Thomas chose as the subject of this poem scintillates with light. The title is a celebration, replete with a sense of wonder. It is first of all a celebration of the human, but the painting is so expressive of light and luminosity that an association with the numinous seems inevitable. What we have here, then, is a painting which is religious in its subject matter almost incidentally, although Van der Leeuw, quoting Jacques Maritain, says:

> Thus did the great masters of the cathedrals build: 'They believed; and as they were so they did. Their work disclosed the truth of God, but without doing so purposely, and precisely because it did not do so purposely.'[57]

It is a representation of a church, but was of interest to the artist only for the effect of the light on its façade. However, in representing that light, Monet has in fact enhanced the religious quality of the painting, and the poet, having begun like Monet, with the façade, goes on to read the religious dimension for himself. We should note here that the title of the poem is an essential, integral part of the poem. Any reading of the poem must give full value to the title as the first line. When we do this, we realise that Thomas immediately turns away from the exterior – which Monet has positively enhanced – to the interior, abandoning the painting in the process. The reader is conveyed not only into the painting but into the depths of the cathedral. Having appreciated the exterior, which is made available to us only through the reproduction, we move to the interior made available through the poem.

> But deep inside

effects the transfer of our attention, not only from exterior to interior, but from the concrete to the spiritual. Thomas has manipulated a profound change of perspective, and created a space inside which he constructs a period of contemplation. The exterior of the cathedral as represented in the painting becomes a kind of icon which leads into meditation on more profound areas of faith.

The first stanza becomes a meditation on the effect of time on the statues in the cathedral; Thomas sees the erosion of the stone as an improvement on art, and this effect of time as involving God in the creative act. A complex metaphor grows out of the image of the 'chipped figures with their budgerigar faces'. The whimsical choice of 'budgerigar faces' might be appropriate to the Gothic[58] style of the carvings, but seems limited, until we see how, in the next stanza, it is generalised into more conventional bird imagery:

> There is
> a stone twittering in

> the cathedral branches
> The excitement of migrants
> newly arrived from a tremendous
> presence.

Now it becomes a flexible metaphor having not only the traditional associations of soul and spirit but of that 'presence' which we see elsewhere in Thomas's work:

> Ah, but a rare bird is
> rare. It is when one is not looking,
> at times one is not there
> that it comes.[59]

The 'migrants newly arrived' of the second stanza might literally be birds, often found in lofty cathedrals, or they might be angels or saints. They might even, as we have noted, represent the 'presence' from which they have come. Thomas skilfully manipulates the metaphor between these possibilities, keeping the reader aware of the literal and spiritual connotations, until at the end the reader is no longer an observer only; through the sliding perspectives of the poem the reader is actually confronted, or challenged, by a personal relationship with or response to the 'migrants':

> We have no food
> for them but our
> prayers. Kneeling we drop our
> crumbs, apologising
> for their dryness, afraid
> to look up in the ensuing
> silence in case they have flown.

The metaphor conveys the image of visitors feeding the birds with crumbs, but in associating the crumbs with 'our' prayers, Thomas changes the tenor of the metaphor so that it effectively literalises itself, becoming a comment on the 'dry' quality of our spiritual lives. (A dryness which might refer to the 'dark night of the soul' (deus absconditus) or to the prevailing modern 'death' of spirit.) In 'afraid to look up' there is again the sense of a delicately held moment of perception, of such fragility as will not survive the slightest distraction. This fleeting moment of communion realised in silence, and compensating for long periods of waiting, is a familiar image in Thomas's work. 'Sea-Watching' again provides a gloss on the situation:

> There were days,
> so beautiful the emptiness
> it might have filled,
>   its absence
> was as its presence . . .

Thomas has succeeded in conveying the reader/viewer from a place outside the painting into its deepest, most imaginative, interior. The realisation of that moment of perception of the Other renders this a religious poem.

'Monet: *Rouen Cathedral, Full Sunshine*' demonstrates Thomas's ability to develop a profoundly religious reading from a painting which is only religious in a secondary way.[60]

If we now consider his treatment of 'Gauguin: *The Alyscamps at Arles*' (Plate 8) we will see how he approaches what is in fact an uncompromisingly secular painting. The surface texture of this painting presents the reader/viewer with what is, in effect, a landscape with figures. Bazin states that the building in the background is in fact the ruins of the chapel of St-Honorat.[61] Thomas ignores this information; he is going to impose his own religious reading of the painting over the secular one of the artist, and decides to use the image of the building to represent a place of worship:

> Shining morning!
> A trinity of figures –
> coming from Mass? They
> have the stiffness of candles.

The short exclamatory opening phrase 'Shining morning!' sets a suitable tone of wonder, which might be a response to the subject of the painting, or to the achievement of the artist – a blurring of the source of inspiration which, Thomas recognises, is essential in experiencing the poem as religious. Interpreting the painting, the poet suggests that the figures might be coming from the Mass, and pursues this initial concept as most appropriate to his design. This is a carefully controlled poem. The sense of control and organisation is first noted in its appearance on the page. Where the majority of poems in *Impressions* are irregular, here we find four neatly arranged stanzas of four lines each. As it moves through the stanzas, the metaphor of the Mass develops the thought a step further. The first stanza expresses the elements of the pictorial composition in the language of religion, turning the three figures into symbols, or icons, for the Trinity, the Mass and the candles. Here Thomas makes the painting represent the sacrament of organised religion, and the rigidity of such religion is implied in the 'stiffness' of the candles. In the second stanza we find a binary opposition is set up. The century's 'convention', which is organised religion and the sacrament of the Church, is 'inside', a word which suggests containment and restriction, while 'out here' suggests space and freedom, and becomes a sacramental vision of nature. In this detail Thomas's flexible attitude to his images is demonstrated: where, in the last poem, the viewer was led from outside to inside the cathedral in order to experience the numinous, here the reverse is true. The sense of the numinous is ministered by nature as the stream becomes the 'living water' and the leaves 'bread'; the sacrament of the Church takes second place to the sacrament of nature. This is a reading of nature we might have expected Thomas to make, but in the third stanza he introduces yet another form of sacrament:

> over them have the crispness
> of bread. Art is a sacrament
> in itself. Now that
> the angelus is silent . . .

The angelus is silent because the moment of communion has been accomplished. In the painting (according to Thomas) the figures are leaving the Mass. But at the same time associations are set up which exercise the imagination, and while the reader has been encouraged to linger over the idea that art is a sacrament, verbal echoes come into play. 'Now that the angelus is silent' is a subordinate clause, the main clause being 'the brush-strokes go on/calling' which begins the following stanza. However it makes such a strong impact on the hearers that the links between Art and the angelus and sacrament and silence linger in the memory. The effect is two-fold: the idea that art is a sacrament, that is, it is capable of mediating God, is suggested, and also the possibility that the present age is a post-Christian age, and, therefore, that in the absence of any call

to worship, Art is the only sacrament available to the present generation. Wallace Stevens makes a similar point:

> The paramount relation between poetry and painting today,
> between modern man and modern art is simply this: that in
> an age in which disbelief is so profoundly prevalent or, if not
> disbelief, indifference to questions of belief, poetry and paint-
> ing, and the arts in general, are, in their measure, a compensation
> of what has been lost. Men feel that the imagination is the next
> greatest power to faith: the reigning prince.[62]

Thomas's apprehension of the painting, then, begins within the
canvas, centred on the elements of its artistic composition. However,

Art is a sacrament
in itself.

stands as a complete sentence and we become aware that a more
distanced position is being taken. It is the painting as artifact which
is now the object of contemplation:

> the brush-strokes go on
> calling from the canvas's
> airier belfries
> to the celebration of colour.

The final stanza makes that outward gesture, which implicates
both viewer and reader in the action of the painting, demanding a
response to the great sacrament of Art. When this happens the
figures in the painting share with the reader/viewer the sublime
moment. For the figures in the painting the silence of the angelus
registers the completion of the feast. For the viewer or reader, the
angelus is silenced not only by the intervening years, but also by
the increasing secularism of our time. Only the brush-strokes continue to call to the celebration of colour. But as we have seen in
'Woman Combing (Degas)', Thomas associates brush-strokes with
the secondary imagination, the echo of God; the canvas itself, literally the 'stuff' of art, becomes the 'airier belfries' replacing those
of the church. We may, then, legitimately infer that the call of this
'angelus' is to the recognition of the Other, which is at the heart of
the response to all beauty.

Thomas's poems regularly contain echoes of medieval and Renaissance religious art. He is clearly familiar, for example, with the practice of including the Donors in the picture, which identified them not only with the painting as artifact, but with the painting as experience. We are not surprised, then, to find that Thomas makes just such a gesture in his poem 'Veneziano: *The Annunciation*'. However, the similar experience applied to Impressionist and Post-impressionist paintings in 'Monet: *Rouen Cathedral, Full Sunshine*' and in the even more secular painting 'Gauguin: *The Alyscamps at Arles*' is not only surprising, but registers a high degree of creative thinking on the part of the poet.

Having considered Thomas's reading of a single image, here 'woman', and of a variety of images drawn from art, we can now move on to reading some of his images of God. Drawing on the experience we have now gained we may expect to find multiple readings of a single image between which the reader is required to arbitrate. We shall anticipate sliding perspectives which continually force us to adjust our own perspectives, and we will not be able to limit our reading to those poems which are conventionally religious. We shall turn now to a consideration of Thomas's use of landscape.

3

Landscape as Image

And God saw everything that he had made, and, behold, *it was* very good.

Gen 1: 31

... cursed *is* the ground for thy sake; in sorrow shalt thou eat *of* it all the days of thy life;

Thorns also and thistles shall it bring forth to thee; and thou shalt eat of the herb of the field;

In the sweat of thy face shalt thou eat bread, till thou return unto the ground; for out of it wast thou taken: for dust thou *art*, and unto dust shalt thou return.

Gen 3: 17–19

The problems of reading landscape as a metaphor for God are numerous; the polar opposites have already been defined, for example, by Wordsworth and Tennyson respectively, in 'nature never did betray/The heart that loved her',[1] and 'Nature red in tooth and claw'.[2] The first quotation sees Nature working to the benefit of the responsive soul. Wordsworth makes no qualifications. A sense of order prevails, intensified by the word 'never'. In so far as Nature provides an adequate metaphor for God, he is represented as a God of order and compassion. The second quotation, however, notes the aggression built into the natural order, and a conflicting image emerges, an image of a fierce God who is indifferent to suffering. Neither can be true in isolation from the other. Somehow these extremes have to be negotiated; Thomas has approached the problem in a number of ways. He has written poems which identify with each of these positions – for example, 'The Bright Field'[3] might be said to epitomise the imaginative, Wordsworthian, stance towards Nature, while 'Rough'[4] is as harshly realistic as the lines from Tennyson. This dual approach has created problems for some readers, who see it as reflecting an instability in Thomas's faith, rather than, as I see it, his determination to explore all possible responses. Indeed, the restriction of the possible readings of Nature to the two mentioned above would seem to Thomas to be simplistic in the extreme; while he acknowledges in his own work these polar opposites, he is aware of many shadings in between. The very long poem 'The Minister'[5] not only meets Thomas's need to find a space in which he can adequately explore the oppositions, but also serves to demonstrate the variety of positions which Thomas recognises and will continue to pursue in later volumes. Unusually for Thomas, the poem takes the form of a 'play for voices', which gives the poet the opportunity to dramatise the variety of responses it is possible to make towards landscape and nature, and through them to God. He does not, however, offer the reader a series of clearly defined attitudes to nature, landscape and God. In a series of connected incidents which are, in the main, open-ended, the narrative reflects the complexity of the problem, and the readers become involved in the debate. They are challenged by statements which swiftly undercut their expectations; by inconsistencies in the voices, and perhaps more than anything else by the denial of an authoritative narrating voice. These strategies serve to illustrate the problematic nature of landscape, and demonstrate how landscape can function as a metaphor for the problematic nature of God. Even in this early work the denial of reader expectations operates in the mode of the *via negativa*, which Thomas adopts as a linguistic strategy. This gives a sense of coherence to the work, as it enacts and echoes linguistic-ally the theological approach to an understanding of God which is Thomas's preferred mode of interpretation. Through the many-voicedness of the text, Thomas implies an objective reality which is other than our interpretation of it, and through a series of conflict-ing readings of the same thing creates a metaphor for the whole problem of interpretation and understanding of anything, and, by extension the problem of saying anything about God.

The characters in the poem are required to make choices which are deeply engaged with the landscape. The text, then, does not present answers; it offers a number of views, partial and selective, through a series of voices, and occasionally a number of views within a single voice. It is the readers' task to arbitrate between the voices and to make their own decisions. This function of the text, to engage the readers in making choices, is paradoxical in that it both is, and is not, what we may expect of a religious text. Religion is about having and making choices, as Thomas reminds us else-where.[6] At the same time, most religious texts do find closure, a point at which writer, reader and religion are in agreement. The best we can find at the conclusion of this poem is a somewhat arbitrary rehabilitation of nature within a greater purpose.

The background which Thomas chooses to use for this debate is that of a bleak moorland. This concentrates the attention on harsh realities and precludes any tendency to sentimentalise nature. It is a landscape within which people live and work without reference to its attractions, associated traditions or God. A strong challenge is presented to the notion that these things are essential, valuable or even desirable; in a life as hard as that presented here, beauty, culture and religion may be dispensable luxuries. It is the strength of this antipathetic voice in a religious text which readers may find disturbing; and that, perhaps, is the point of the exercise. The value which the peasants – the word is Thomas's – set on this landscape is governed by how well it can supply their needs. They do not project any symbolism onto the landscape; it does not speak to them of God. It is a hostile world, and they in turn are hostile to ideas of God. This response of the peasants challenges those more traditional readings of landscape in which beauty is inscribed as an inherent quality. The peasants do not take note of any beauty, their pragmatism suggesting that such a reading is only a construct, what one of the characters, Job Davies, might have called 'a fad'. They read the landscape in economic terms, which results in the 'logic of the Smithfield' with hard people who 'treat their ministers as they treat their horses'. In this bitter little community God is restricted to the confines of the chapel, from which the people receive only such things as they choose. Through the peasants we find a partial reading of nature and of religion.

In this poem, to repeat, the relationship of the people to the landscape is a painful one. The problems they encounter daily are starkly presented; nowhere are they romanticised. The poem opens with the narratorial voice defining the difficulties:

> In the hill country at the moor's edge
> There is a chapel, religion's outpost
> In the untamed land west of the valleys,
> The marginal land where flesh meets spirit
> Only on Sundays and the days between
> Are mortgaged to the grasping soil.

In this account of the nature of the land, the paucity of the soil, and the effort required to make a living, certain phrases stand out, suggesting more than the purely physical. The land is itself marginal, existing between the hill country proper and the valley. The demands of this land exert a grip on the people which is relentless, leaving little time or energy for the contemplation of spiritual things, hence the irony of the phrase 'The marginal land where flesh meets spirit'. This phrase may at first suggest to the reader a condition of spiritual wholeness, a mystical union between body and spirit, 'man' and nature, which is one possibility, but the notion is a fleeting one; the narrator deliberately undermines this reading and replaces it with its negative, suggesting not only the difficulty of keeping body and soul together but also the marginalising of religion itself – flesh meets spirit 'only on Sundays'. The reading slides from the Wordsworthian to the Tennysonian by the addition of that one phrase; physical hardship is reflected in spiritual exiguity. Vision interacts inevitably with the environment, so the people cannot be blamed if their vision is limited. It is worth noting that the long description of the land in this stanza is a subordinate clause; the main clause reads: 'In the hill country there is a chapel.' The chapel, then, is the subject, but it is overlooked because of the impact the description of the bleak landscape makes on the reader; the narrator identifies with the peasants, and as the voice re-enacts, in language, their experience it involves the reader in that experience too.

Although the narrator seems to identify with the peasants, the narratorial voice also takes a judgemental stance towards them. We are told that 'They chose their pastors as they chose their horses', and this is confirmed when the narrator's voice gives way to that of Job Davies:

> But ay, he must be young.
> Remember that mare of yours, John?
>
> Too old when you bought her; the old sinner
> Had a taste of the valleys first
> And never took to the rough grass
> In the top fields.

Davies has learned a kind of wisdom from the moor, a crudely unsentimental attitude which is necessary to, or one way of, survival; he defines the mare as an 'old sinner' (p. 21) because she is unable to adjust to the rigours of life in the hills. His use of religious language here indicates a mind-set in which values have been adjusted – we might even say distorted – to reflect experience. But this he has learned from the moor. Comparably flawed is the reading of the landscape offered by Buddug (p. 25), whose language has no religious reference:

> I know the place, under the hedge
> In the top meadow; it was where my mam
> Got into trouble, and only the stars
> Were witness of the secret act.

Here the language of the girl is played off against language of a higher plane, not so much biblical as Shakespearean. The romance in the echoes of 'I know a place where the wild thyme grows,'[7] and the witness of the stars, are quickly undercut by the pragmatic attitude of the girl:

> They say her mother was the same.
> Well, why not? It's hard on a girl
> In these old hills, where youth is short
> And boys are scarce; and the ones we'd marry
> Are poor and shy. But Job's got money,
> And his wife is old. Don't look at me
> Like that, Job; I'm trying to listen
> To what the minister says.

Buddug's soliloquy takes place in chapel, but the only indication we have of this comes in the phrase 'I'm trying to listen to what the minister says'. This, of course, merely alerts the reader to the ineffectiveness of the religious language of the minister on this occasion. For Buddug nature does nothing to enhance life or to inspire 'finer' feelings. Nor is religion enlisted in rationalising her response. As with Davies, survival is all that is aspired to, and the enforced discipline of nature is more effective in shaping lives than the self-imposed discipline of chapel-going. Where Davies wrests life into conformity with the harsh conditions in order to survive, Buddug, by contrast, manipulates the situation so that it works to her advantage.

The narratorial voice recognises the partial reading of the moor that the peasant makes:

> And Job was right, but he forgot,
> They all forgot that even a pastor
> Is a man first and a minister after.

The narrator can see the flaw in the wisdom Job has acquired.

Thomas often appears to look back to a time when 'man' and nature seemed to coexist in harmony; a time when man was close to nature and to God. But it is not always the Christian God who holds together the culture and creates order in life. The voice of the narrator takes on the tones of Job Davies to illustrate the breakdown in this alternative order:

> Harvest! harvest! the oats that were too weak
> To hold their heads up had been cut down
> And placed in stooks. There was no nonsense
> Plaiting the last sheaf and wasting time
> Throwing sickles. That was fad of Prytherch
> Of Nant Carfan; but the bugger was dead.
> The men took the corn, the beautiful goddess,
> By the long hair and threw her on the ground.

Here Thomas recognises that pagan ritual, through its ceremony and gaiety, could give more significance to life than the cold pragmatism into which the religion of these people has degenerated. The exclamations with which the lines open suggest joy and celebration, but the voice soon degenerates into the tones of Job Davies, with his coarse language and the logic of the Smithfield. The practices of their ancestors which might have helped them to retain a sense of mystery and awe in the face of nature have not just been neglected; nature, in the form of the beautiful goddess, has been abused and insulted.

Those individual voices which we have considered so far have been relatively uncomplicated. They have reinforced the image of the character Thomas wishes to convey to the imagination of the listeners, and identified their attitude to the landscape. Thus the voice of Job Davies is recognisable by his consistent use of bad grammar, a coarse mode of expression and colloquial diction. Davies's relationship to people is the same as his relationship to nature – it is exploitative and, as the narrator says, uses 'the logic of the Smithfield'. The attitude ascribed to Buddug is different only in degree. For her the hills militate against her finding economic security 'It's hard on a girl/ In these old hills, where youth is short/ And boys are scarce; and the ones we'd marry/ Are poor . . .' Nature is reduced for Buddug to the hedge in the top meadow where her adulterous relationship with Davies will, she hopes, secure her future. Both of these voices are consistent in themselves; their reductive attitude to the landscape is reflected in their reductive attitude to God; we find Davies responding to the minister's challenge:

> Adultery's a big word, Morgan: where's your proof?
> . . . .
> Take a word from me and keep your nose
> In the Black Book, so it won't be tempted
> To go sniffing where it's not wanted.

In their reading of landscape the peasants do not find God at all; but neither do they find God in the chapel. However, these voices occupy only a marginal place in the narrative.

The voice of the minister is much more complicated. He introduces himself, somewhat pompously, as 'The Reverend Elias Morgan, B. A.' (p. 23). He came, he says, 'In April':

> It was the time when curlews return
> To lay their eggs in the brown heather.

We might suppose from this that he is a man who has a close relationship with the natural world; that this voice is going to be set against that of the peasants, representing a positive stance against their negative one. But in fact, this voice says:

> But I didn't even know the names
> Of the birds and the flowers by which one gets
> A little closer to nature's heart.

The sliding perspective reveals further possibilities through the 'negative way'; it challenges the reader, presenting an image of the minister as someone who has an intimate knowledge of nature, only to negate the impression immediately.

This voice has already said that when the minister arrived in the hill country,

It was the time when curlews return.

It has demonstrated a countryman's awareness of nature: the voice recognises the bird, knows its name, recognises its song and is familiar with its habitat. Similarly, later in the poem, the same voice says that a thrush sang in a cypress morning and evening ('early and late'). This voice recognises the bog cotton, and, paradoxically, engages with the language of nature to express the attractions of the town:

> And the girl in the green blouse,[8]
> Fresh as a celandine from the spring meadows,

It is the 'celandine' which draws our attention to an awareness of nature on the part of the speaker in these lines; the name of the flower has been chosen deliberately. (If the choice had been the anticipated one, 'fresh as a daisy', it would have registered as mere cliché, and clearly been 'in character'.) How, then, can we reconcile the differing points of view registered in this voice, and what is the purpose of this inconsistency? One approach might be to suppose the text to be uttered retrospectively: that the minister is speaking from a position of acquired knowledge, but this may be to expect something of the text which it cannot supply. There is nothing in the narrative to suggest that the minister ever won his 'long fight with the bare moor', and to anticipate this is to read the text as a realist fiction. In introducing himself, then, it seems to me that the voice of the minister is taking on a dual function, like that of a Greek chorus. He is introducing his own character objectively, complete with faults and failings, and this avoidance of the snares of realist fiction is significant for Thomas's religious project.[9]

This voice is, in effect, both the narrator's voice and the minister's voice; we can hear the narrator's voice informing the minister's voice. And the narrator, in using his own language to express a position which he ascribes to the minister, is able to juxtapose the narrative position with a contrasting understanding of nature, thus giving the reader/listener once more the responsibility of choosing between them. The difficulties of reading landscape as a metaphor for God are thus crystallised.

The minister's voice, then, reveals that he is aware of the gaps in his education which are going to make life difficult for him:

> my knowledge
> Would have been complete, had it included
> The bare moor, where nature brooded
> Over her old inscrutable secret.
> But I didn't even know the names
> Of the birds and the flowers by which one gets
> A little closer to nature's heart.

This makes a strong contrast with the acute observation and precise denotation of plants and birds which we shall see the narrator displaying:[10] a careful and appreciative observation of, and interaction with, nature which will not only underline the deficiencies in Morgan's position, but through the textual interfacing will alert us to the literariness of the text we are reading.

The relationship of the young minister to nature is a problematic one. For him nature has 'an old inscrutable secret', and he also believes that through a knowledge of birds and flowers one gets 'A little closer to nature's heart'. But as we have seen, his voice is inconsistent, and closely informed by that of the narrator. We may expect him to attempt to resolve the place of nature in the scheme of things, but because of the chorus-like effect of the voicing we cannot be sure. Having revealed something of the minister's alienation from nature through his confessed ignorance of the names of things, Thomas reiterates this alienation in the image of the minister's house:

> Unlike the others my house had a gate
> And railings enclosing a tall bush
> Of stiff cypress.

The house is firmly separated from the moor by the gate and the railings (p. 24). (This is an image not only of self-protection but also of control and of imposition upon nature that Thomas will return to again and again.)[11] It represents for Thomas not only a futile setting of the will against nature, but also a failure to interact with and enjoy the natural world.

This is emphasised by the rigidity of the 'tall bush of stiff cypress' which seems to be the only thing allowed to grow inside the railings. However, the minister's relationship to nature is complicated still further, and perhaps unexpectedly, by his religion. The remaining lines of the paragraph demonstrate the point. In view of the minister's acknowledgement that through the birds and flowers 'one gets/ A little closer to nature's heart' we might anticipate a sacramental attitude to nature. Instead, resistance to pleasure is manifested in his response to the thrush's singing, and in the conflicting language in which it is expressed. The minister says that the thrush takes the tall bush as its 'pulpit'; so he, like Job Davies, uses his own, religious, language set, but he fails to make the connection between the pulpit and the proclamation of the word of God. He uses the cliché of the bird singing in praise of God,[12] but fails to see its significance. The conflict in his language demonstrates that, like his parishioners, the minister 'lost the parable and found the story' – or, as Eliot says, 'we had the experience but missed the meaning'.[13]

The narrator will tell us that 'God is in the throat of the bird' (p. 20); but the minister is beset by Calvinistic fears. Surely it is a pantheistic, pagan idea, that God is in the throat of the bird? The theory is both attractive and a threat to his faith. But it is not only a 'pagan' theory. It is a distinctly orthodox, non-puritanical sensibility which is being registered here (cf. Hopkins, 'The Windhover' – 'my heart in hiding stirred for a bird' – where the Jesuit happily sees Christ in the perfection of the bird).

Speaking of this sensibility Barrett[14] says:

> In the Divine Comedy the whole of nature is merely a canvas upon which the religious symbol and image are painted. Western man has spent more than five hundred years in stripping nature of these projections and turning it into a realm of neutral objects which his science may control . . . Protestantism unveiled nature as a realm of objects hostile to the spirit and to be conquered by puritan zeal and industry. Thus Protestantism, like science, helped in the despiritualisation of nature, emptying it of all the symbolic images projected on it by the human psyche.

The idea of God present in nature is the tune which 'John Calvin never heard' and it is a tune which makes 'The Book's black letters[15] dance'. The compression in this line invites a number of readings. The pejorative rendering of 'black' suggests an implied criticism of the book, or at least a negative association.[16] Simultaneous readings of 'dance' must also be made – either the letters 'dance' because the minister is distracted by the bird's song and does not concentrate, or the letters of the book 'dance' as though for joy as the bird's song rehabilitates the word of God in nature. Again the voice of the narrator can be heard informing that of the minister, rendering the text unstable.

Where the peasants are indifferent to nature, whether recognised in a Christian or pagan mode, the minister is afraid. Fear of nature, fear of the pagan, fear of ceremony and symbolism, burden the minister with guilt. The sunlight is a new temptation, and in a telling phrase he says: 'I closed my eyes and went on with my sermon.' Like the railings around the house, the closed eyes are an attempt to protect himself from the reality which is nature; but where the railings give protection from a nature which is threatening, the closed eyes give protection from a nature which is seductive. Morgan's resistance to nature is underlined by the voice of Davies speaking in his own uncouth language:

> You who never venture from under your roof
> Once the night's come; the blinds all down
> For fear of the moon's bum rubbing the window.

Davies's language demonstrates that he has recognised the fear of sensuality in Morgan, and registers his contempt.

There are moments when Morgan seems to accept the sensuality of nature, the moor in its 'moods of softness when the white hair/ of the bog cotton is a silk bed/ for dreams to lie on' (symbolic images projected on it by the human psyche);[17] but, where the peasants have a selective response to religion and nature, so he has a selective relationship with nature, controlled by his subjective responses. His brief acceptance of the moor's beauty is very closely connected with an act of kindness he has received. As Morgan goes to bed 'happy for once' the moon too is mellowed, softening the 'moor's harshness'. He seems to be on the brink of a discovery, and determines that 'Tomorrow will be different'. But when he wakes to 'the ancestral fury of the rain/ spitting and clawing at the pane' the resistance is still there. As the poem progresses Thomas uses a variety of means to demonstrate the minister's alienation from nature. Where a woman had planted some flowers, finding consolation in nature, Morgan pulls them up and sprinkles cinders there instead, in a reversal of the old prophetic promise to give 'beauty for ashes'.[18] As the seasons revolve and August brings a holiday, Morgan is found at the seaside, not being restored by nature, but walking 'the smooth Pavements of Aber'. Later, with 'the old pallor' back in his cheeks, we read:

> In his long fight
> With the bare moor, it was the moor that was winning.

As time proceeds, nature itself becomes a depressing metaphor for Morgan's life, reflecting in terms of its landscape the time before he came to this place, and the time that lies ahead:

> Morgan was part of the place now; he was beginning
> To look back as well as forwards:
> Back to the green valleys, forward along the track
> That dwindled to nothing in the vast moor.

Morgan does not find his answers. He does not succeed in making sense of nature. His life, like the track, dwindles to nothing on the vast moor.

The peasants read the landscape as a powerful, negative force to which they must adapt; but this leads them to marginalise God. For them landscape represents a God who is indifferent to them. If the peasants read God at all it is as nature first and then as an irrelevant superstructure. For Morgan it is the landscape which must be marginalised, because its attractions are seductive and threaten his relationship with God. Morgan does not see nature as 'red in tooth and claw', but neither does he have the freedom required to embrace Wordsworth's premise that 'nature never did betray/ The heart that loves her'.[19] For Morgan, nature might very well betray him into compromising his faith. It is in the problem of the moor that Morgan is lost. It offers him no fulfilment. Morgan fails to read God (as the narrator reads God) as positive, mediated through nature. He reads God as set over against nature. Morgan's failure is therefore different from that of the peasants, and may be worse, since he has the possibility of integrating the two positively where they do not.

The concept of 'dwindling' is enacted in the form of the poem itself. It does not move towards closure, to a consensus on the relationship between man, God and nature. Having set the negative of the moor against the negative of Morgan's religion, it has effectively set nature against God. 'Man' (and the reader) must somehow try to arbitrate between the two.

An intimation of a possible solution is hinted at in the lines:

> He never listened to the hills'
> Music calling to the hushed
> Music within . . .

The narrator in his omniscient mode, resorts to the philosophy of the Romantics as he offers yet another way of reading nature. We are reminded, perhaps, of Coleridge:[20]

> so shalt thou see and hear
> The lovely shapes and sounds intelligible
> Of that eternal language, which thy God
> Utters, who from eternity doth teach
> Himself in all, and all things in himself.

Or maybe of Wordsworth:[21]

> And I have felt
> A presence that disturbs me with the joy
> Of elevated thoughts; a sense sublime
> Of something far more deeply interfused,
> Whose dwelling is the light of setting suns,
> And the round ocean and the living air,
> And the blue sky, and in the mind of man:
> A motion and a spirit, that impels
> All thinking things, all objects of all thought,
> And rolls through all things.

However, for Morgan it is not to be; where for the Romantics the mind was enlarged and refined by their apprehension of nature, for Morgan the experience of dwindling we have already noted is all that is available to him. In the most scathing of all his rebukes to Protestantism, Thomas shows that it is the narrowness of Morgan's religion that has deprived him of a positive engagement with nature, and thus with God:

> Protestantism – the adroit castrator
> Of art; the bitter negation
> Of song and dance and the heart's innocent joy –

The sense of restriction and spiritual deprivation echoes that of the peasants who are 'mortgaged to the grasping soil'.

Most of what we know of the peasants and the minister comes from the narrator. The peasants, as expressed in their own voices, are consistent, but are placed at the edge of the narrative. The narrating voice sometimes identifies with the peasants and sometimes takes an omniscient stand, which suggests that this voice recognises the problem and can resolve it. The minister carries a larger share of the narrative; he represents a more complicated reading of landscape as a metaphor for God and, perhaps as a consequence of this fact, his voice is inconsistent. Yet the inconsistency which the portrait of the minister dramatises is containable, as we have seen, inside the frame of an authoritative understanding – here, that of the omniscient author. The peasants and the minister, then, in their own voices, register a kind of stability. In striking contrast, the narrator's voice is seriously unstable, and unreliable in a way very different from that of his protagonist, and it is to an examination of the narrator's voice that we now turn.

The voice of the narrator is impersonal and the land and its inhabitants are, in the early stanzas, observed from a slight distance. However, this voice has already influenced the readers' perception of the situation in a number of ways. The resistance of the peasants to religion is inscribed in the language of the first stanza, which uses pioneering terms – 'religion's outpost', 'untamed land'. The narrator's voice now influences reader response in a different way:

> This is the land of green hay
> And greener corn ...

The opening words of this stanza encourage the reader to anticipate a green, perhaps romantic, world, a notion as swiftly undercut as by the opening words of 'The Waste Land' – 'April is the cruellest month'.[22] Things are not what they seem. When the green is that of corn and hay that has failed to ripen, there is little cause for joy in the 'green' land. The anaphora in the last three lines of the stanza enables the narrator's voice to work ironically, dispelling any sentimental attitude the reader may have to nature. 'This is the land where they burn peat' – the statement is again qualified by the lines that follow. The exposition again takes on the form of a *via negativa*; we are allowed to suppose that things are what they seem, that they fit in with our preconceived ideas, then a strong negative revision must be made before we move on:

> This is the land where they burn peat
> If there is time for cutting it,
> And the weather improves for drying it,
> And the cart is not too old for carrying it
> And doesn't get stuck in the wet bog.

Far from presenting a sentimental picture, the slow reiteration and heavy rhythms of the knowing voice suggest the kind of bitter stoicism with which the peasants endure their labour.

Sometimes language and syntax suggest meanings which may be applied to the people as much as to the land which they try to cultivate:

> This is the land where men labour
> In silence, and the rusted harrow
> Breaks its teeth on the grey stones.

Here, in the personification of the rusted harrow, we feel that the men too are being broken, and the echoes of Ecclesiastes[23] in the rhythm and language of these lines serve only to emphasise the futility of the effort and the hardship of the life. Biblical echoes and religious language are used in a number of different ways in this text, but, with one significant exception, never promote an explicitly religious point of view. Here, the religious undertones serve to emphasise difficulties; elsewhere they are used ironically, undermining a religious response. Alternatively, religious language demonstrates the peasants' indifference to, or ignorance of, the Scriptures. It is for the reader to decide if, and how, religious language can work, and how it can be used appropriately, in such a climate. Indeed, the problem of language persists throughout that part of the text which is focused through the narrator.

The narrator does not offer a single or consistent view of nature within that portion of the text which he speaks; in the third stanza the valleys are momentarily contrasted with the hill country, but the narrator's voice, as we have seen, swiftly undercuts the favourable impression:

> Below the valleys are an open book
> Bound in sunlight; but the green tale
> Told in its pages is not true.

In the tension between appearance and reality in the landscape, resolution is found only in the way of negation, and 'appearance' is judged unfavourably in terms of fictionality. The phrase 'the valleys are an open book' is misleading in itself, for it encourages the presumption that the scene is transparent, when 'the green tale' is in fact a fiction. Elsewhere, the indifference of nature to moral laws

is clearly registered in, for example, 'the unchristened wind' which
blows the preacher's words to pieces:

> 'Beloved let us love one another,' the words are blown
> To pieces by the unchristened wind
> In the chapel rafters . . .

This is the only occasion on which the words of the Bible are quoted
directly and allowed to stand without being distorted by irony. Yet
if the meaning of the text is not undermined on this occasion, the
text is undermined in its articulation. The words represent an ideal
which is challenged by actual circumstance. The image of words
being destroyed by elements which do not acknowledge a higher
power is a particularly striking evocation of the frailty of language
in collision with experience; of ideas in conflict with facts; the idea
of a God of love is challenged by the harsh reality of life. The image
is repeated later when the narrator informs us that while Morgan
preached, 'Out in the fir-tree an owl cried/ Derision on a God of
love'. (A reversal of this is seen in the reference to Luther throwing
his bible at the devil – here the sunlight.)

This conflict between the word in the book and the word uttered
is reiterated immediately. The word in the book is referred to now
as 'love's text'; again, the abstract is set against the concrete:

> love's text
> Is riddled by the inhuman cry

Here a simultaneous double reference encourages the listener to
respond to these lines as if they expressed all the pain of these suffering people, the 'inhuman cry' of their anguish fragmenting the
ideal of 'love's text'; but the inhuman cry is not that of the people;
it is the cry of the predatory buzzard. As with the 'unchristened
wind' and the owl's cry, it is nature itself, not human pain, which
is challenging the Word. It is

> the inhuman cry
> Of buzzards circling above the moor.

In the image of the text 'riddled by the inhuman cry', religious
language becomes 'a puzzle', and also riddled in the sense of 'shot
through with holes' reinforcing the earlier phrase 'blown to pieces'.

Early in this text, then, strong negative revisions deny the reader a firm position; the language of religion does not work, and the language of nature is not true. A direct conflict between words and the Word is illustrated in the antipathy between text and voice. The difficulty of 'saying' is focused, and begins to be explored in the remaining lines. Fictionality, tale-telling and a preoccupation with words and language are now foregrounded. Early paragraphs have acted like a preface to a novel, and the narrator as storyteller has given the poem the feel of a realist fiction. The first three paragraphs have set the scene. At the beginning of the fourth paragraph there is a shift of perspective as the scriptural text comes across with a sense of immediacy, and then there is an abrupt shift in the timescale as well, as the narrator's voice intervenes. A curious affinity with George Eliot[24] results:

> Come with me, and we will go
> Back through the darkness of the vanished years
> To peer inside through the low window
> Of the chapel vestry,

In the line 'Come with me, and we will go' the voice sounds as stable and authoritative as anything we find in George Eliot. The relationship between the voice and the 'we' of the text seems quite clear: the author/poet/narrator will conduct the reader/listener through the experience of the poem. But an omniscient author needs a consistent voice throughout a work, and must seem to be in complete control of the point of view, a point of view which is shared with the reader. However, this authorial voice is not consistent, and the author/reader relationship soon breaks down. On page 21, the narrator's voice at first takes the reader into his confidence: 'Did you notice the farm on the hill side?' The voice also raises questions on behalf of the reader: 'What has that to do with choosing a minister?' it asks, and answers itself: 'Nothing, nothing.' As we move on to consider the 'choosing of the minister' further complexities emerge.

Thomas uses the order of the seasons as a controlling frame for his treatment of the minister; the seasons not only follow the minister's experiences with the hill people, but also create a metaphoric pattern of his life-span, as if his arrival in April were in some way also his birth. This is registered when the deacons, heads together choosing their new minister, are represented as a group of farmers huddled over the delivery – as in parturition – of some farm animal (p. 22). A sense of the momentous is created, as the language of advent merges the biblical images of darkness[25] with images of Yeats's 'The Second Coming'.[26] These apocalyptic passages prepare the way for Thomas's introduction of the minister. The bald facts of the daily life of the hill farmer are reiterated between:

> Thick darkness is about us, we cannot see
> The future, nor the thin face
> Of him whom necessity will bring . . .
> But we can see the faces of the men
> Grouped together under the one lamp,
> Waiting for the name to be born to them
> Out of time's heaving thighs.

The image which is created in this paragraph is significantly a painterly one, lit from the centre in the manner, perhaps, of Caravaggio. The central image represents the human dimension, the men 'grouped' together under the one lamp. But fused with this image are other, half-realised images; images which suggest the cattle-shed not only of the Welsh hill-farm but also of the Nativity. 'They choose their minister as they choose their horses . . .' The anticipated arrival is that of the minister, but it might be the birth of an animal or, coloured by the Yeatsian language, of something Other and far more portentous. The minister himself is reduced to a 'thin face' and a 'name'. ('Waiting for the name to be born to them' raises the whole problem of language and of naming, and in the implicit context of the Nativity even of 'naming' the Other.) Various language sets foreground various possible readings. The passage juxtaposes the human and the animal, the mundane and the biblical, and no particular reading has precedence over another.

In the first line the omniscient voice falters, and the relationship between the narrator and the reader becomes confused. Is the 'we' still that of the narrator/reader relationship of 'Come with me and we will go'? The situation is complicated further when we read: 'But we can see the faces of the men.' In the first part of this paragraph the 'we' seems to refer to figures who exist within the text – 'thick darkness' surrounds them. But in the last part there has been a change of perspective. The 'we' who can 'see the faces of the men/ Grouped together under the one lamp' are external to the projected image or even to the text. Like the minister's, the narrator's voice begins to read like the chorus in Greek drama, acquiring a surprising flexibility.[27]

In the face of its increasing instability and loss of control as the narrative proceeds, readers must continually adjust their perspective. We have already noted how the apparently stable authorial voice addressed the reader earlier, in the lines 'Come with me and we will go', and we saw that the relationship between the narrator and the reader at that point seemed quite clear. If we pursue this feature of the text we find that the voice becomes increasingly ambiguous, eventually requiring a very careful reading to follow its intricacies. This linguistic instability perfectly focuses the various attempts the poem makes to reconcile the opposed and opposing faces of landscape. (We shall see how these sliding perspectives manifest themselves.)

The problems of the relationship of the narrator to the 'we' or the 'you' of the text become even more difficult as the poem proceeds:

> Did you dream, wanderer in the night,
> Of the ruined house with the one light
> Shining; and that you were the moth
> Drawn relentlessly out of the dark?

Now the voice is addressing the minister, and returns to its omniscient mode, qualified only by the question in the opening lines. The voice presumes to know the feelings of the minister, his fears and emotions, as they are registered in his dreams:

> And when you tried to cry out, the cry got stuck
> In your dry throat, and you lay there in travail,
> Big with your cry, until the dawn delivered you
> And your cry was still-born and you arose and buried it,
> Laying on it wreaths of birds' songs.

The two 'voices', as we now see them to be, complicate the text with grotesque images of birth and the inversions which arise as one image grows out of another. At first the minister was 'being born'; now he 'gives birth'. But his cry of resistance is stillborn and the dawn chorus becomes a symbol of mourning.

A short meditative passage of three lines follows, omniscient and full of foreboding:

> But for some there is no dawn, only the light
> Of the Cross burning up the long aisle
> Of night; and for some there is not even that.

This becomes a kind of meditative interlude, the religious language being used figuratively, but seriously; then a further change of mood occurs:

> The cow goes round and round the field
> Bored with its grass world, and in its eyes
> The mute animal hunger, which you pity,
> You the confirmed sentimentalist,
> Playing the old anthropomorphic game.
> But for the cow, it is the same world over the hedge.
> No one ever teased her with pictures of flyless meadows,
> Where the grass is eternally green
> No matter how often the tongue bruises it,
> Or the dung soils it

The ambiguous 'you' reappears. It is not clear who is being addressed, the 'wanderer in the night' of the earlier stanza or, as I think more likely, the reader. The pity of the 'confirmed sentimentalist' is misdirected. Animals do not worry or ask questions about the meaning of life. It is man who desperately needs an answer. The passage ends with a sombre expression of despair.

The multiple, sliding, perspectives, which it is possible to adopt in reading nature as a metaphor for God, preclude any kind of stability in the voice. God is like these things – and he is not. Again, the *via negativa* seems to be the only way out of the impasse. The paradox of a landscape which is at once beautiful and cruel, simultaneously benefiting and indifferent to humanity, is one that haunts Thomas; while his religious sensibility would like to see landscape as sacramental, his scrupulous honesty forces him to recognise other, opposed, readings. In this exploration of 'man's' relationship to his surroundings Thomas needs another voice, one which can register nature as not only indifferent and hostile but also sacramental. What we may not expect is that Thomas will use the same persona to register completely different points of view. But this is precisely what he does.

If we retrace our steps we notice how, as the poem proceeds, the language becomes increasingly rhetorical, until in the seventh paragraph, the narrator, apparently affected by his own rhetoric, allows a new, different voice to burst through the frame of the poem; at the heart of the poem a subjective response to nature is introduced:

> O, but God is in the throat of a bird . . .

Having already used the predatory buzzard as a negative image of God, the narrator now uses the songbird as a positive one: 'love's text/ Is riddled by the inhuman cry/ Of buzzards' is juxtaposed with 'God is in the throat of a bird'. In the image of the buzzard nature cannot be reconciled with God – the cry of the buzzard is a challenge to the word. In the image of the songbird, however, nature articulates God. Images for God have to be drawn from our experience, and the question of choice, of what we decide is an appropriate image, is fundamental. In the choice of an image or symbol we not only extend but also limit our apprehension of what is being symbolised. If we say that God is in the throat of a bird, meaning – as Thomas seems to here – a songbird, we are choosing one image of a bird in preference to another – the buzzard. We are choosing to make what seems to us to be a positive reading. But that is to ignore the image of the buzzard. In reading landscape as a metaphor for God, it is precisely this tension which engages Thomas, and forces him to use the *via negativa* as a medium of arbitration between two opposing readings. It is the *via negativa* which enables us to say that God both is, and is not, like a bird. This approach complicates the (apparent) simplicity of the readings formerly offered: those of a nature indifferent to humanity and therefore unable to mediate God, and of people who, in turn, are indifferent to nature.

In introducing the songbird as an image of God, then, the narratorial voice now introduces as a matter of urgency not only a God who is intensely present in nature, but also the possibility of an individual response to Him. Subjectivity is emphasised as the release of repressed emotion sounds in the narrator's voice:

> O, but God is in the throat of a bird;
> Ann heard him speak, and Pantecelyn.
> God is in the sound of the white water
> Falling at Cynfal. God is in the flowers
> Sprung at the foot of Olwen, and Melangell

Felt his heart beating in the wild hare.
Wales in fact is His peculiar home,
Our fathers knew Him.

The warmth in this voice contrasts strongly with the cold realism
of earlier stanzas. A strong affirmation of faith appears in the reiterated phrase 'God is in' – God is in the throat of a bird, in the
sound of the white water, in the flowers, in the wild hare; the
immanence of God in this localised landscape is emphasised by
the appeal to the Welsh folk memory, to the great hymn-writers
of the past and the figures of history and folklore. Greatly daring,
the narrator claims the possibility of a 'Welsh epiphany' – 'Wales in
fact is his peculiar home,/ Our fathers knew him.'[28]

Here the narrator claims that the voice of God which is the
'well kept secret' (p. 20) is in fact audible to everyone – the hymn-
writers and folk-heroes of Wales were familiar with it – and it is
most clearly heard in nature. This is a traditional reading of nature
already made familiar by the Psalms of David:

The heavens declare the glory of God,
and the firmament showeth his handiwork.
Psalm 19.1

But instead of employing a Hebrew thought-form, Thomas has
rooted the experience in the Welsh culture and offers it as an
immediate and accessible experience to the people of Wales in general and to these people in particular. Having demonstrated how
the harshness of nature has deadened the sensibilities of the peasants
to God, the narrator's voice is now making an eloquent plea on
behalf of nature and its ability to mediate God.[29]

But the representations of Welsh responsiveness to God and nature which Thomas has selected need to be examined closely.
Ann, Pantecelyn and 'the water at Cynfal' are all associated with
an almost mystical awareness of God – Olwen is a legendary figure
from *The Mabinogion*, and Melangell is an early Welsh saint. How,
then, are we meant to read this assembly of disparate figures? The
narrator appears to find nothing difficult or incongruous about them.
The figures from recent history, Ann Griffiths[30] and Pantecelyn[31]
were hymn-writers, and early Methodists; Morgan Llwyd of Cynfal[32]
was a Puritan who had been deeply influenced by the Quakers
and Jacob Boehme. Each has a flair for expressing a deeply personal

apprehension of God which rises out of a familiarity with the mystical. Yet the Methodism of Ann and Pantecelyn proves a problematical element: Calvinist influence, with its sharp opposition of (fallen) nature and grace, sits uneasily in their work with their presence as examples of those who heard God's voice in nature; they are not the most immediately obvious or even appropriate representatives of those who find God in nature. The nature they use as metaphor in their writing is often closer to the nature seen by the minister when trying to write his sermon than the nature here celebrated by the narrator.

Ann's most famous hymn, for example, ends with these lines:[33]

> Beth sy imi mwy a wnelwyf
>   Ag eilunod gwael y llawr
> Tystio'r wyf nad yw eu cwmni
> Yw cystadlu a Iesu mawr;
>   O am aros,
> Yn ei gariad ddyddiau f'oes.

> What can weigh with me henceforward
>   all the idols of the earth?
> One and all I here proclaim them,
> Matched with Jesus, nothing worth;
>   O to rest me
> All my life-time in His love!

Similarly in Pantycelyn's hymn *Cariad at Grist*, we read:[34]

> I gaze across the distant hills,
>   Thy coming to espy;
> Beloved, haste, the day grows late,
>   The sun sinks down the sky.

> Love that the sensual heart ne'er knew,
> Such power, such grace it brings,
> Which sucks desire and thought away
> From all created things.

Nature is commanded by Ann and Pantecelyn to the service of poetry, not as sacramental in itself but merely as the source of powerful metaphors to express something which is to them more urgent, more important. Thus we have Ann saying:

O blessed hour of rest from my labour, in my lot, in the midst of a sea of wonders with never a sight of an end or a shore; abundant freedom of entrance, ever to continue, into the dwelling places of the three in one, water to swim in, not to be passed through, man as God and God as man.[35]

(Verse translations of this hymn do not demonstrate the point as strongly as the paraphrase.)

It is clearly the paradox of the three in one which is engaging Ann's attention here, not a preoccupation with nature or with God in nature. Again, we find Pantecelyn saying:

> Tan y don yr wyf yn llefain
>   Mae mynyddau ar fy mhen,
> Haen ar haen sydd o gymylau
>   Duon rhyngof fi a'r nen
>
> Sunk beneath the waves I languish,
>   Whelming mountains weigh me down,
> Clouds that hide the face of heaven,
>   Layer on layer, above me frown.

In spite of the language employed, Pantecelyn, too, is preoccupied with something other than nature. Nature is used here as a metaphor for separation from God rather than as an indication of God immediately present.[36]

We may gather, then, that it is not for their sacramental approach to nature that these hymn-writers find a place in this paragraph, but for their acute perception of God and their own mystical natures. Morgan Llwyd, however, fulfils our expectations of one who heard the voice of God 'in the throat of a bird'.

The Rev. W. Meredith Morris says of Morgan Llwyd:

He communed with nature; he worshipped at her inmost shrine, and she repaid him by disclosing to him the secrets which she confides only to those who are called to be seers. In our opinion, he is the only Welsh writer who has penetrated to the eternal through the transient and gazed upon the face of the Ineffable.

And again:

It is the holy fellowship with Nature which the author so constantly maintained that makes him appear mystical.[37]

There is, in Morgan Llwyd, more than the nature mystic. There are facets of his character which one imagines would have great appeal for R.S. Thomas. According to R. Tudor Jones:[38]

> There is no escaping his burning concern for the spiritual life. No Welsh Puritan expressed that concern with greater vigour and brilliance than he did. . . . The promotion of true piety was the master concern of his life.
>
> Believing, for Llwyd, is receptive attention to what God says. 'Your first task is to be quiet and to silence absolutely every other noise in your heart . . . and think of nothing but God.' Man should seek of God 'the silent heart within . . . to sink down into thyself and so out of thy self into God thy root'.

(A further quotation from Morgan Llwyd, however, which seems particularly pertinent to a reading of 'The Minister' apostrophises the Welsh for 'lying in the bonds of falsehood on the bed of Babel, grazing in the devil's meadow to feed the flesh, without knowing the God who made them'.)[39]

It is little wonder that he finds a place in Thomas's pantheon. Morgan Llwyd, then, may represent that harmony between 'man', nature and God which Thomas sees as desirable, reinforcing the mysticism of Ann and Pantecelyn with an acceptance of Nature as mediator of God.

Thomas's inclusion of Olwen in this litany is even more radical. In 'the flowers sprung at the feet of Olwen',[40] Thomas is effectively transposing a secular myth into a Christian icon, and indeed, the paragraph from *The Mabinogion* which Thomas has in mind is not unlike some parts of the 'Song of Songs'.[41] It is a passage which, in appropriating nature as a metaphor for Olwen's beauty, absorbs the very beauty of Nature itself into her person:

> Yellower was her head than the flower of the broom, whiter was her flesh than the foam of the wave: whiter were her palms than the shoots of the marsh trefoil from amidst the fine gravel of the welling spring. Neither the eye of the mewed hawk, nor the eye of the thrice-mewed falcon, not an eye was there fairer than hers. Whiter were her breasts than the breast of the white swan, redder were her cheeks than the reddest foxgloves. Whoso beheld her would be filled with love of her. Four white trefoils sprang up behind her wherever she went; for that reason she was called Olwen.[42]

God is in the flowers

Thomas uses his typical mode of carefully curtailing line endings to make his point. 'God is in the flowers' reiterates the theme of God present in nature, but

God is in the flowers
Sprung at the foot of Olwen

embraces the whole of Welsh folklore and claims it as a revelation of God. However, the trefoils speak more of magic than of miracle, and Olwen's inclusion in this stanza is not justified by her personal response to nature. Rather, Olwen *is* nature, nature personified. We begin to see not only how hard Thomas has to work to appropriate these legends to his cause, but also how partial a reading of the nature/God debate they really are.

Melangell is hardly more convincing:

and Melangell
Felt his heart beating in the wild hare

The story of Melangell tells us that she hid a hare beneath her mantle in order to save it from the hounds of Brochfael Ysgithrog, Prince of Powys.[43] Melangell's act of compassion is interpreted by Thomas as her recognition that God is in all living things; while he does not manipulate her story, he gives it extended meaning or significance by applying an imaginative reading to it; her inclusion in this list is really based on the fact that she is a Celtic saint.

In drawing on these figures from Welsh history and culture, however, Thomas has made each of them available for a richly metaphoric treatment of the interaction between God and nature. This appropriation of Welsh culture is not so much a Christianising of the tales as an appeal to the peasants; if they cannot see God in nature as it appears around them, surely they might recognise him in the beauty of nature as presented in their own culture?

All these responses to nature, then, imaged in things Welsh, appear to register a spontaneous heartfelt cry, but we have seen how in some parts they are laboured and in others fragmented. The narrating voice offers a number of partial views of nature, none of which seems to appeal to the peasants. The negative tone which pervades the text seems to deny any means of imaging God; yet, paradoxically, there is in the range of positions taken up an awareness of inter-action between the self and the other as it is registered in nature, in God and also in religious language. Thomas tries to bring all these possibilities together in his list of those who, in their different ways, recognised or represented God. The list is a comprehensive one: Ann and Pantecelyn represent the Welsh Methodist tradition; Morgan Llwyd the nature mystic; Melangell is the Celtic saint and Olwen is almost an earth-spirit. Their unique Welshness is a crucial element in Thomas's project.

The various experiments which Thomas has made in voicing and the constantly shifting perspectives on nature, God and religious language operate both to affirm and to deny the adequacy of any one of them as a representation of God.

The text of 'The Minister' elaborates ways of seeing and speak-ing landscape. They all prove to be imperfect and inconsistent, the voice of the narrator focusing the conflict most directly. Few of Thomas's poems are as elaborate as this. In the shorter poems the oppositions and inconsistencies are largely maintained between the poems. We find that the narrating voice in these poems presents the peasants, the minister and other country dwellers as variously as the narrating voice in 'The Minister'. However, the expectations which the character of Job Davies could never fulfil are now projected onto the peasant, often represented by the figure of Iago Prytherch. (Prytherch is a composite of the peasant farmers whom Thomas knew in his various ministries, and the narrating voice is closely identified with that of the priest.) These expectations may seem at times to be unrealistic. In 'Soil',[44] for example, there is an appear-ance of harmony between the man and nature. Hands and feet, bones and blood are in intimate contact with the soil:

> This is his world, the hedge defines
> The mind's limits; only the sky
> Is boundless, and he never looks up;
> His gaze is deep in the dark soil,
> As are his feet. The soil is all:

The peasant seems to be not only integrated with the landscape but barely distinguishable from it. This might portend the most integral harmony between the man, nature and God, a condition hoped for but never realised in 'The Minister'; but the opening lines of this stanza are pregnant with criticism. 'The mind's limits' create a problem for the poet. He simply cannot accept the degree of unselfconsciousness manifested in the peasant. It is the poet who recognises and articulates the symbolism in the spilt blood, not the peasant. As we have seen, whenever the peasant is allowed to speak the language is uneducated and the sentiment is sometimes crude or shallow.[45] This element prevents a Wordsworthian conclusion to the scene for there can be no 'lofty utterance'[46] from this peasant: unlike Wordsworth's leech-gatherer, 'Prytherch' can offer no 'choice word and measured phrase'. Over and over again, Thomas is frustrated by the inarticulacy of the peasant, as if a verbal acknowledgement of the presence of God in nature is essential. In some of these poems he seems to presume that the most valid way of experiencing God is through the mind, and since he does not recognise any intellectual acumen in the peasant, he assumes that there can be no experience. In the opposition between reason and imagination, or intuition, we might have expected Thomas to come down firmly on the side of imagination and intuition as valid methods of perception, but in his treatment of the peasant he seems to overlook the intuitive response and demands an intellectual one which the peasant cannot give. On the whole, Thomas is mystified and disappointed with the peasant, suffering a kind of frustrated romanticism. 'Valediction',[47] the poem which, in Song at the Year's Turning, follows 'Soil' begins:

> You failed me, farmer, I was afraid you would

and continues:

> The two things
> That could redeem your ignorance, the beauty
> And grace that trees and flowers labour to teach,
> Were never yours, you shut your heart against them.

In the early poem 'Autumn On The Land'[48] the Wordsworthian principle is rejected:

> ... You may look in vain
> Through the eyes' window; on his meagre hearth
> The thin, shy soul has not begun its reign
> Over the darkness. Beauty, love and mirth

And joy are strangers there.
                    You must revise
Your bland philosophy of nature, earth
Has of itself no power to make men wise.

Thomas's response to the peasant in these early poems is based
on values which suggest the Cartesian 'I think, therefore I am', and
because he cannot discern that the peasant is thinking he finds it
difficult to acknowledge the validity of his existence and therefore
fails to see him as a metaphor for God. But the 'You' of this poem
is also being satirised. The philosophy of the 'You' is 'bland' and
must be revised. So who is this 'you' which the poem addresses?
The voice is very like the narrator's voice in 'The Minister', seem-
ing, as it does there, to attack both sides at once. Interestingly, the
'You' of 'You may look in vain' is even more ambiguous than that
of 'You must revise'. It could easily be replaced with 'I', and this
suggests that it is in fact a distancing device, which in fact refers
to Thomas himself, and is a self-criticism. If he valued the action
of the body as much as he does that of the intellect, then Thomas
would have less of a problem in seeing the farmer as a metaphor
for God. God incarnated in Christ takes the form of the suffering
servant, and the actions of the body are of infinite importance in
the divine economy. But in elevating the intellect over the body,
the poet diminishes the whole man. The paradox here is not least
one of values and is explored further in 'The Country Clergy':[49]

I see them working in old rectories
By the sun's light, by candlelight,
Venerable men, their black cloth
A little dusty, a little green
With holy mildew. And yet their skulls,
Ripening over so many prayers,
Toppled into the same grave
With oafs and yokels . . .
                    . . . God in his time
Or out of time will correct this.

Many readers note the satirising of the 'yokels' here, and resent
the suggestion that they are not worthy to share the same grave
as the priests, but fewer recognise the satirising of the priest in the

phrases 'a little dusty' and 'holy mildew'. These, together with the reference to the skulls 'ripening' and finally toppling, create a metaphor of decay, not just in death, but in life as well. As we have seen him do so many times before, Thomas indicates within the density of his language both the positive and negative modes of being. For the priests the positive side in this poem rests in those lines omitted above:

> They left no books,
> Memorial to their lonely thought
> In grey parishes; rather they wrote
> On men's hearts and in the minds
> Of young children sublime words
> Too soon forgotten. God in his time
> Or out of time will correct this.

Again, echoes of 'The Minister' reverberate, as these 'positive' intimations of genuine spirituality are set up in immediate juxtaposition with the 'negative' signs of decay. A negative reading suggests that the intellect of the priest, ultimately, achieves no more than the ignorance of the peasants, being 'toppled into the same grave', but a positive reading sees achievement in the 'sublime words' written on 'men's hearts and in the minds/ Of young children'. We must ask, then, what is the 'this' that God will correct?

We might say it is the fact that the words are too soon forgotten; readers who take exception to what they see as intellectual snobbery will interpret it as supporting their case. But if we interpret the tension as lying not between the 'yokels' and the priest, but between the priest as representative of decay and priest as representative of the word of life, then we may recognise that this paradox is something only God can correct, in so far as the priests are representatives of mortality in their flesh but of eternity in their calling. It seems there are as many readings of the priest as there are of the peasant.

As the Prytherch poems continue Thomas acknowledges this possibility of making multiple readings of his subjects. He experiments with the various readings of the peasant open to him in 'Which':[50]

> Could I have said he was the scholar
> Of the fields' pages he turned more slowly

> Season by season, or nature's fool,
> Born to blur with his moist eye
> The clear passages of a book
> You came to finger with deft touch?

Thomas acknowledges his own manipulation of his observations. He can make the peasant into a metaphor for God, sometimes painting tentative, ethereal pictures as in 'The Gap in the Hedge':[51]

> That man, Prytherch, with the torn cap,
> I saw him often, framed in the gap
> Between two hazels with his sharp eyes,
> Bright as thorns, watching the sunrise
> Filling the valley with its pale yellow
> Light, where the sheep and the lambs went haloed . . .

and sometimes creating more overt images of God as in 'Absolution':[52]

> Prytherch, man, can you forgive
> From your stone altar on which the light's
> Bread is broken at dusk and dawn . . .

In 'The Gap in the Hedge' the imagery creates references to Calvary of such obliqueness that we may or may not make the associations, but in 'Absolution' the peasant is clearly a sacramental figure; a priest who can pronounce absolution on the poet. Someone whose soul has been

> made strong
> By the earth's incense, the wind's song.

The poet does not choose now to see the rags and the empty mind of the peasant; he sees a figure who has been consecrated by his patient sympathy with the earth:

> It was you who were right the whole time;
> Right in this that the day's end
> Finds you still in the same field
> In which you started, your soul made strong
> By the earth's incense, the wind's song.
> While I have worn my soul bare
> On the world's roads . . .

Thomas has deliberately elevated the situation into an explicitly religious frame, avoiding all his reservations about the peasant.

As 'The Minister' offered a number of readings of the peasants and the landscape in a variety of voices, so in these poems we are offered a number of possible readings from a variety of viewpoints. However, just occasionally, the narrowest point of authentic 'contact' between the farmer and the landscape is acknowledged by the poet, based in the peasants' experience and not on the poet's imagination. Consider 'The Parish':[53]

> There was part of the parish that few knew.
> They lived in houses on the main road
> To God, as they thought, managing primly
> The day's dirt, bottling talk
> Of birth and marriage in cold eyes;

The people in the first stanza are not the peasants of 'The Minister'. While it is the same rural landscape, this part of the parish is a village, and we may note here that 'the main road' is often a pejorative term with Thomas, a metaphor for worldliness not unlike that of the 'broad way' of the Scriptures.[54] By means of the carefully organised line-ending the main road is both actual and metaphorical, displaying Thomas's distaste of the narrow, inward-looking lifestyle represented – another aspect of the kind of Protestantism Thomas so dislikes. These people are unaware of, or conceal their knowledge of, the primitive power of the natural world around them, represented here by the force of the grass. (The tenuous nature of civilisation and the ever-present power of the natural world which always threatens to take back its territory is a feature of Thomas's work.) In this narrow domestic environment then, ignorance of God in nature takes a different, more petty form than that of the isolated hill farmers. But we find here that narrow point of contact between the farmer and the poet which was not acknowledged in 'The Minister':

> But you knew it, farmer; your hand
> Had felt its power, if not your heart
> its loveliness.

The farmer is not totally unaware of at least one aspect of God manifest in nature; he has first-hand experience of nature's power, and this partial, but real, response is preferable to that of the people who live 'on the main road'. The contradictory aspects of nature are merged in tacit acceptance in the lines:

> Somewhere among
> Its green aisles you had watched like me
> The sharp tooth tearing its prey,
> While a bird sang from a tall tree.

Paradox is registered in the setting for the action – the sharp tooth tears its prey within an arena which might be a church. The 'green aisles' not only form an aural pun (isles) but anticipate the sentiment of the opening line of 'The Moor':[55] 'It was like a church to me.' The bird which sings 'from a tall tree' while the action takes place heightens the paradox as it does in 'The Minister.' (The birdsong accompanies the action as music might in a church; also the tree is usually linked to the crucifixion in Thomas's symbolism. These images set up wider resonances, embracing the whole idea of sacrifice, nature and worship.) Images of God, then, and the difficulties inherent in them, are intensely compressed in these lines. The paradox of nature is mirrored in the paradox of religious practice. The Protestantism which is critiqued here finds a different exposition in the later poem 'The Chapel':[56]

> A little aside from the main road,
> becalmed in a last-century greyness,
> there is the chapel, ugly, without the appeal
> to the tourist to stop his car . . .
>
> But here once on an evening like this . . .
> . . . a preacher caught fire
> and burned steadily before them
> with a strange light, so that they saw
> the splendour of the barren mountains . . .

Here, interestingly, the Protestant ethos, so often criticised by Thomas, is a positive one. Seen in relation to the tourists, Puritanism is valued, while in the context of 'The Minister' its narrowness identified Puritanism as bad. The chapel on this occasion enables people to see the presence of God in the landscape, something it was not able to do in 'The Minister'. This flexibility of the symbol is a recurring feature in Thomas's work and it has an honourable provenance. We may note how Julian of Norwich refers to that cardinal religious symbol the Blessed Virgin:

> Also God shewid in party the wisedam and the trueth of hir soule, wherein I understood the reverend beholding that she beheld hir God and maker, mervelyng with a greate reverence that he would be borne of hir that was a simple creature of his makeyng. And this wisdam and trueth, knowyng the greteness of [her] maker and the littlehede of hirselfe that is made, caused hir sey full mekely to Gabriel: 'Lo me, Gods handmayde.' In this sight I undestoode sothely that she is mare than all that God made beneath hir in worthyness and grace; for aboven hir is nothing that is made but the blissid (manhood) of Criste, as to my sight.[57]

Here the Blessed Virgin as handmaid is defined in relation to both a lower and a higher order, and a double perspective is registered.

We have already noted the significance of 'a little aside from the main road'. This little chapel has been left behind by events; traffic, river and clouds pass it by. But it has something to contribute to an understanding of how God can be mediated.

The experience described in the second stanza has much in common with 'The Minister': the isolated chapel, the 'darkness' about the hearers, which may or may not be metaphorical. However, if we look at the passage in 'The Minister' which corresponds with the experience described in 'The Chapel', we find that it is almost a parody:

> Narrator
> The moor pressed its face to the window.
> The clock ticked on, the sermon continued.
> Out in the fir tree an owl cried
> Derision on a God of love.
> But no one noticed, and the voice burned on,
> Consuming the preacher to a charred wick.

> The Minister
> I was good that night, I had the hwyl.
> We sang the verses of the last hymn
> Twice. We might have had a revival

If only the organ had kept in time.
But that was the organist's fault.

In 'The Minister' no one notices the cry of the owl; the voice burns, and the preacher is reduced to a charred wick. This contrasts strongly with the image of the preacher in 'The Chapel' who 'caught fire/ and burned steadily before them/ with a strange light', and a significant part of the people's response is that they 'saw the splendour of the barren mountains around them'. A positive response to the natural world is an integral part of their response to God. This is the significant omission in 'The Minister'. As early as 1955 we find a poem which suggests to the reader that Thomas has given up his quest to find some affinity between human beings, God and nature. In 'No Through Road'[58] we read:

All in vain. I will cease now
My long absorption with the plough,
With the tame and the wild creatures
And the man united with the earth.

But he never does abandon this 'long absorption'. The sentiment expressed in 'The Parish' (published in 1961) is just another facet of the same story, not a further step towards resolution, and *Laboratories of the Spirit*, while introducing a more overtly religious dimension to the poems, is still preoccupied with 'man united with the earth'.[59] Far from resolving the issue it sometimes presents an even harsher reading of people than any we have considered so far. Consider 'The Reception',[60] which opens:

The clouds were brown
like the landscape. Sullen men
worked there, fingering their
scars. The brown
got into their minds
so that they could not see
God.

Here the tension is expressed clearly, without ambiguity. It is the problem that we have already identified in 'The Minister'. There the priest's difficulty with the people, his inability to understand them, and the source of his constant soul-searching, resulted precisely because, in the landscape, the people do not see God. 'Reception' mythologises the situation.

The landscape literally 'colours' the peasants' view of life; everything takes on its colour. The pain which in 'The Minister' is imaged in the phrase 'mortgaged to the soil' is represented here by the scars of the 'sullen' men, scars which, one may infer, were inflicted by the landscape.[61] The landscape prevents the men from seeing God. The opening lines reiterate the view of an omniscient onlooker, but as the poem continues it is complicated by an important shift in perspective:

> It concerned him
> at times. He arrayed himself
> in bright green, but the winds of that place
> burned him;

The situation is now looked at from God's point of view. Where, in those opening lines, the landscape was integrated with the men, the language now makes it impossible to separate the landscape from the Passion. It is imaged in the seasonal change from brown to green and then in the falling leaves. God is in the green, which is a moving attempt on his part to engage the sympathies of the men. If the landscape cannot image God to men, then God will change the landscape. The nuances of the next three lines are complex and subtle. The two images of God which we find here are both scriptural, and are overlaid one on the other. The first image we might consider is that of the Crucifixion.

The 'body nailed to a dead tree' needs no gloss, but 'the winds of that place/ burned him' is less familiar. I think we might be justified in associating these lines with Julian of Norwich, as Thomas makes oblique reference to her work on a number of occasions. In her account of the crucifixion Julian says:

I saw iiii maner of dryengs: the first was blode-less; the secund was payne folowyng after; the thred, hangyng up in the eyr as men hang a cloth to drye; the forth, that the bodily kynd asky[d] licour and ther was no maner of comfort mynystid to hym in al his wo and disese. A! herd and grevous was his peyne, but mech more hard and grevous it was whan the moysture faylid and al beganne to drye thus clyngand. These were the paynys that shewdyn in the blissful hede: the first wrought to the deyng whyl it was moyst; and that other, slow, with clyngyng dryand, with blowing of the wynde from withowten that dryed him more, and peynd with cold, than myn herte can (thyngke).[62]

The other image of God which we may read in these lines is that of God the Holy Spirit – or, as the Authorised Version has it, the Holy Ghost. God the Holy Ghost is manifest in Scripture in powerful images of wind and fire.[63] Submitted to the blindness of the peasants,

> the winds of that place
> burned him; he was a ghost
> unnoticed . . .

God the consuming fire is here burned by the incomprehension of the people. The image of God presented in the green landscape, then, is no more successful than that presented in the brown. The green is just 'flimsy integument/ of the hard soil' – a light outer covering of the same hard world which lies underneath. This is perhaps the most cynical reading of landscape and God which we have yet encountered, and the cynicism is attributed to the peasants. The story of redemption is just the 'sugar on the pill' in a hard and painful world.

At this point the sliding perspective adjusts itself again; in a retreat from the realistic narrative the poem begins to operate in the mode of the myth. (This sudden shift of perspective is a familiar feature of the Psalms.)[64] Here Thomas has God withdraw to consider what he will do next:

> He withdrew to
> consider, rejuvenating
> himself at the mind's
> sources. White, he thought;
> I will visit this people
> as a white bird, my feathers
> their winter. They perceived
> him then; fell upon him
> in silence, seeking for the brown soil
> he deprived them of,
> trampling him into it.

This almost naive identification of God with landscape and with season serves to express the poet's own conviction that there is a deep and much more complex connection between the two, and also frames that conviction in a way which is meaningful and accessible. This is, of course, the form and purpose of all myth. Thomas universalises the experience of the peasants in their inability to see God in Nature by identifying it with God's offering of himself. It recognises that humankind generally is unwilling to recognise God in whatever mode he reveals himself.

While there are a number of poems in the mode of the *via positiva* which register the response of the poet,[65] there are few in this mode which take on the persona of the farmer or peasant. Interestingly, one which does so is the last poem in *Laboratories of the Spirit*. 'Good' attempts to reconcile many of the tensions which have been set up in earlier poems:

> The old man comes out on the hill
> and looks down to recall earlier days
> in the valley. He sees the stream shine,
> the church stand, hears the litter of
> children's voices. A chill in the flesh
> tells him that death is not far off
> now: it is the shadow under the great boughs
> of life. His garden has herbs growing.
> The kestrel goes by with fresh prey
> in its claws. The wind scatters the scent
> of wild beans. The tractor operates
> on the earth's body. His grandson is there
> ploughing; his young wife fetches him
> cakes and tea and a dark smile. It is well.

This is an attempt to harmonise all those disparate images of nature, and thus of God, which have exercised the narrator in 'The Minister'. Here landscape and church are in harmony. Nature is held in a healthy balance: the herbs growing in the garden and the kestrel with its prey are now two sides of the same coin. Death and life are both accepted, and, in another echo of Julian of Norwich, we are told: 'It is well'.[66]

Through the things that he sees, the farmer perceives that 'all is well', the things of the earth symbolising God, for him, in his own *via positiva*. However, this is only a temporary resolution. The exploration of tensions continues; conflict is foreshadowed in the presence of the tractor, and the clinical terms which describe its action. With hindsight we know that in Thomas's imagery the tractor will become a symbol of the materialistic, rational and scientific attitude to life which is in conflict with the imaginative, intuitive, spiritual life.

The many voicedness of these texts and the multiple readings of the figures within them demonstrate not only Thomas's awareness of the difficulties of imaging God, but also the inadequacy of language as we use it to express our perceptions of God. Unsurprisingly, therefore, the images that Thomas uses in these early poems often contradict one another.

Brian Wren has remarked: 'No image is adequate. . . . Allowing God-images to clash is important, because it reminds us that we are approaching that which is beyond all images.'[67]

Thomas, as we have seen, is happy to create multiple images for God, and the 'clashes' are always significant, always reminding us of the impossibility of naming 'that which is beyond all images'. The impossibility of finding adequate images leads Thomas, in some poems, to reject language as a medium of revelation altogether, so that in 'The Moor' we read:

> What God was there made himself felt,
> Not listened to, in clean colours
> That brought a moistening of the eye,
> In movement of the wind over grass.

The refusal to identify God in an image is emphasised here in the indeterminacy of 'What God was there' – though inevitably, the use of the masculine pronoun limits the intended broadness of the concept. Nevertheless, a mode of perception other than that which relies on language is insisted on as the line continues:

> What God was there made himself felt,
> Not listened to . . .

So God communicates his presence through a means other than language, and the priest responds also without resort to language:

> There were no prayers said. But stillness
> Of the heart's passions – that was praise

> Enough; and the mind's cession
> Of its kingdom. I walked on,
> Simple and poor, while the air crumbled
> And broke on me generously as bread.

If praise is a positive response to the Ultimate Reality, then in this context the stillness – which is without language – is praise.

This is an early encounter in Thomas's *oeuvre* with the mystical tradition, with that intuitive response to God which relies neither on knowledge nor on language. It is an intuition which, we note, he rarely ascribes to the peasant.

Ironically perhaps, like most mystics, he must turn back to language in order to express the inexpressible, to share his experience of God.

The experience of God as we have seen it to be in these poems is one which says this is what God is like, and also what he is not like. In the farmer and the priest, the hymnist and the mystic, the effective and ineffective modes of Protestantism, Thomas discovers images of God. There is a built-in weakness in all of these images, but it is a weakness which is not only inevitable but desirable. It is the inadequacy of images of God which prevents them from becoming idols.

4
Myth and Science as Images of God

Among the many images of God which Thomas presents, two recur frequently. These might be figured as God present and accessible, and God absent but in a relationship defined by that absence. These images of God find their origin in traditional theology and mysticism. But a further body of poems, while still drawing on orthodoxy as a source, deals with its informing myths in a disturbing, radical way. I will identify poems which operate in this way as 'mythic poems'. In the mythic poems Thomas seems to set his face steadily to look at the challenging possibilities which present themselves on an objective appraisal of the experienced world: challenging particularly to faith and religious belief. The mythic poems offer an image of a God who is often indifferent, frequently objectionable and altogether unlike the God of popular imagination. In these poems subjective experience continually pushes against objective reason. Hence the two *vias* – the *via positiva* and the *via negativa* – are, in this new frame, on the same side, set against an imaginative construction based on reason. But the subjective experience which is challenged by these poems is that of the reader. The challenging, objective stance is set up by the poet, and this has confused many readers, not to say some critics.[1] In his interview with R.S. Thomas, J.B. Lethbridge wondered whether he detected some despair or discouragement in the poems published since *Frequencies* (1975). Thomas explains: 'I think there's a certain amount of misunderstanding of my work, a lot of my work is ironic, which possibly some people wouldn't always get. What I'm tilting at is not God, but the ideas of God.' It seems to me that the mythic poems fit into this category of 'tilting at ideas of God'. We cannot approach these poems with the same expectations that we bring to other Thomas poems. They are an entirely different genre. They rely on our discomfort for their effect. The readers' response to these poems inheres in the *via positiva* and the *via negativa*, for in rejecting the image Thomas presents us with, we claim to know what God is, and is not, like. In the act of protest we are forced to reappraise our own, perhaps simplistic, notions of God. The mythic poems, then, find their origin in questions such as, 'What if God?' 'Suppose God . . .' Or again, 'Given this experience God is . . .' A myth is a way of explaining the world to ourselves, of ordering apparent disorder. According to Wellek and Warren,[2] a myth is 'any anonymously composed story telling of origins and destinies: the explanations a society offers its young of why the world is and why we do as we do, its pedagogic images of the nature and destiny of men.' Thomas invents his own myths or distorts canonical ones, and presses them into the service of explanation. Given the world I observe, he seems to say, is this myth any less likely than any of the other stories we tell ourselves? The mythic poems engage readers on a more subjective level than many others. While other poems allow them to observe the painful fight for faith of one man, these involve the readers themselves.

The mythic poems emerge as a specific group within the Thomas *oeuvre* in *H'm* (1972), but they are anticipated from the earliest collections. In *Song at the Year's Turning* (1955), and included by Thomas in *Selected Poems 1946–1968* (1986) we find 'Pisces'[3] a deceptively simple song in the mode of the nursery rhyme, but with a sophisticated content.[4] In keeping with its early appearance in *Song at the Year's Turning*, 'Pisces' registers primarily as a nature poem, raising those questions about the availability of nature as a possible image for God which we have considered in the previous chapter. However, it demonstrates techniques which become crucial to an understanding of the later mythic poems. In this particular case Thomas operates a triadic structure, the simple two-stanza poem addressing three distinct questions, the answer to each provoking further and more critical questions. Typical of the mythic form, a question is being raised and an explanation proffered, but where in many of Thomas's mythic poems the question is covert, here it overtly forms the structure of the first stanza. It falls into the category of myth defined by Wellek and Warren as 'the explanations a society offers its young of why the world is and why we do as we do'. But there are a number of complications.

If we consider the question which is raised literally in 'Pisces' – 'Who said to the trout,/ You shall die on Good Friday' then the question the myth tries to answer is the child's question of 'Why do we eat fish on Good Friday?' The poem is addressing a received tradition which has lost much of its import in an affluent and secular world, having etiolated from an astringent discipline of Lenten self-denial[5] into a nominal observance of a prescribed food. But the simplicity of the question is complicated by the strength of the associations we make between the second and third lines:

> You shall die on Good Friday
> To be food for a man

This leads us to the second part of the triadic structure, as the question is extended, by association, to the death of Christ on Good Friday and to the institution of the sacrament or Eucharist – Take, eat; this is my body.[6] The question the myth now addresses is a theological one. Who decided Christ should die 'to be food for a man'? It will be helpful to pause a little here and consider the reinforcement of the association from other points. The association we make between the figure of Christ and the trout lies uncomfortably in the imagination as it fails to accommodate itself to a traditional icon, but if we think of the trout in terms of 'the fish', then the title illuminates the problem for us. The fish as a symbol for the Christian faith pre-dates that of the cross, the letters of the Greek word for fish – *Icthus* – being an acrostic for Jesus Christ God's Son Saviour.[7] The term *Icthus* has fallen out of recognition, except in circles of religious devotion, but another term for fish – *Pisces* – is immediately recognisable to any number of readers, owing to the proliferation of interest in astrology, itself a kind of secularised faith. *Icthus* has been replaced in the modern consciousness with *Pisces*. It is this forgetting of the religious significance of the icon that underpins the first stanza:

> To be food for a man
> And his pretty lady?

Now the man/woman set is disrupted by the choice of 'lady', and creates a new, romantic frame for the poem, reminiscent of courtly love. This in turn suggests early Marian poems in their merging of sacred and secular images.[8] In the context of myth, then, this stanza poses the question which the myth is supposed to answer, but the question has been complicated well beyond that implied by its nursery rhyme form. The answer, when it comes, does so with the same apparent immediacy as the question:

It was I, said God,
Who formed the roses
In the delicate flesh
And the tooth that bruises.

The third part of this triadic structure, then, questions the role of God in the act of sacrifice. The second stanza draws out the implications for the Godhead, and raises questions of morality and mystery. As the words spoken by God are not signified by inverted commas there is considerable ambiguity in the voice. If we read God's response as limited to the first three words of the stanza, then God acknowledges in a simple and straightforward way that *he* 'said to the trout', and this reading returns us to the nursery rhyme form of question and answer – 'I, said the sparrow'. In this reading the remainder of the stanza becomes a gloss on 'God', spoken by the narrator. But if we read the whole of the stanza as being in the voice of God, two further readings emerge. In one reading it is possible that the whole stanza is a *non sequitur*, limiting God's action to that of creation. A more challenging reading remains, in which God seems to justify his actions on the ground that he is the creator. He created both the 'flesh' and the 'tooth'. At this point 'Song for Gwydion' [9] provides a gloss. Where 'Pisces' refers to the 'roses/ In the delicate flesh', 'Song for Gwydion' has 'the beautiful blithe garland/ of stipples' and the reference to the distinctive markings of the trout is clear. In 'Pisces' the implied savagery of 'the flesh' in juxtaposition with 'the tooth' is modulated by metaphor and adjective: 'the roses in the delicate flesh' distances the harsh reality, reminding the reader of the alterations in consciousness effected by a deliberately selective use of language. In this reading God also takes responsibility for the 'tooth that bruises', thus compounding the problem of suffering, of predator and of prey. There is no explicit moral concern expressed in God's voice.

Though the first level of reference is to the fish, the choice of metaphor and adjective have the effect of adding a wider reference. The question which is now raised is 'Whose flesh, and whose tooth is meant?' In keeping with the romantic tone of 'His pretty lady' and the conventions it suggests, it is possible to attribute the roses to the 'pretty lady', and the tooth to the man, or to both man and woman. Humans comprise in their own selves both the roses in the flesh and the tooth that bruises, and these too, the lines imply, were created by God.

But we have already seen that the trout stands as an icon for the Christ. The 'roses/ in the delicate flesh' take on an even more affective significance when applied to Christ. Can God be taking responsibility for the wounded flesh – the stigmata? Can the stigmata be the 'roses in the flesh'? Is God responsible for both the victim and the aggressor? The concept of sacrifice is made very clear in 'Song for Gwydion' where the trout is 'the first sweet sacrifice I tasted'. 'Pisces' offers no answers to the moral and theological problems it raises. Like many of Thomas's mythic poems, it raises questions of profound theological import and leaves the conclusion to the reader.

The significance of this little poem is considerable. The majority of Thomas's mythic poems appear after 1972 and are collected in *H'm* (1972) and *Laboratories of the Spirit* (1975). They were hailed as a new departure by some critics,[10] but in this poem, published in 1955, the concerns which were to preoccupy Thomas so much later are already in evidence. 'Pisces' contains in miniature the agenda and structure which emerge so clearly in the poems of later collections. A careful examination of the publications of intervening years will reveal that the theme has inconspicuously prevailed throughout, culminating eventually in that body of poems which I have referred to as the mythic poems.

The subject matter of these poems, then, is not new. They are concerned with the problem of suffering. Like the nature poems they raise the classic theological question of whether God is good, or powerful, and whether he can be both. But there are important differences between the nature poems and the mythic poems. A brief look at a nature poem of the 1950s will illustrate this. In 'January',[11] for example, we note the interfacing between beauty and suffering:

> The fox drags its wounded belly
> Over the snow, the crimson seeds
> Of blood burst with a mild explosion
> Soft as excrement, bold as roses.
>
> Over the snow that feels no pity,
> Whose white hands can give no healing,
> The fox drags its wounded belly.

The questions which challenge us are typical of those which are raised in the nature poems, but the manner in which they are raised is quite different from the mythic poems. For example, 'January' appears initially to be a completely objective statement. Its painterly qualities require no additional verbal exposition to make a case, and the voice is carefully distanced in the manner of the realist novel.[12] The metaphysical questions are latent in the images and must be foregrounded by the reader, whereas the mythic poems not only foreground the metaphysical questions, sometimes stating them explicitly, but directly involve the persona of God. Across the surface of the mythic poems we see the play of cause and effect, of desire and consequence, often complicated by that arbitrary action so characteristic of myths. In them God plays many roles and has many voices. He is not only anthropomorphised, but protean – he adopts differing forms and personas, fitting into whatever scenario has been prepared for him. (In this respect the poems operate a similar strategy to that by which all cultures create their gods in narrative.) In 'Rough'[13] he is a classical deity or a fairytale giant: the grass curls 'like God's beard'. In 'The Tool'[14] his image merges with that of Adam and the voice is complicated. Occasionally, as in 'At It',[15] the voice is entirely subjective. The image of God in the mythic poems then, is fabulous, often whimsical. We need to remind ourselves of Thomas's admission that it is 'not God I am tilting at, but ideas of God'. While they find their focus in the problem of suffering, it is the perceived image of God, and its informing logic, which is always being challenged. The key feature of the mythic poems lies in the way that revelation and observation fail to support one another. We are reminded of the tension that the artist found between 'observation' and 'vision'.[16] The myths are created from an objective appraisal of the world as we know it. Where revealed truth is not concomitant with perceived experience, it is distorted, wrenched into conformity. The mythic poems actually operate in the gap between lived experience and spiritual perception. This may be demonstrated by a reading of the poem 'Rough'. Here echoes of the nursery rhyme persist, conferring authenticity of the kind awarded to folklore:

> God looked at the eagle that looked at
> the wolf that watched the jack-rabbit
> cropping the grass, green and curling
> as God's beard. He stepped back;
> it was perfect, a self-regulating machine
> of blood and faeces. One thing was missing:
> he skimmed off a faint reflection of himself

in sea water; breathed air into it,
and set the red corpuscles whirling.

We note a triadic structure at work again. The poem operates in the nursery rhyme mode, with a traditional, incantatory use of repetition. The rhyme which springs to mind – This is the house that Jack built – serves as an ironic counterpoint to the creation myth. God is figured rather like a giant in a fairytale, observing the scene from a height (I see this figure bending over oceans and whirling man into being, rather in the manner of David bending over the brook selecting his pebble and whirling his slingshot at the giant Goliath – a curious reversal of scale) and having a beard which may be not only curling but green.[17] This reading is in the mode of 'How the world began' – 'those stories we tell our young to explain . . .'. As an imaginative reworking of the Creation myth, however, it is surprisingly comprehensive, drawing on a variety of sources. The Genesis story is elaborated to accommodate both the scientific and the mythic accounts.

Not only does this remind us that life is believed to have generated first in the sea, but it also bears echoes of the myth of Aphrodite. From the macrocosm (sea, air) to the microcosm (red corpuscles) the whole of creation is represented. In the Genesis mode, the creation of man results from a perceived absence – 'one thing was missing'. The principle of cause and effect operates, complying with those expectations we expressed earlier. We may therefore expect a further complication to ensue.

We recognise, as we did in 'Pisces', a nursery rhyme form which begs a question: in 'Pisces' the question was explicitly framed; in 'Rough' it is implied. As in 'Pisces', the reading progresses from the innocent question to the more profound – from the question of origins to the problem of suffering. In 'Rough', suffering is not registered as a problem when it is part of the natural order, the 'self-regulating machine'. (They only 'look'.) It is the arrival of 'the creature' that complicates and disrupts the situation:

It was not long
before the creature had the eagle and the wolf and
the jack-rabbit squealing for mercy

This is no prelapsarian Eden. This is the myth of the creation of the 'world as we know it'.[18] In 'the self-regulating machine/ of blood

and faeces' a more sophisticated agenda is implied than a reworking of the Creation myth. The inverted, hierarchical organisation,
from God through the eagle, and downwards from wolf to rabbit
to grass is suggestive of two orders of being, one natural and one
metaphysical. The first, with God as onlooker, ends in the 'self-
regulating machine of blood and faeces' and is clearly the order of
what we now call the food chain. There is one conspicuous absence,
as the poem notes.

However, it can also be read, with very little adjustment, as the
scala naturae,[19] the ladder of nature, or the chain of being. In both
these readings, what is missing is the figure who holds 'the central
position in the scale of nature' – 'man'.

The second part of the triadic structure develops from the nursery
rhyme form and the innocent question into the complications of differing cultural responses (most notably, the problem of suffering).
We have noted in passing how the received myth of the Genesis
story has been distorted. In the Genesis story the capacity for pain
comes after an initial act of disobedience and the consequent separation from God. There cause and effect are very clear. No such
clarity is available here:

> God took a handful of small germs,
> sowing them in the smooth flesh . . .

We can read this passage as indicating cause and effect if we
choose. We may say that God introduces suffering as a way of
correcting the creature's capacity to dominate; it then becomes a
punishment for crime, Thomas's version of the Old Testament
narrative of Genesis. But the sentence structure can be seen as signifying a purely arbitrary act. There is no qualifying preposition such
as 'so' (. . . God took). In this case it is rendered merely the last in
a sequence of acts which are expressive of power without responsibility. This response corresponds to the second stanza of 'Pisces',
where we also found that God's responsibility was problematic.

This is Thomas's challenge to that simplistic attitude which he so
deplores, the point at which so many readers demur. Revelation
insists that God is love. The cosmology that underlies the chain of
being insists that God 'moves the cosmos through his active love of
creation'.[20] Lived experience, however, is not convinced and challenges those ideas and notions of God which fail to interrogate the
questions.

At this point the poem as myth of 'how the world began' or 'how suffering began' has achieved its end. But Thomas objects to simplistic understandings of God, even, we might suppose, those invented by himself. So there is an added complication which might even become explication:

> There was the sound
> of thunder, the loud, uncontrollable laughter of
> God,

Now God takes on the image of the Olympian god whose laughter is the thunder and whose playthings are mortals. This, the third part of the structure, repeats an image of God which is often implied in Thomas's poems – that of the creator who is distanced from, or indifferent to, his creation. A God who has no compact, no covenant with 'men'.[21] But here, with the laughter there is an acute juxtaposition of pain:

> and in his side like an incurred stitch, Jesus.

The image of the Olympian god is sustained as Christ is conceived within the body of the father – a parody of the myth of Pallas Athene who sprang from the head of Zeus.[22] But the whole structure of redemption is turned on its head. Christ is not the fulfilment of God's love, but is involuntarily 'incurred'; not the response of compassion to the plight of humankind, but the product of God's laughter.[23] Only the pain in the side reminds us of the conventional image of Christ; it is not possible to separate the pain from the laughter. The significant placement of the final word, 'Jesus', suggests that he is the product of both. It also suggests that this is the point to which the whole poem has been working. That the question we should have asked in the beginning was not how was the world made, nor even why suffering, but rather, why Jesus? In some way he seems to be the answer to the first two. That to a series of events, some arbitrary, some cause and effect, the inevitable consequence should be Jesus.

In *H'm* we find two poems which also approach the theme of creation and which have certain elements in common with 'Rough'.[24] 'Echoes' (p. 4) appears before 'Making' (p. 17), but we will look at 'Making' first as it is, superficially at least, a far simpler poem. However, the naiveté it assumes is misleading:

> And having built it
> I set about furnishing it
> To my taste: first moss, then grass

As in 'Rough', the earth is something which God has 'built', but this narrative tells a different story. It follows the traditional biblical account closely, elaborating on the received myth, but not radically distorting it, telling the story through the subjective 'I' which is God's voice. The frame is smaller and less alienating than that of 'Rough'. This is achieved in a number of ways. A human scale is achieved through the domestic language employed – 'built', 'furnishing' 'to my taste' – as if God were a householder. The careful distinction of elements, 'first moss, then grass', and the rhythm thus created, might even suggest a child 'playing house'. This is supported by the simplicity of certain phrases – 'I set about', and later, 'I thought up'. There is a disinclination to note discord, so that even the bacteria are rehabilitated, called out of darkness into light, the archaic language echoing the language of Scripture.[25] There is an irony, a touch of whimsy even, in the bacteria providing a metaphor for humans. The tension between revelation and observation generally found in the mythic poems is moderated here by the implied innocence of God. This God takes an almost childlike pleasure in the act of creation. We might say it is God at play.

The account of Creation follows an evolutionary pattern, proceeding from simple to more complex organisms. The inanimate things are furnished to God's taste. The animals are to 'divert' him. In other words, they are created to give him pleasure. But something is missing.

As in 'Rough', God notes an absence, but the paradigm here is not classical but Miltonic. Thomas identifies God's experience with 'man's' and complicates it, through a Miltonic allusion. We read: 'I slept and dreamed/ Of a likeness'. This is reminiscent of Adam's dream. In *Paradise Lost* we read:

> whereat I wak'd and found
> Before mine Eyes all real, as the dream
> Had lively shadowed . . .
>
> VIII. 309ff

And also:

> Shee disappeered, and left me dark, *I wak'd*
> *To find her*, or for ever to deplore

> Her loss, and other pleasures all abjure:
> When out of hope, behold her, not farr off,
> *Such as I saw her in my dream,*
> > (VIII. 478ff; italics added)

The image of God is merged with that of Adam. The perspective is complicated. To appreciate it fully we need to refer to the canon. In Genesis[26] God says that 'it is not good for man to be alone'. God recognises, on behalf of the man, the need for companionship. He causes a deep sleep to fall on Adam, and from his rib creates Eve. When we turn to *Paradise Lost* we find that Adam dreamed, and woke to find it real. (We are reminded also of Keats's observation in his letter to Bailey – the Imagination may be compared to Adam's dream – he awoke and found it truth.) Thomas merges these sources; in making God both the dreamer and the creator, he makes them new. The evolutionary order persists however in 'fashioning it,/ when I woke, to a slow/ music.' which implies the long passage of time, the 'slow music' referring, perhaps, to the 'dance to the music of time':[27]

> > in love with it
> > For itself, giving it freedom
> > To love me; risking the disappointment.

The image of God now expresses tenderness which finds its counterpart in human experience – that of the lover or the fond parent.[28]

This is a return from the extended myth of Thomas's creating to the biblical analogue of God as lover or Father, and is one of the reasons why this poem is less alienating than others in this genre. (God as lover, in the tradition of the Song of Songs, does not often appear in Thomas.)[29]

The simplicity of the language, the naiveté of the persona, at first reading, renders this God a hopeless romantic, a divine optimist. This is qualified by the closing phrase. In spite of the lightness of touch a seriousness is perceived in the rhythm which gives a solemn ending to the poem. After the semi-colon, the emphasis falls on 'risking' and the phrase becomes portentous. 'Risking the disappointment' falls away like a voice trailing off into wistfulness. There is sympathy for the hopes and fears of this God. In stark contrast to this playful, loving God, as we shall see, is the God of 'Echoes'. In 'Making', the creating God participated in the human experience in being identified with Adam's dream. The question the poem answers there is 'why people'? (why 'man'?). The answer seems to be that humans were created to satisfy a need for companionship on God's part and that creation is an act of love. Pain does not appear. Bacteria are just a part of creation, with no special significance for man. In 'Echoes' we return again to the question of suffering, and reach a very different conclusion. The poem operates by suspending the line endings and inviting the reader to anticipate what follows. Every line carries a burden of condensed meaning:

> What is this? said God. The obstinacy

– of what? is the obvious response. Of God perhaps? Though the next line immediately locates the obstinacy in an unnamed other – 'the obstinacy/ of its refusal' – God's rage in the third line (the rage of a child) certainly seems to support the possibility. The reader is also unsure what 'this' is. Whatever 'it' is, it seems either to pre-exist God, or to exist without his knowledge. The suspense is held over seven lines, and even then the reader must deduce that 'it' is the earth. The persona represented is one who uses force and has no scruples in exacting pain. Frustrated by 'its' refusal to answer,

> He struck it
> Those great blows it resounds
> With still . . .

The echo of a blow. Set in motion then, not by love, but by a blow of anger, the world turns on a 'slow axis of pain'. This might be an explanation for the pain of the earth, but it is not clear whether the 'slow axis of pain' was already in existence before the blow or was the result of it. The idea of the earth suffering as though in pain is not original. For example, we read in Romans 8. 22: 'For we know that the whole creation groaneth and travaileth in pain together until now.' And if we turn to Milton again we find:

> So saying, her rash hand in evil hour
> Forth reaching to the fruit, she pluck'd, she eat:
> *Earth felt the wound*, and Nature from her seat

Sighing through all her Works gave signs of woe,
That all was lost.
                    (*Paradise Lost*, IX. 780ff; italics added)

In 'Making', God was associated with Adam in his dream. Here, in the hand which reaches out and contrives pain, he is associated, obliquely, with Eve and – more directly, perhaps – with Cain. There is a reaching out of a hand which confers pain on the world. The effect in this instance is to transmute the action of original sin into the act of creation.

We are reminded of other poems where Thomas explores the whole complex of pain, truth and beauty:

> Seeking the poem
> in the pain, I have learned
> silence is best . . .
>   One thing I have asked
> Of the disposer of the issues
> Of life: that truth should defer
> To beauty. It was not granted.[30]

This association of sin with creation is far-reaching. Is suffering, rather than love, at the heart of creation? We are invited to demur, to explain why, given our observations, this is not as likely an explanation as any other. The interfacing of suffering with beauty is remarked again, as 'Nature bandaged/ Its wounds'. Nature here is kinder than God. (The equivocation of 'Its' complicates even this reading. Does nature bandage 'Its' own wounds, thus identifying nature with the earth which then becomes an independent, self-sustaining object, or does nature bandage 'Its', that is the earth's, wounds, implying that nature is a benevolent force independent of the earth?) Whichever reading we choose, it seems that the beauty of the natural world is not the intended creation of a loving God but a contingent act of nature, and beauty emerges from the suffering at the heart of the universe. It is almost like fair skin emerging where once there was an ugly wound. But the beauty reminds God of 'an intention'. What follows is an act of creation which seems to occur in spite of his spoken word rather than through it. 'They shall answer for you.' The tone might be that of a threat or a promise. The new creation, trees, birds, animals, seems to rise spontaneously from the ambiguous word, and it, also, is beautiful. However, there is again something missing, and it is registered this time by the animals who

> wandered, drinking
> Their own scent, conceding
> An absence.

We have seen that challenged by God to speak, the earth refuses to answer. It exercises a choice which fails to satisfy God. The new creation – the animals – give some sort of reply, meeting God's demand for an answer up to a point, but this is still not satisfactory. They cannot offer anything positive, they can only concede 'an absence'.

This absence, familiar to us from so many poems as the primordial metaphor for the human relationship with God, is no easier to understand than the earlier details of the poem. J.P. Ward sees this absence as something into which the shapes come: 'Later birds and animals appear, in apparent contentment, along with an "absence" *into which* "the shapes came, slender/ as trees, but with white hands,/ curious to build"' (italics added).[31] This reading sees absence as a space into which something – here, the shapes – might move. In Ward's reading, the absence is a place, a location. It seems to me, however, that the absence is not positive, as in Ward's reading, but negative, signifying a lack. In other words, the absence signifies the shapes. The 'shapes' *are* that which is absent – the perceived 'other' which is missing:

> Where are you?
> He called, and riding the echo
> The shapes came,

The spoken word interfaces with the canonical text again, recalling Genesis 3.9: 'And the Lord God called unto Adam, and said unto him, Where *art* thou?' Adam responds reluctantly, having been hiding from God as a consequence of disobedience. But here the shapes are called, not into account, but into being:

> riding the echo
> The shapes came, slender
> As trees . . .

The phrase conjures up elusive images which we can barely form but can recognise as being beautiful. They are created by the word of God and come riding into being on the echo of that word. We notice that it is by their 'otherness' that the shapes are recognised. They are like that which is already known – trees – but also not like, having hands 'slender/ As trees, but with white hands'.

But there are two 'echoes' stated or implied in this poem. We have read 'riding the echo' as riding the echo of God's voice. The other echo is that resonance of the initial blow with which the earth was sent reeling. Does it make a difference if it is the echo of a blow that the shapes are riding, rather than the echo of a voice? If the former, they would then, presumably, be created as part of the pain of the universe, perhaps the outcome of that travailing and groaning we noted earlier:

> On the altars
> They made him the red blood
> Told what he wished to hear.

The earth maintained a silence, the animals conceded an absence. The 'shapes' demonstrate a wish to acknowledge the sacred – the other – but the God who is figured here, who insists on being answered, uses violence to abstract what he wants to hear. Ultimately it is blood which speaks, and the association with Cain is strengthened. The cycle of pain which *this God* set in motion in the first place is complete.

We have noted how Thomas enjoys subverting expectations, and in these poems he has often reversed the relationships which are usually held to exist between God and 'man'. In 'Echoes' the reversal of roles is cleverly and effectively employed. Here the creation is responding to God in much the same way as God is seen to be responding to 'man', or perhaps, more specifically, to the poet. The poet has persisted in asking questions of God which God refuses to answer. He is a God who does not speak. He is a God who hides himself. The animals, answering for the earth, concede only an absence. Similarly, in the poet's experience, when creation speaks for God it is usually to 'concede an absence' (as we have already seen in the previous chapter). In this poem it is creation which takes to itself the role of silence and absence, leaving God, rather than the poet, frustrated and angry.

Origins, pain, absence. These are the elements that shift and change with kaleidoscopic variation across the mythic poems. Perspectives alter with disconcerting swiftness and we are required to adjust our

focus rapidly to keep up. Consider 'The Tool'. Published three years
after *H'm*, this poem from *Laboratories of the Spirit* is still engaged
with creating appropriate metaphors to describe creation and primeval beginnings. It demonstrates the whole complex of ideas which
continue to preoccupy Thomas. He wrestles with the idea of creation
ex nihilo, and the idea of absence carries many nuances.

The poem opens with the affirmation of primeval emptiness, of
nothing, in the form of dialogue. One voice enquires while the other
appears to know the answers:[32]

> So there was nothing?
> Nothing. An echo?
> Who spoke? There was emptiness
> And a face staring

This voice confirms what there was and what there was not, but
even so the voices are not easily distinguished throughout. We
are reminded of the way the voices slide into one another in 'The
Minister'.

The implied situation defies images and resists expression. Thomas
attempts expression in terms of questions and negatives – there is
'nothing', 'emptiness', 'absence'.[33] But an echo insists on a voice, and
a thought on a mind; the disembodied 'face' creates a surrealistic
atmosphere, but whose voice, thought and face they are is deeply
ambiguous.

The echo might be the echo of the initial creating word, or it may
be the first intimations of human speech:

> There was thought
> probing an absence. God

Here the placement of 'God' at the end of the line can be read as
signifying God as, in apposition to 'absence', the object of thought's
quest. We might read 'There was thought probing an absence –
God', until the next line resolves this by making God subject: the
source of the voice and of the thought which probes the absence.
We could read God, that is, as a noun in apposition to 'thought' or
to 'absence'. (Once again, momentary ambiguities in the syntax show
how subject and object blur confusingly in the religious experience.) This reading would suggest that it is God who is scrutinising
emptiness, seeking a likeness. Out of the void God searches for
something; something other:

> God
> knew he was naked and
> withdrew himself.

God's need of an other renders him vulnerable. This is signified in the nakedness. Aware of his vulnerability God withdraws.

If we pursue this reading and make the voice that of God, then God speaks twice more, and we must accommodate the idea of pain again:

> Pain, said
> the voice, and the creature
> stood up, its mind folded
> on darkness.[34]

'Pain' becomes the word which calls man into being, is, even, the condition of his being. The second occasion of speech is unambiguous. Unable to communicate through the wholeness of creation, God speaks directly in his own persona:

> 'Forgive me',
> he said . . .

This is the reading we make if we refer to God the echo, the thought and the face. We can, however, produce a quite different reading by taking a different perspective. Certain elements of 'The Tool' might remind us of 'Making', where faces 'stared in from the wild', as though willing themselves to be created. If this poem operates from the same perspective as 'Making', then the face is not that of God staring out, but that of the first man staring 'in', and the absence which his thought probes is the absence of God. It is this probing of the absence which is felt by God to be a threat. His vulnerability is expressed as nakedness and he withdraws – that is, he 'hides himself'. Language is the means by which the human searches out God. The space between them, that God seeks to maintain and which the language of humans seeks to bridge, represents both God's resistance and the inability of the human fully to experience his presence.[35]

The introduction of language, the articulation of the first word, is a response to the stimulus of pain – 'the germs/ swarmed' and 'Pain, said/ the voice'. The first word, the beginning of self-consciousness, an awareness of pain, the ability to recognise the 'other' – in this reading, both God and the creature are vulnerable and the mystery of pain is an integral part of the relationship.

Whichever reading we prefer – and man as subject is probably the most convincing version in the light of the remaining lines – the image Thomas uses to express the vulnerability of God is complex. It is again taken from the Genesis account of the Creation.[36] There God walks in the garden in the cool of the day and calls Adam, but Adam has sinned and knows he is naked so he hides himself. Human nakedness is an effective image of vulnerability, powerlessness even, and in applying it to God, Thomas not only ascribes to God the frailty and tenderness of the human, but in this context strongly identifies God with Adam. The significance of this emerges later in the poem.

In the sequence of the poem, then, God withdraws himself when he recognises the intention of man to probe the absence. As we read in Isaiah 45, he is 'a God who hides himself', who is unwilling to be discovered.

As it develops, the poem folds back on itself, extending meaning by engaging the reader in reading which becomes re-reading:

> and the creature
> stood up, its mind folded
> on darkness. It put out a hand,
> as though to implore
> wisdom, and a tool
> gleamed there. The alternatives
> of the tree sharpened.

'Its mind folded on darkness' is ancillary to 'the creature stood up', but on reading 'folded' we immediately refer to the preceding lines and see the body, too, unfolding as man evolves from his primitive posture. Similarly, when we read 'the alternatives of the tree sharpened', the word 'sharpened' alerts us by association and we refer to the tool, and it in turn becomes sharp, threatening the tree, which becomes an image of God.

The images roughly follow a line of historical development – the creature stands, pronounces the first words, makes the first tools.[37] The myth of the creationist is interwoven with the theory of the evolutionist: the prehistoric figure is set in a metaphysical context. The creature whose first word is 'pain' and whose mind is 'folded on darkness',[38] puts out a hand 'as though to implore/ wisdom' and engages our sympathy.

The 'alternatives/ of the tree' carries a weight of meaning.[39] It represents, among many other things, the initial choice presented in the creation myth, where the tree represents the knowledge of Good and Evil. There, Eve put out a hand to the tree when she 'saw that the tree was good for food, and that it was pleasant to the eyes, and much to be desired to make one wise.'[40] Here the hand is put out 'as though to implore/ wisdom' but, as if by magic, the tool 'gleamed there'.

The juxtaposition of the 'tree' with 'sharpened' is ominous. The question of choice becomes crucial once man has the tool. It can be creative or destructive. 'The tree's wholeness' suggests nature in its perfection; here it is an image of God which can speak to the man if he will hear. He does not hear because 'the sound/ of the tool drowned him'. The conflict between nature and mechanistic science is defined. So the tree can be the Tree of Life from which God speaks to the man, or it can be the cross on which God is crucified. The choice is bound up with the use of the tool, the ultimate, de-structive power of which is figured in the Crucifixion.[41]

The image of God as Adam is developed further with the archaic phrasing of 'He came forth'.[42] In the nakedness which is the vulner-ability of God, God presents himself to the man. Where God had formerly hidden himself in order to maintain his own mystery, here he comes forth in his nakedness – vulnerability – to submit to the freedom which he has given to the man. In one of Thomas's typic-ally complex metaphors, the Christ figure merges with that of Adam – the first and second Adam. Of course, to blend the image of Christ with that of Adam is not original. It is a Pauline practice, which has become a commonplace. As Donne has it in 'Hymne to God my God in my Sicknesse':

> We thinke that *Paradise* and *Calvarie,*
> *Christs* Crosse, and *Adams* tree, stood in one place;
> Looke Lord, and finde both *Adams* met in me;
> As the first *Adams* sweat surrounds my face,
> May the last *Adams* blood my soule embrace.

What is particularly arresting in Thomas's use of the image is the transposition of language which he effects. The precise words spoken by God here should be noted. The word from the Cross, spoken by Christ, is not 'Forgive me', but 'forgive them'.[43] Placing the words in inverted commas, subjecting them to the ordinary rules of grammar, intensifies our perception of the vulnerability of

God. In Thomas's reworking, God takes the responsibility for the pain of creation. The 'disappointment' which was 'risked' in 'Making' has here become a reality. A further gloss on this is to be found in 'Covenant'.[44] There we read:

> I feel sometimes
>   we are his penance
> for having made us. He
> suffers in us and we partake
>   of his suffering.

Wisdom and wholeness and communion with God are represented by the tree. Suffering and division are represented by the tool. These are the 'alternatives of the tree' which sharpen with the appearance of the tool.

Before the arrival of the tool the 'other' is referred to as 'the creature' or 'it'. We have 'its mind' and 'it put out a hand'. Only after the tool appears does the creature take on gender, as though its identity were somehow defined in its possession of the tool. It is the sound of the tool that prevents 'him' from hearing God's voice. An even more profound effect of the arrival of the tool is suggested in the mode of expression: 'the sound/ of the tool drowned him'. God seems to be totally submerged by the tool. His role as 'other' is threatened.[45]

The mythic poems, which as we have seen are largely preoccupied with questions of origins, of creation and of suffering, are also concerned with the alienation of humans from God because of their grasp of science. Thomas's attitude to science proves extremely important to an understanding of his perceived relationship of humans to God. Before we explore this most important point, we need to note two significant points which have emerged from our reading of these mythic poems.

They have all had something to say about the relationship between God and suffering. The poet cannot find a satisfactory answer to the problem of pain. What he does do is recognise that God himself does not escape the implications of pain. In these poems he ranges over the possibilities, presenting us with the many faces of God. In 'Rough' suffering is problematical. Pain cannot be separated from laughter. In 'Making' the bacteria take their place alongside the rest of creation and have no particular significance. The enormity of their ability to disrupt the relationship between God and humankind is not registered. In 'Echoes' God is a monster who is unmoved by pain. Where in 'Making' he gave humans freedom to love him, in 'Echoes' he cannot tolerate freedom, and pain is the result of opposition. The childlike God of 'Making' is willing to 'risk . . . the disappointment'. In 'Echoes' he punishes the earth so that the blows reverberate 'still'.

And it is in 'The Tool' that the complexities of pain manifest themselves most clearly. The effect of the tool has been to force God into surrender. At the beginning of the poem God knew he was naked and withdrew himself, but the possibility of the loss of himself as 'other', drowned by the noise of the tool, forces him to reveal himself.' 'He came forth in his nakedness.' It seems that the man only achieves selfhood in opposition to the 'Other' and the tool is the symbol of his own claim to otherness. The separation is profound, signified in the 'alternatives of the tree'. Submitting to the tool, God is included in the suffering. While this does not resolve anything, it does perhaps have the effect of reducing the alienation. God himself is rendered vulnerable and in this a relationship of sorts is restored:

> 'Forgive me,'
> he said, suffering the tool's
> insolence in his own body.

This is the nearest Thomas comes to the resolution of a problem which is by its nature insoluble.[46]

These poems also explore the perspectives of absence. The God who hides himself – the *Deus Absconditus* – is a familiar image for God in the iconography of R.S. Thomas. His is a God who is known largely in terms of what he is not, who is recognised by hints, shadows, spaces, absence. He is the Other, the Being who is not a Being. But the kaleidoscopic refractions of the poems we have considered open up other possibilities, shed new light on the situation.

In 'Rough' we read:

> One thing was missing:
> he skimmed off a faint reflection of himself
> in sea water . . .

God, contemplating his creation, steps back and observes that something is missing. It is a purely objective observation. The creation of 'the creature' has no more significance than the rest of creation, nor is God engaged with it in any more subjective way.

But in 'Making' we have a different image. God is now 'disturbed' by 'an absence'. The significance of this phrase should not be underestimated. It challenges the apparent naiveté of the poem and brings it into line with other poems which find their theological centre in the *via negativa*, for here Thomas seems to suggest that God is disturbed by an absence much as humankind is disturbed by an Absence in the *via negativa* poems. God is subject to emotion. Thomas has created a kind of *Deus Absconditus* in reverse, in which God, rather than man, searches for the other. Man is the 'hidden'.

If we look again at 'Echoes' we shall see that even greater complexity develops. We have already noted occasions where Thomas has developed his theme by reversing traditional roles, or by identifying God in images more usually associated with man. (Such is the case, for instance, in the earlier noted 'God knew he was naked and withdrew himself'.) In 'Echoes' there is an exchange of positions which is extra-textual, for we can stand outside the text and observe that what is going on inside it is a mirror-image of the relationship between the poet and God. Outside the text the poet seeks to know God. He challenges the resistance of God through language.[47] Inside the poem God seeks to know 'It' – the earth, the creation? – we must decide. But he tries to know it through language. He insists that it speak to him. He challenges its resistance and only achieves anger, frustration and pain. God is placed in the position more usually occupied by the poet, or, more generally, by the seeker after truth.

At the heart of the poem, and of the experience, there is an absence:

> and through the trees
> Animals wandered, drinking
> Their own scent, conceding
> An absence.

The 'absence', the lack of an 'Other', is noted by the closed circuit of the animals' senses. There is no human scent for them to notice. In placing the awareness of the absence in the consciousness of the animals, Thomas creates a comprehensive need for the other.

In 'The Tool', God anxiously withdraws as he recognises thought 'probing an absence'. This is the conventional image of the human recognising the Absence, the 'Other', the 'transcendental signified', which we call God.

In these poems we may now note, God, 'man' and animals all concede an absence. Each to each is the 'other'. There is an implied necessity for the existence of the human. As Thomas notes elsewhere:

> He needs us
> as a conductor his choir
> for the performance of an unending
> music.[48]

John Wheeler makes a similar point. He tells a story of a conversation between God and Abraham: 'Without me', God says, 'you would not exist'. 'But without me', replies Abraham, 'you would not be known.'[49]

The concept of the 'Other' then, at this point is basically one of necessity, but one which can be read as harmonious, each figure/component needing the other in order to define itself. But there is another element in the equation, which Thomas addresses with less composure. We might well begin by looking at the poem which addresses the problem head-on – 'Other'.[50] What emerges here is something more completely 'other' than anything registered in the relationships we have so far explored.

We have seen that the human is identified by the otherness of God: that in conceding an absence the humans perceive themselves more clearly. The 'Other' is necessary for identity, even for God. In this poem the perception of the 'Other' has broken down. God sees everything in terms of himself:

> It was perfect. He could do
> Nothing about it. Its waters
> Were as clear as his own eye. The grass
> Was his breath. The mystery
> Of the dark earth was what went on
> In himself.

This might be an ideal, God inherent in his universe, figured by the things he has made and necessary to its continued existence. But this creation is also separate from, and independent of, him and God refuses to accept this. The metaphor of parenthood and the growing independence of the child, which Thomas uses to develop the theme, is a sensitive critique of human relationships. But good parents learn that their children are not extensions of themselves, that they must achieve 'otherness'. The God in this poem is unwilling to concede this. He is the 'jealous' God[51] of the Old Testament:

> There were trysts
> In the greenwood at which
> He was not welcome. Youths and girls,
> Fondling the pages of
> A strange book

The natural responses of the young to each other are expressed in terms which suggest disloyalty to the God. While the initial purpose of the archaic language is to suggest a distant time and place, the 'trysts in the greenwood' at which God is not welcome also reminds one of Herrick's 'Corinna is going a-Maying',[52] with its suggestion of dalliance with older gods, and the 'olde opinion' of the Wife of Bath's Tale, according to which the elf-queene 'Daunced ful ofte in many a grene mede'.[53]

God plans the destruction of the place. The flood myth is distorted to accommodate his jealousy, and the means of destruction which he *apparently* chooses is the machine. (The qualification is necessary as this reading could be a *non sequitur*. The relationship of God's plan to the appearance of the machine might be one of cause and effect but it might also be a simple unrelated temporal sequence. I am pursuing the idea of cause and effect.)

This is one of Thomas's most potent symbols for the estrangement of humans from God. It is responsible for the destruction of the 'long peace/ Of the place'. The machine appears 'in the distance'. The image created suggests a pastoral landscape whose people are looking forward to the advent of the machine, who hear its seductive music in the distance. It sings, and it sings of money. It is apparently singing to itself; the suggestion is that it is innocent, self-contained and limited. But it sings, or perhaps, to anticipate a change of metaphor, 'spins' a siren song, and soon men and women together are caught in its web. A sinister note is introduced in the image of the predacious spider. (There is a hint of the earlier Welsh poems in 'The villages were as flies/ To be sucked empty', for this is indeed what Thomas sees one effect of the machine to be, as it lures people away from the countryside to the towns in pursuit of work and wealth.)[54] Once invented, the machine cannot be uninvented. The effect reduces God to tears. The reading we have produced by assuming the machine to be the effect of God's plan finds its conclusion in God regretting his action. However, had we followed the line of thought which sees the machine as an unrelated sequence, then God is rendered passive and helpless. Perhaps to have just one explanation for the proliferation of the machine and its effect would be too simple a conclusion for Thomas.

We have said that the mythic poems are concerned with the alienation of humans from God because of their grasp of science. This is not seen as an exclusively modern problem. It is signified in the potential for independence from God and rendered universal in the symbols of hand, tool and machine. We have already considered the implications of 'The Tool'. There is another poem which is of value in tracing Thomas's line of thought on this subject, and that is 'The Hand'.[55]

In this account of confrontation with God, the story of 'Wrestling Jacob' provides the matrix. Thomas will elaborate and distort this story so it is as well to remind ourselves of certain details as they appear in the biblical account.

When Jacob wrestles with the 'man' at the brook – the man is a symbol for God – he is so tenacious in his fight that in order to maintain supremacy God dislocates Jacob's thigh. This becomes the 'joints of the hand' in the poem. In the biblical account God asks Jacob his name but refuses to reveal his own name to Jacob. In the poem it is the hand which demands to know God's name. In the Genesis story God blesses Jacob, but he does not do so in the poem. The 'I am' of the last line is borrowed from Exodus where God reveals his name to Moses:

> And God said to Moses, I AM THAT I AM: and
> he said, Thus shalt thou say unto the children
> of Israel, I AM hath sent me unto you.
> (Exodus 3. 14)

Clearly, Thomas sees this story of a tenacious, persistent opposition to God as a suitable vehicle for conveying an impression of the acute 'otherness' which is symbolised in the hand:

> But the hand wrestled with him. 'Tell
> me your name', it cried, 'and I will write it

in bright gold. Are there not deeds
to be done, children to make, poems
to be written? The world
is without meaning, awaiting
my coming.'

The boisterous, confident, energetic address of the hand is superficially attractive, but its vision of itself is a vision which is in danger
of deposing God. The whole of the contest in the story of Wrestling
Jacob rests on the principle that to know a man's name is to have
disarmed him to some extent, is to be able to exercise some kind of
power over him. However charmingly 'the hand' expresses itself,
this is a power struggle. God looks down the years and sees where
this leads:

he saw cities
the hand would build, engines
that it would raze them with. His sight
dimmed. Tempted to undo the joints
of the fingers, he picked it up.

The potential to be destructive as well as creative is present.
Because of this God is tempted to weaken his adversary, and the
battle becomes a battle of conscience for God, a battle with himself.
In 'Other' it was the sense of otherness which God resented and
decided to destroy. Here, in a nice play on the Genesis story, he
wrestles with himself. Not only is the right of the 'other' to exist at
all in question, but also the effect of the 'other' on God. Thomas uses
his technique of careful line-breaks to demonstrate the tensions:

But God, feeling the nails . . .

Habits of association direct our thought immediately to the Crucifixion, and we assume that God sees the Crucifixion as the ultimate
opposition made possible by his creation of the hand. (The poem
'Earth'[56] says: 'The machine replaces/ the hand that fastened you/
to the cross'.) The decision to 'undo the joints' seems imminent. But
the poem proceeds:

But God, feeling the nails
in his side . . .

1. Monet: *Lady with Parasol*

2. Cassatt: *Young Woman Sewing*

3. Degas: *Mademoiselle Dihau at the Piano*

4. Degas: *Musicians in the Orchestra*

5. Toulouse-Lautrec: *Jane Avril Dancing*

6. Renoir: *The Bathers*

7. Degas: *Woman Combing*

8. Gauguin: *The Alyscamps at Arles*

This has the effect of confusing us momentarily, as 'his side' also has associations with the Crucifixion, but of course, the logic is at fault. Christ did not suffer the nails in his side. Even so, the phrase has had its effect. The image of the Passion has been reinforced and the possible consequences of otherness emphasised. We become aware that the 'nails in his side' also bear connotations of the hand reaching out in order to identify the Christ. But the Passion image represents only one of the polarities suggested in these lines:

> But God, feeling the nails
> in his side, the unnerving warmth
> of the contact . . .

From this perspective the nails are those of the hand wrestling with God, and the fear, if such it is, is not that of alienation but of contact. The reality of contact is not what God had anticipated. Previously we have read:

> It was a hand. God looked at it
> and looked away. There was a coldness
> about his heart, as though the hand
> clasped it.

The coldness indicates a dread of consequences, but is also projected onto the hand as if it too were cold.[57] But actual contact reveals the hand to be warm and God is unnerved by it. For him, the warmth of human contact is another source of vulnerability. While the touch of the hand might at the moment be gratifying it holds a frightening potential – the delivery of the first tool. Resolution is found in a reversal of the outcome which we find in the canonical myth:

> 'I let you go',
> he said, 'but without blessing.'

In realising its potential for good and for evil, the hand can produce only 'mixed things'. All that God can do is to require that he should be known as separate from the 'mixed things'. (Ironically, 'mixed things' describes precisely the problematics of imaging God, the meeting place of the *via positiva* and the *via negativa*.)[58] God uses the formula for himself-as-other that he gave to Moses – 'I am':

> Messenger to the mixed things
> of your making, tell them I am.

The hand retains the freedom to operate independently of God, and it is this independence which is signified in the tool, in the machine, and in science. The greater the degree of independence which science provides, the less God is needed. Thomas sees this as a tragic reduction of human experience. For him, the loss of the numinous is too great a price to pay for the advantages science has conferred. The machine despoils nature[59] symbolising an alienation of the human from nature; it has emptied the villages as people go in pursuit of money, alienating people from their roots and from each other, and it has rendered humans independent of God, the ultimate alienation. In spite of the strength of these feelings Thomas confesses the impossibility of finding a resolution, seeing two sides to the problem. On the one hand, he regrets the passing of the age of faith, but on the other, he recognises that much of the faith was based on helplessness and ignorance.[60] As science has pushed back frontiers, so, for some, God has been pushed further and further out of the frame. This is what John Tripp was missing when he remarked that 'the agricultural tractor can't really be that significant in the scheme of things'.[61]

Thomas has said:

> One of the great motifs of my later works has been the wrestling with the machine, which has transformed our life, has really led to a loss of faith of a great many people; because religious faith and dependence are so closely linked and the machine in all its aspects has made man more or less independent. You know, if you've got an illness these days you don't kneel down and pray; you go to hospital and a surgeon or a physician cures you, so there's no need to pray to God. These things are available in other ways. There are a thousand aspects of the machine. I took the machine as a symbol of all sorts of technology and scientific curiosity . . . it's the over-use of technology in service of the libido, this unquenchable desire for more and more material goods and material pleasures and so on. That is the enemy, and it's that that I see the machine as being the provider of, and in the process, of course, enslaving man. In the process of giving man these things the price it asks is enslavement. The great saying of Christianity

about God is that his service is perfect freedom, whereas to me the service of the machine is perfect enslavement.[62]

The role of the priest and the poet are complementary in Thomas and the effect of the machine on religion is reflected in its effect on poetry. In his poem 'The Other',[63] his most ferocious image of the machine demonstrates the Coleridgian phrase Thomas has sometimes referred to, that the opposite of poetry is not prose, but science.[64]

In a poem remarkable for its density, the machine appears here as a Frankenstein's monster, dominating its creators. 'They did it to me.' The voice is that of the machine and its first utterance is to disclaim responsibility for its actions. We are reminded how often the metaphor of the tool is used to do just this. But when it is invented, brought forth out of the mind as it were, the machine takes on a life of its own. The creators seem helpless to control it. Its advent is announced in jarring, ugly language – the 'screech of steel', the 'cogged smile', the 'iron hand'.[65] While it is welcomed as a release from drudgery, the effect of its arrival is in fact to deprive the people of work. Deceived by the smile they put out trusting hands, only to have them broken. Having welcomed the machine as a release from drudgery they find their skills are rendered obsolete. Resistance to the machine is expressed in a Luddite-type revolt (they rose), but the machine is insuperable, cropping them 'like tall/ grass'. We note how easily the voice might be transposed to that of 'war'. The imagery is modernised with the reference to oil:

> A little oil,
> I begged in conspiracy
> with disaster.

The implication of war increases, reminding us of the vast changes which have been effected in global politics and economics by the machine's appetite for oil.[66] The resistant voice now is that of the poet, who can find, in the machine, nothing to celebrate. So the machine is the poet's undoing too. The language of the machine is not a poetic language – it challenges the poet – and the effect of the machine on the modern consciousness has been to deprive the poet of those subjective and emotional resources on which he habitually drew.[67] The voice of the machine, somewhat unnervingly, expresses the recognition:

> I took him apart
> verse by verse, turning
> on him my x-ray
> eyes to expose the emptiness
> of his interiors.

It was out of the 'mind's mortuary' that the machine came in the first place. It is a nice irony that the poet's mind is also the mind that created the monster. In the technological age the machine is a kind of perverse poem. Those human needs which were once met by the poet (and priest) can now be provided by the machine which in so doing deprives the poet of his resources. 'The emptiness/ of his interiors' anticipates the closing lines where the image of the house with no hearth can be read both literally and metaphorically. Reading in a literal mode we see that the machine has supplanted the need for the living flame on the hearth with a mechanical form of heating, against which the figure of the poet huddles for warmth. But read metaphorically, we see the poet, deprived of the warmth of poetic language and theme, struggling to survive by trying to draw on the machine for his material. The problem has been expressed in a more wistful manner in *H'm*, where, in 'The Hearth', a poem not often remarked upon, we are offered a helpful gloss on the interplay between poetry and science. Here the hearth is opposed to the scientists outside. It is the hearth which controls and focuses the scale of life in this poem:

> In front of the fire
> With you, the folk song
> Of the wind in the chimney and the sparks'
> Embroidery of the soot – eternity
> Is here . . .

The metaphors are beautiful in themselves but they are also suggestive of the ambience – the style of living and the values – which is prized in this house, folksong and embroidery evoking a way of life which is rural, traditional and almost lost. The whole of life is contained in the small room and eternity becomes a present reality in the achievement of wholeness. (Thomas subscribes to the scriptural understanding of eternity as a quality of life, as well as of life hereafter.)[68]

'Outside' is the world of science and technology, of a restless people moving, time-ridden, in pursuit of a new saviour who may be science itself. The suggestion is that 'outside' is not just outside of the house, or of the room with the hearth, but outside the couple. It is outside 'us':

> and outside
> Us is time and the victims
> Of time, travellers
> To a new Bethlehem, statesmen
> And scientists with their hands full
> Of the gifts that destroy.

The poem consists of one long sentence, and we notice how much more colourful is the poetry of the first half than that of the last. The image of the Magi has itself lost the vibrancy associated with the Nativity. Their hands are full but they are full of the 'gifts that destroy'. The lyricism of the first half of the sentence is balanced by the austerity of the last. Poetry here is denying itself, it is seeking a language which is appropriate to desolation. It is a self-referential irony that the poet has succeeded. The poem not only demonstrates the poet's antipathy to the age of technology and his doubts about its inherent values, but also reflects Thomas's awareness of the difficulties in producing authentic poetry in an age whose language is the language of technology.

The advent of the machine, the poet's need for an appropriate language and the loss of the numinous are closely related in Thomas's thought. How does the poet (or the priest for that matter) come to terms with the language of science? Is it possible to produce poetry from this language, and if so is it religious poetry? Can the language of science be adapted to praise God? Can science stand as an image of God? These are just some of the questions raised by the image of the machine in Thomas's work. A further question presents itself in the poem 'Reply'.[69] Has science itself become a religion?

The interfacing of science with religion and the comprehensive treatment of the components make this one of Thomas's most metaphysical poems, which works by a deliberately self-conscious elevating of the elements into a religious frame. Just as, in the Prytherch poems, he occasionally, and knowingly, romanticises the peasant, so here Thomas plays with the possibilities of rendering science an expression of praise. But what at first appears to be a willingness to consider the potential of science to stand for an image of God quickly becomes a critique. Embracing all the symbols of technology, from the simplicity of the wheel and of bolts and rivets to the sophistication of strontium and plutonium, space exploration and the computer, Thomas parodies the Scriptures. The wheels seem to fulfil the function which in Job belongs to the stars – 'The morning stars sang together'[70] – and in the Gospels to the star of Bethlehem.[71] The travellers and gifts refer to the Magi[72] and the anthem and choruses refer, with the Song upon Patmos, to the vision of Revelations.[73] The positive images of science glorifying God are persistently undercut by pejorative language. The wheels proceed in 'unnecessary' directions. The travellers hold out 'thin' gifts. The chorus of the bolts and rivets is 'expensive' and expectations of the computer to reinstate communication with God is futile. But there is more here than a critique of modern technology. There is a sense of enormous loss, which increases as the poem proceeds. The pattern is not just that of salvation history but is also the pattern of conventional worship, with images of worship being produced as the languages of religion and science are interfaced with each other. We find intimations of praise, images of genuflection and offering, and the 'clerestories' remind us of the church building, but by the time we come to the anthem the sense of loss deepens with the realisation that none of these things achieves communication with God. A profound sadness permeates these lines:

> What anthem have our computers
> to insert into the vacuum caused
> by the break in transmission
> of the song upon Patmos?

There is a sense of movement in the poem which describes an upward and outward motion, which might reflect an aspiration towards God as much as a movement through time and space; but as the progression moves it passes from 'thin', through 'high', to 'blind space'. The pejorative use of 'blind' qualifies what might otherwise seem to be a positive progression, and a sense of failure is confirmed when what might have been a goal is realised as a vacuum. It is as much a critique of prayer as of science. Thomas seems to be saying that while modern communication systems can make connections previously unthought of, not only is there now a vacuum at the heart of modern life which science cannot fill, but science has undermined that mode of communication which we once found satisfying, and we feel the ache for the old mystical experience of John on the island of Patmos. So the experiment with science, and with the language of science, to express a modern understanding of God has succeeded only in demonstrating its inadequacy in functioning as an image of God. But if God is the God of science too, what image can the poet create for him? Thomas offers us 'At It'.[74] where 'he' is imagined sitting at Eddington's table 'that is not a table' – God the scientist. The poem begins:

> I think he sits at that strange table
> of Eddington's, that is not a table
> at all . . .

And moves on to:

> I imagine his
> face that is more the face
> of a clock . . .

but these phrases are emotionally neutral. A variation in rhythm draws attention to the second paragraph:

> And I would have
> things to say to this God . . .
> . . . storming at him,

This is a good place to begin as it introduces the point of opposition. The emotion evoked, largely through the rhythm, stands in marked contrast to the objective, neutral observations of the poem as a whole. It is the point where morality intrudes and a human scale and human values are registered. Where the voice has formerly been cool and distanced, now it is angry and involved, and the unspecified 'things to say' suggests an inarticulacy promoted by anger, a wry contrast with Job who stormed with the 'eloquence' of the abused heart. But this voice, formerly cool, is capable of storming too. The passage reveals a depth of anger unimagined and unprepared for by the earlier lines. It sets up the opposition between the objective, scientific understanding of the world and the human understanding of notions of right and wrong which that scientific view does not address. The heat and the anger of this paragraph contrast strongly with the remainder of the poem. Contained within the emotional, rhythmic structure of the paragraph is the 'human condition' and outside it is the indeterminate, the unknown.

Superficially, the images create a picture of God as a scientist who is sitting at a table writing, working out the calculations that constitute the universe. God is anthropomorphised in that he sits and he writes, but closer reading demonstrates that he is not really defined at all, and there are no concrete images. Description is invalidated by negatives and what at first appears to be an image is rendered abstract and unstable.[75] The table is not a table, the handwriting is invisible; what we thought was a face is 'more the face of a clock' and the perspective of time encompasses empires 'not yet begun'. The poem has all the signs of a classic *via negativa*.

The 'Eddington' referred to is the scientist A.S. Eddington, the first expositor of the theory of relativity in the English language and a practising Quaker, and the poem is informed by his book *The Nature of the Physical World*.[76] In the Introduction to this book we read:

> I have settled down to the task of writing these lectures and have drawn up my chairs to my two tables . . . my scientific table is mostly emptiness. Sparsely scattered in that emptiness are numerous electric charges rushing about with great speed; but their combined bulk amounts to less than a billionth of the bulk of the table itself. . . . There is nothing substantial about my second table. It is nearly all empty space . . .

Eddington's style is intended to make his subject accessible to the lay person, and his use of images is very appealing. Thomas makes good use of them: 'I think he sits at that strange table/ of Eddington's' suggests that God presides over the interiors and intricacies of science. As the creator-God, he writes 'the instructions the genes follow' rather than creates man from the dust of the ground. It is very much a late twentieth-century concept of God. But as we have already noted, if we read closely we find that, in fact, there is no image of God at all, and this is in keeping with Eddington's rejection of the notion of substance in his own field. Thomas finds in Eddington's concept of eliminating substance a mode of apprehending God which is free of preconceived ideas. Eddington refers to our notion of substance as 'a traditional

picture-gallery of conceptions which convey no authentic information of the background and obtrude irrelevancies into the scheme
of knowledge'. Thomas's growing impatience with conventional
images of God could be described in just those terms.

We might expect that pure science can mediate God and stand
as an acceptable image of God; Thomas has acknowledged this to
be so,[77] but the God of science in this poem fails to inspire either
awe or rapture. The contemplation of this God gives rise to an
apparently unprovoked outburst – the passage we looked at above,
which, in context, seems to be almost a *non sequitur*: 'And I would
have/ things to say to this God . . .' It is to this God, the neutral,
abstracted figure, that the voice would have 'things to say', would
storm at him as Job stormed. The reference to Job implies that the
crux of the opposition lies in the question of suffering, but this
question is not overtly raised. It has no place in the scientific discourse, and it is only in the sub-text of the 'abused heart' that the
inference may be discerned. Eddington acknowledges the relationship of suffering to the scientific discourse in this way:

> In the world of physics we watch a shadowgraph performance
> of the drama of familiar life. The shadow of my elbow rests on
> the shadow table as the shadow ink flows over the shadow paper.
> It is all symbolic, and as a symbol the physicist leaves it. Then
> comes the alchemist Mind who transmutes the symbols. The
> sparsely spread nuclei of electric force become a tangible solid;
> their restless agitation becomes the warmth of summer; the
> octave of aethereal vibrations becomes a gorgeous rainbow. Nor
> does the alchemy stop here. In the transmuted world new
> significances arise which are scarcely to be traced in the world of
> symbols; so that it becomes a world of beauty and purpose – and,
> alas, suffering and evil.[78]

This suggests that there is an important aspect of being human
which science cannot address. There is then an inadequacy in the
scientific concept. The human mind is not satisfied with the world
of scientific theory. It 'need(s) a technique/ other than that of physics'.[79] But in this poem God is imaged only according to the technique of physics – he is a 'shadowgraph performance'. In so far as
he is, he is entirely self-contained and self-absorbed, and it is the
implied indifference to the human condition which links the God of

science with the God of Job; the God who also created marvels and wonders is barely represented.

Emotion is confined to the central passage and nowhere is it applied to God. God belongs to that unstable discourse outside the passage and outside the human scale. The passage anticipates a time when a relationship between God and humans will allow for a human response to be heard. In the phrase 'the abused heart' there are implications of injustice, of questions of right and wrong, but there is nothing in the rest of the poem to suggest that this is a moral universe. There are no implicit moral criteria in the actions of the scientist-God, only the efficacy of his methods is registered.

The rhetoric of the passage we have foregrounded would suggest that there is a time of reckoning, a time when questions will be answered and wrongs righted. We might even anticipate a typical Thomas inversion of biblical precedent in which God becomes the one judged and man stands in judgement. This is coldly undermined in the concluding lines – there will be no judgement other than his

>   abstruse
> geometry that proceeds eternally
> in the silence beyond right and wrong.

The moral question is put on one side, and we are returned to the dilemma suffered by Job. The scientist-God re-emerges in the pragmatic language of the earlier lines, language which, relying on the discourse of science, empties them of all moral content. This enables Thomas to elevate the apparent indifference of God to a dimension which can no longer be challenged by human values. God operates in the silence 'beyond right and wrong'. The words confirm our premise that the poem is engaged with notions of justice. But there is also the implication that our values are temporal and spatial; that there is a context other than that which we know, a different dimension which is outside of human experience. Once again, Thomas underlines his conviction that God is other than that which we can imagine, and he places God firmly outside the limitations of human knowledge and values. It is a bleak resolution, an emotionless reconciliation of moral and scientific values. But it is yet another possible image of God.

The depersonalising of God which occurs when the language of science is employed, the greatest challenge of all to conventional religious belief, is further evidenced in *Later Poems*. 'Gradual'[80] makes a useful gloss on 'At It'. The liturgical title suggests that the poem is a hymn, or psalm, of praise, but unlike a hymn it does not find satisfactory closure. The 'borders of the understanding' and the minds whose 'instruments are beside the point of their sharpness' remind us both of the cleverness of the scientists and of their failure to meet our spiritual needs. Thomas says:

> I need a technique
> other than that of physics
>
> for registering the ubiquity
> of your presence.

The language of science will not do, but what is the alternative? Language which is constructed around ordinary human experience will not do either, for it cannot help anthropomorphising God. Thomas recognises that God is free of human senses and finds liberty in that freedom. For the human, however, the senses are life. Without them we die. This sense of the otherness of God, the challenge it presents to the intellect and the need to define who, or what God is, elicits the plea:

> Call your horizons
>
> in. Suffer the domestication
> for a moment of the ferocities
> you inhabit.

The request reveals the poet's own apprehension of God; we catch a glimpse of his personal mode of dealing with the problem. The unlimited 'horizon' which represents God is as difficult a concept as God being 'beyond right and wrong' in 'At It'. The request to 'call in' the horizons and to 'suffer the domestication' of the ferocities, is a request for accommodation to the human scale, for God to be brought within the limits of our understanding and our language. The poem escapes the 'technique of physics', but it does not escape the problem of human language. To 'call', to 'suffer' (note two meanings of 'suffer') and to 'inhabit' are all firmly oriented within the human experience; domestication is imposed on the God by necessity.

'Suddenly',[81] in the same volume, provides a brief respite from struggle, and may therefore be used to bring this section to a close. This poem appears to find closure as the final lines gather together nature, science and the machine, and allow them all the ability to mediate God. The fusion of the language of science with the vernacular in an expression of praise is at last accomplished. But there is something which is not entirely convincing in the tone of this poem. It begins well, in the manner of a psalm:

> He addresses me from a myriad
> directions with the fluency
> of water, the articulateness
> of green leaves; and in the genes
> too, the components
> of my existence.

Here God's 'language' is fluent, it is articulate, but it is indirect. The poetry is successful because the images work hard; the metaphors not only suggest the manner of God's speech but also present the reader with the means – here the natural objects – by which that speech is mediated. In other words, we realise that God speaks fluently and articulately, but that he does so through water, leaves and genes. The poem is less successful when the metaphors become more direct: 'The rock,/ so long speechless, is the library/ of his poetry.' 'The weather/ is his mind's turbine . . .' The ideas are apposite, but we cannot help feeling that they have not been sufficiently assimilated by the poetic imagination before finding their place on the page. They lack the elegance of the earlier passage. A further problem is raised by the lines which suggest that God sings in the chainsaw. The image of the chainsaw is clearly an attempt to rehabilitate the machine, but it is not convincing. In other poems the machine 'sings', but it does not sing of God. It sings of money.[82] Here we are asked to accept that God speaks, or rather 'sings', through the chainsaw, just as he does through the water and the green leaves. Readers must make a conscious effort to see the chainsaw as a constructive, friendly object, rather than a destructive and potentially harmful one. They must also accept the notion that God 'sings'.[83] (The awkward possessive in 'the skin's parchment' doesn't work very well either.) The problem here is of a subtly different kind. The poem's self-conscious elevation of disparate features into a religious frame demonstrates the actual problems the religious poet has in an age of technology. We noted a similar technique applied in 'Reply'. That poem was successful because there we were *meant* to note the ironies of elevating technology into a religious frame. 'Suddenly' does not work like that. It purports to be a serious resolution of the tensions between science and religion, and although the closing lines do achieve something like an acceptable resolution, it is not wholly successful. Its placement at the end of this chapter is not to confirm the possibility of finding successful images for God in science, nor to affirm its centrality in Thomas's work. Rather, it serves to reiterate the difficulties, and to recognise our own need to resolve the increasingly abstract and problematical images which Thomas has created.

5

The *Via Negativa*

During our reading of 'The Minister' we discovered that the relationship between the narrator and the reader was an uneasy one. Readers are unsure of what they are expected to bring to the reading of the text. The narratorial voice is constantly shifting between various positions; sometimes it is authoritative, sometimes interrogatory, often unreliable. The reader can at no time afford to be passive, but always must be making judgements and assessments as the reading proceeds. A similar process pertains in the shorter poems. They are, perhaps, less self-reflexive texts than 'The Minister', but often they lack the movement towards closure which has generally been supposed to be the project of the religious text. If we consider some of Thomas's poems on prayer, we note how he complicates the relationship between the narrator and the reader, and how this becomes almost a critique of the act of prayer itself. Inscribed in the reading, of course, is the relationship between the narrator or implied persona and God.

An early poem on prayer is 'In a Country Church'.[1] Here the narrator is distanced from the persona by the use of the impersonal 'one' in the first stanza, but the narrator is still authoritative. The first stanza is at pains to demythologise the popular concept of prayer. It opens with an unambiguous statement: 'To one kneeling down no word came.' There are no illusions to be entertained here, and any expectations of a visionary nature are sharply, even satirically, undercut by the narrator:

> . . . the dry whisper of unseen wings,
> Bats not angels, in the high roof.

This earthing of the experience, rendering it mundane, represents a different sort of closing of the gaps in the text; the reader is permitted no private interpretation. We can contrast this with the lines in 'The Minister' where a rather different effect is produced:

and love's text
Is riddled by the inhuman cry
Of buzzards circling above the moor.

As we saw, the enjambment here prolongs the speculation and invites the reader to define the source of the 'inhuman cry', only to undercut any religious reading by the words of the following line. In the opening lines of 'In a Country Church', however, no such mystery is encouraged. There is no sense of the numinous and in the absence of a 'word' a serious sense of lack might be registered. As St Ignatius has it (in Simon Tugwell's formulation),[2] 'God is one, in a mystery of his own being; but from his primordial Silence there comes a Word.' Yet this is precisely the expectation which the opening lines of the poem deny. In fact, the whole of the first stanza creates an antithesis to the experience of Pentecost.[3] Instead of the gift of language, 'no word came'. Where at Pentecost there was the sound of a 'mighty rushing wind' which certainly stirred the saints, here the wind's song is only 'saddening the lips/ of the grave saints' who are 'rigid in glass'. The 'unseen wings' are bats, not angels. The key words which influence the reader are 'sad[dening]', 'grave', 'rigid' and 'dry'; the action is frozen in a moment of time, and the image of prayer which registers is desolate. While this stanza is emphatic, leaving little room for the reader to make a private reading, the reader's response is still a dynamic part of the poem. These bleak images, which occur frequently in Thomas, often disappoint the reader, who expects him to claim ease of access to the ear of the Almighty.[4] Readers, then, are forced into the position of enacting a response to this stanza, which parallels a possible response to prayer. They may be irritated by the lack of communication, expecting something more positive, or, while identifying with its honesty, may find the experience bleak and unsatisfactory. A sudden shift of position introduces the second stanza, and the narrator moves from the authoritative to the interrogatory mode:

Was he balked by silence?

The question provides a space in which the reader may anticipate the response of the persona, but, more significantly, it reveals that the narrator too has difficulty in making sense of the situation. (Paradoxically, in pre-empting the question, the narrator undermines the interrogative mode. Such is the authoritative tone of the question that it verges on the rhetorical.) The phrase 'He kneeled long' suggests both delay, and the time within which the first stanza operated.

We might expect the poem to continue in the negative mode, but the apparent desolation of the period of waiting in the first stanza sees the flowering of intuitive understanding in the second:

> He kneeled long,
> And saw love in a dark crown
> Of thorns blazing, and a winter tree
> Golden with fruit of a man's body.

In this image the paradox inherent in all mystical experience is demonstrated. The intuitive response obviates the need for language – the lack of which is regretted in the first stanza – but in returning to language in order to express that intuitive experience, the poet/ mystic must rely on paradox and metaphor. These by their very nature conceal as well as reveal the mystical experience. In the first stanza the narrator has carefully unpicked any knots, leaving the reader with no possibility of misapprehension; the metaphors clarify the subject. The second stanza challenges the first with its mystical experience couched in ambiguities, and here the metaphors re-mystify the vision. There are many things here which are far from clear. The images slide between the concrete and the abstract, blurring distinctions and demanding readjustments as we read. The lines consist of a number of startling juxtapositions. At first love appears to be in a 'dark crown', but that is adjusted in the next line, to a 'dark crown of thorns'. The thorns appear to be 'blazing'; a further adjustment of the sense produces the understanding that it is in fact 'love' that is 'blazing', so that love and thorns are insepar-ably linked. In the first image then, we have an abstraction finding a form, a presence, 'he' saw 'love blazing'. In the second a concrete image reinforces the implications of the abstract one, and introduces some paradoxes of its own. The cross is presented as a 'winter tree', a recurring image with Thomas, but here the tree is 'golden with fruit'.[5] 'Golden' suggests plenitude and fecundity, pleasurable response, until the line is completed – 'golden with fruit of a man's body'. The clarity of language employed in 'a man's body', the lack of euphemism in the phrase, has the strange effect of defamiliarising the religious image, raising the consciousness to an awareness of an actual human figure, and of human suffering. It now takes a great effort of the imagination to accept the image of the golden fruit as an appropriate metaphor for the 'man's body'.[6] Not only must these two images be held in tension, but the images of 'love blazing' and 'a man's body' must also be reconciled. 'To one kneeling down no word came.' The term 'word' is used here in its normal sense to indicate a linguistic means of communication. No verbal communication is received by the figure kneeling. But communication of some sort is realised in the second stanza. To quote Tugwell again: 'From the mysterious silence there comes a Word.' This 'Word' is the Logos, God's expression of himself in Christ,[7] and it is through this Word that communication is effected in the second stanza. The image of God which is received is that of the man's body; in this poem God communicates only through the experience of suffering.

Simon Tugwell's reference to St Ignatius continues:

and the Word is himself One, coming from the One without being separated from the One . . . his disciples must enter into this unity, by responding both to his words and deeds and to his silence, and this means reproducing in themselves the conjunction of silence and word, of faith and charity, of flesh and spirit.

The conjunction of silence and word occurs in this poem, but the language of the first stanza suggests that the silence is suffered rather than desired, that it is a lack, rather than a fulfilment, of revelation. God, then, does not communicate through words, but he does communicate through the Word and through silence. Paradoxically, then, God is remote and uncommunicative and prayer is cold and unproductive, but God is also intensely near and prayer is effective and fruitful. We are reminded of the words of Ruysbroek:[8] 'Tranquillity according to His essence, activity according to His nature: *perfect stillness, perfect fecundity*' (my italics).

This paradox is registered not only within the poems but between the poems as well. Consider 'In Church.'[9] Where in the last poem the silence was suffered, here it is explored. The voice admits its own puzzlement over the situation and offers no authoritative lead to the reader. The arena in which God must be found is silence, and the silence holds within itself the possibility of being fruitful and productive or merely empty. The poet expresses 'the quality of its silences' in a way which animates them, as if he is predisposed to anticipate a positive element. A close reading reveals an almost Dickensian skill in animating the inanimate. The air recomposes itself.

It waits. Stones have grouped themselves about it. Shadows advance and take possession of places the light had held. Pews are uneasy, and, as before, there are the bats. Within this silence, then, there is a life which inheres, which is not dependent on the presence of a human figure to animate it, which has an independent existence, a life of its own. In this emptiness, this silence, this absence, the narrator implies, God dwells; the air becomes a metaphor for God, but in so doing it ceases to be empty, silent absence. Set in contrast to this is the need of the human to be a creative part of this transformation. The stones, for example, already have implied life because they have 'grouped themselves' around the air, but to the narrator they are the hard ribs of

> a body that our prayers have failed
> To animate.

(The line end at 'failed' is, of course, significant.) The man breathing has tried to fill this air with life, but already it is alive, and it becomes an appropriate symbol both for prayer and for God. The idea implicitly stated, of the merging of the air (God or prayer) with the breath (or prayer) of the man so that neither can be separated from the other, holds within itself a delicately held uncertainty, a kind of positive doubtfulness about where the 'I' of the poem ends and the Other begins. The ambiguity precisely focuses the experiential quality of the moment.[10] Uncertainty continues in the images of emptiness and waiting. Images of man and emptiness and waiting are familiar in the work of R.S. Thomas, but their significance varies.[11] Here the untenanted cross as emptiness is ambiguous. It may be empty because the myth is untrue and therefore meaningless, or it may be empty because Christ is risen, in which case it is a symbol of resurrection and faith is justified in its waiting. The questions may be nailed to the cross, demanding answers, like Luther's treatise nailed to the church door, or they may be 'nailed' to the 'untenanted cross' as a sign that they have been dealt with forever in the death and resurrection of Christ. The popular concept of the religious text as closed, or even of seeking closure, is challenged; the options are kept wide open. The poem can remain poised in a state of unresolved equilibrium, or it can embrace the *via negativa* and find God in the absence, in the emptiness.

The tension between the silence and the word which manifests itself in 'In a Country Church', and the ambiguities of silence as we read them in 'In Church', are fundamental to the mystical way. It is a way paved with paradox. Through the *via negativa* the mystic hopes for a purer apprehension of what God is, an apprehension which transcends created things; but in expressing that apprehension the mystic of necessity draws on created things as metaphor, thus acknowledging the possibility that the creature might function as a reflection of God. In other words, the *via positiva* is an essential complement to the *via negativa*, and without it the *via negativa* cannot express its intuited knowledge.

'In Church', 'In a Country Church' and the further poem 'Kneeling'[12] all have a similar theme. They all register moments spent in the church waiting on God and have been considered repetitive by some readers. It seems to me, however, that the very nature of the project demands this multifaceted approach. The poet is engaged in exploring the experience of a man waiting on God, trying to find a means of communion, of communication. He is trying to discover exactly what is going on in this act, and noting that no two experiences are quite the same. The mode of consciousness in the persona varies, affecting the outcome, so that it becomes necessary to state and restate his apprehension of God. The experience is never quite fully told. Often these poems start with an objective awareness of surroundings, or with a position of straightforward self-consciousness:

> To one kneeling down no word came,
> Only the wind's song
> > 'In A Country Church'

> Often I try
> To analyse the quality
> Of its silences.
> > 'In Church'

Between them they register various approaches to God but two elements seem to recur. There is the awareness of the self, which may dominate for most of the poem, and there is the (sometimes momentary) loss of this awareness. Sometimes self-awareness blurs into vision ('In a Country Church'), or there might be a movement of the consciousness away from self towards God. This may be so momentary as to be barely perceptible ('In Church'), or it may be more sustained as in the poem considered earlier, 'The Moor':

What God was there made himself felt,
Not listened to . . .

There were no prayers said. But stillness
Of the heart's passions – that was praise
Enough; and the mind's cession
Of its kingdom.

We note here the paradox which is permanently in attendance on the religious poet, that of expressing as though immediate an awareness which by its very nature could only be perceived in hindsight – an awareness of a lack of self-consciousness. The poem 'Kneeling', on the other hand, appears to be totally self-conscious throughout:

Moments of great calm,
Kneeling before an altar
Of wood in a stone church
In summer, waiting for the God
To speak . . .

The components in the scene are itemised with the precision and clarity of a set of stage directions – the 'hero is discovered kneeling before an altar of wood in a stone church in summer . . .' This is in harmony with the image of the priest as actor which is being developed. Self-consciousness is epitomised in 'the sun's light/ Ringing me, as though I acted/ a great role'. The theatrical imagery develops, blending the presence of the congregation, or even of angelic spirits, with that of an audience awaiting a performance. It is that moment of tension before the priest/actor delivers his words. The prompter is in attendance. At the same time there is in the precise language a heightened awareness of the nature of things, a sensitivity to the fundamental being of those things which compose the surroundings; the nature of stone and wood, of summer and sunlight and of their contribution to an apprehension of God. We may note the further paradox that this sensitivity, expressing itself only in bare statements of 'stone' and 'wood', makes no attempt to represent poetically their 'fundamental being' as, perhaps, Hopkins would have done. The language, more akin to Wordsworth than to Hopkins, generates a sense of the massive solidity of the features and refuses to etherealise them. The significance of this will be noted in due course: for now, we note that the deliberately organised line ending 'as though I acted' does not support the view that this is only role playing. And, indeed, the earlier line describing the air as 'a staircase/ For silence', has pointed in a different direction: the latter is a means of access to communion, a concourse along which God – who is perceived in the silence – might venture, and the possible play on sun/Son further inscribes God's presence.[13] The theatrical and the religious merge, as, in a parody of St Augustine, the priest addresses God:

> Prompt me, God;
> But not yet.

There is a movement from the outer to the inner, from the tangible 'isness' of the theatrical setting to the numinousness of God. A mode of acute self-consciousness lies in the image of the priest as actor. The awareness of physical surroundings and of the self as a figure in these surroundings represents the response of the senses to the tangible world. But a second mode of consciousness is registered in an act of recollection:

> Moments of great calm,
> Kneeling before an altar
>
> Prompt me, God . . .

Here, in spite of the involvement of the first person, the attention is diverted away from the self in a strong movement towards God, and we see that the scene which has been set is more than the stage on which the 'actor' will deliver his lines. It is valid in itself as an intrinsic element in the act of prayer. This act has embraced the entire position of the man: his self, his awareness and his surroundings, and all these elements make a contribution to his communion with God. There is a sense of stillness in the poem which is created by the evocation of such words as 'calm', 'silence', 'still'; in the repetition of the word 'waiting', and in the meditative pace achieved by simplicity of phrasing. In this particular approach, physical silence is a necessary complement to the act of communion. God is waited on for that moment of communion which is also communication. While there is a profound lack of self-consciousness, manifested in the degree of self-naughting which is necessary for such communion, paradox persists in the ability of the intellect, at the same time, to discern the fact that communion and communication may prove inseparable. The need to receive (not to compose) a significant word is focused, and an awareness registered that in the transposition from experience to expression something crucial will be lost.

The essence of the meaning cannot be transposed because it is fixed in something other than language. It inheres in the moment of recollection, embracing the place and the moment and the man. What is experienced is an intuited apprehension of God which precedes and transcends language and therefore cannot be adequately transcribed. God can be experienced but he cannot be told. Or, as the author of *The Cloud of Unknowing*[14] tells us, God 'can certainly be loved, but he cannot be thought'. Evelyn Underhill describes a similar situation:

> The full spiritual consciousness of the true mystic is developed not in one, but in two apparently opposite but really complementary directions . . . . On the one hand he is intensely aware of, and knows himself to be at one with that active World of Becoming, that immanent Life, from which his own life takes its rise. Hence, though he has broken for ever with the bondage of the senses, *he perceives in every manifestation of life a sacramental meaning; a loveliness, a wonder, a heightened significance, which is hidden from other men.* . . . On the other hand, the full mystic consciousness also attains to what is, I think, its really characteristic quality. It develops the power of apprehending the Absolute, Pure Being, the utterly Transcendent: or as its possessor would say, can experience 'passive union with God'. (my italics)[15]

While Thomas modestly denies that he is a 'true mystic'[16] his religious poetry has much in common with the characteristics of mysticism. In the refusal to etherealise his surroundings, accepting their solidity, their 'isness', he 'perceives in every manifestation of life a sacramental meaning'. But he also recognises that the experience which is being so delicately held will be disrupted and diminished by articulation, hence the plea 'Prompt me, God;/ But not yet'. The play on the words of St Augustine are particularly appropriate, for Augustine knew well the elusive character of such moments of heightened awareness:

> And then at last I saw Thy invisible things understood by means of the things that are made, but I could not sustain my gaze: my

weakness was dashed back, and I was relegated to my ordinary experience, bearing with me only a loving memory, and as it were the fragrance of those desirable meats on the which as yet I was not able to feed.[17]

So, as in the poem, there is a sense of a position being held, but being held delicately, tenuously, with a sense that the communion may at any moment be broken, and when it is broken no language can then express adequately what has been received. In the experience of this poem, then, the site of the 'meaning' says the priest, is 'in the waiting'. In the first poem we considered, 'In A Country Church', the expectation of receiving a 'Word' was initially denied. The expectation was paralleled as earlier noted in the words of St Ignatius:[18] 'God is one, in a mystery of his own being; but from his primordial Silence there comes a Word.' In the experience of that poem the Word which was eventually given was received in the form of an image, the 'winter tree/ Golden with fruit of a man's body'. This is typical of the *via positiva*. In the second poem, no word is expected. Rather, silence itself is explored as a possible locus of communication. While the animation within the church suggests some kind of presence, no visual image is used to represent God. He is represented only by air and silence. These refuse the imagination any substance to hold on to, and this approach is much nearer that of the *via negativa*. It does not actually achieve 'passive union with God' but hovers tentatively on the brink of the leap of faith. However, these poems do recognise the different means by which communion with God has traditionally been found. We might say that the first represents speech (the expected Word was received through the image) and the second, silence. What the poet-priest seeks in 'Kneeling', then, is that 'conjunction of silence and Word' which was recommended by St Ignatius. In 'Kneeling' the silence seems more meaningful to the poet because speech involves loss, but in fact the waiting and the speaking are the *via negativa* and the *via positiva* to each other. The *via negativa*, and the experience of its silence, cannot be sustained; it can only be defined imperfectly through the *via positiva*. What is actually required is a 'speaking' which is informed by silence and a silence which 'speaks'. 'The meaning is in the waiting' is only partially true. We might very well refer again to that quotation from St Ignatius which we used above: 'His disciples must enter into this unity, by responding both to his words and deeds and to his silence, and this means reproducing in themselves the *conjunction of silence and word*, of faith and charity, of flesh and spirit' (my italics).

In all our references to God we are of necessity drawing on language which has its roots deep in human experience, and by which it is limited. 'Revelation', says Brian Wren, 'is not disembodied, but incarnational: if God reveals Godself to us, it has to be in language drawn from the particularities of our physical makeup and our political, economic and cultural experience.'[19] It is clear, then, that to express a sense of union, or even communion, with God stretches the resources of the poet. He/she must attempt to find a language which can convey the sense of that which is beyond description because it is always outside of human experience.

Thomas acknowledges this in 'The Combat':[20] 'your resistance/ is endless at the frontier of the great poem.' This resistance of the Infinite to expression in terms which are finite raises some interesting possibilities. For example, a question very much in focus at the time of writing is that of gender-oriented religious language. Images of God in religious poetry lean heavily on the patriarchal system. Wren points out how dependent hymn-writers are on such images of God, and he illustrates his point by organising such images into the cumulative phrase: 'King-God-Almighty-Father-Protector'.[21] The *via negativa* recognises that God is not like anything that we can know; that language is always inadequate. It therefore follows that language which refers to God in patriarchal terms is not only inadequate, as all language is, but also is not innocent. It colours our perception of what God is like, as we draw on our own experience of patriarchy in interpreting the metaphors. There have been some interesting attempts to express an understanding of God which embraces the concept of the female rather than, or as well as, the male, from the spirituality of the Middle Ages[22] to the consciousness-raising of modern feminist writers.[23] Great care must be taken in any project to find new models for God; there is always the danger that in looking to female images the result will be not to enrich our concepts of God, but merely to shift the problem from one gender to the other, or simply to reinscribe a stereotype; the treatment of women in chapter 1 has already alerted us to the problem. However, as patriarchal images leave woman invisible and not represented in the God-image, so female imagery for God can in turn serve to exclude the male. The case for an inclusive reading might be found in Genesis 1.27 where we read:

So God created man in his *own* image, in the image of God created he him; male and female created he them.

This indicates that the first use of the term 'man' in the text is the so-called inclusive, referring to both man and woman; it suggests that God is like man but is also not like man. God is like woman but is also not like woman. 'Feminine' qualities applied to God in an effort to redress the balance raise problems of their own, for 'feminine' qualities also are based on a cultural construct just as those we might instance in the patriarchal approach. To find an image for God which does not rely on either male or female imagery but is both satisfying and appealing, difficult though it is, would seem to be one way of dealing with the problem. Brian Wren does this by moving between the genders, trying to achieve a more satisfying concept of God which does not marginalise women.[24] He challenges stereotypical images of man and woman by applying to one gender attributes which are usually associated with the other. Another option might be to avoid gender altogether, and to refer to God as 'It',[25] but this is not a popular solution. In Judaeo-Christian thought God is personal, so many believers find it offensive to refer to God as 'It' because it suggests to them a thing rather than a person. The use of the impersonal 'It' also raises problems of the adequacy of the images through which we can then understand what God is like, for, as we have seen, such images must relate to human experience and perception. However, there are some examples of a successful use of the impersonal pronoun in this context, notably by Pseudo-Dionysius. By referring to God as 'the universal Cause' in the first instance, he is justified in using the impersonal pronoun throughout the ensuing paragraph:[26]

We therefore maintain that the universal Cause transcending all things is neither impersonal nor lifeless, nor irrational nor without understanding: in short, that It is not a material body, and therefore does not possess outward shape or intelligible form, or quality, or quantity, or solid weight; nor has It any local existence which can be perceived by sight or touch; nor has It the power of perceiving or being perceived; nor does It suffer any vexation or disorder through the disturbance of earthly passions, or any feebleness through the tyranny of material chances, or any want of light; nor any change, or decay, or division, or deprivation, or ebb and flow, or anything else which the senses can perceive.

None of these things can be either identified with It or attributed to It.[27]

Thomas has negotiated the problem with admirable dexterity. I
would not suggest that he has set out deliberately to produce a successful gender-neutral text, but in employing the *via negativa*, with
its distrust of images, Thomas has coincidentally, perhaps, achieved
just this. In 'The Presence',[28] for example, he is primarily concerned
with the difficulty of imaging God, of expressing the experience of
the numinous in terms which are finite. While we concentrate on
the degree of his success, we must also note that one of the effects
of his skilful use of the term 'It' is effectively to neutralise gender
as applied to God. Thomas anticipates Wren and emulates Psuedo-
Dionysius in this beautifully judged piece. Here the elusive nature
of that which we call 'God' is reflected in the absence of proper
nouns. After the reference in the title to the 'Presence' there is no
naming of God. 'The Presence', like 'the universal Cause' of Pseudo-
Dionysius, is of course gender-neutral and this allows Thomas to
apply the impersonal pronoun 'it' throughout the poem without
giving offence. He can construct a whole range of images which
appeal to the modern temperament, exercised as it is by concepts of
male power as applied to God. He creates an image of God which
is neither masculine nor feminine but which is wholly desirable
and a triumph of expression. 'The Presence' is imaged as elusive,
shy, gentle, affectionate and willing to communicate without con-
descension. The terms which construct this image and the method
of their application will become clear as we continue the analysis of
the poem.

We have seen that R.S. Thomas has been preoccupied not only
with finding adequate images for God, but also with finding ways
of expressing that elusive moment of union with God. In 'The Presence' he creates a fine balance between the *via negativa* and the
via positiva which demonstrates the complementary nature of the
two. What we might call negative or insubstantial forms – silence,
invisibility – are given shape through verbs and adjectives which
suggest positive forms of being and substance. It is the reader
who, noting these verbs and adjectives, and working by a process
of association, constructs the image of 'The Presence'.

Using the *via negativa*, then, as a linguistic strategy, Thomas
creates a fluidity of movement which gently urges the reader along,
reflecting the urging of the poet by 'The Presence' as it

> catches me
> by the sleeve, nudging
> towards the long shelf

From the outset the reader is gently pressed into a series of readings and revisions which demonstrate that 'The Presence' is other
than we thought. This denial of expectations embodies a reflection
of meaning in form – God is other than we think:

> I pray and incur

The line ending invites speculation and clichés come to mind –
'wrath', perhaps ('incur' always suggests something unpleasant).
The dictionary definition is '1. 'To make oneself subject to (something undesirable) 2. bring upon oneself.' What is 'incurred' proves
to be 'silence'. Not only are one's expectations undercut, but the
normal use of the word has been challenged in a surprising way.
Because the silence has been 'incurred' there is a sense of 'givenness'
or of imposition, which implies that this silence has a quality which
differs from that of the silence in which the prayer may be pre-
sumed to be taking place. This 'givenness', it seems, is not always
recognised:

> Some take that silence
> for refusal.

We note the deliberate placing of line endings, the sudden break in
communication. 'Some take that silence' implies an affirmative and
accepting response to the silence, but the abrupt line ending 'for
refusal' indicates that for those who do not recognise the nature
of this silence there is nowhere else to go, nothing left to say. But
for those who 'take the silence' the experience expands. From 'I
pray' they move on to 'I feel'. There is an unspoken 'But' preceding 'I feel':

> Some take that silence
> for refusal.
> I feel the power

This could be the old patriarchal language emerging again, for patriarchy *is* power, but the line continues with the tentative encouragement of 'catching' and 'nudging'. This is not patriarchal language,

language of subjection and oppression. This is gentle, almost tentative in its quiet encouragement, and while the image which ensues reverts to the traditional one of God present in his Word (the long shelf that has the book on it) and God as the antidote to the world's ills, it is an image which has been defamiliarised by the context. The reader might be surprised by the juxtaposition of power with tentativeness, but it is clear that the poet is not. His position moves from the earlier 'I feel' to 'I know'. 'I know its ways with me' – the mystery is developed in terms which are so delicate that the reader is barely aware that an image is being formed at all, again a reflection of content in form. In terms of the invisible and the elusive the poet's experience develops. 'The Presence' is recognised from its familiarity – 'I know its ways with me'. The willingness for communion on the part of the presence is endearing, denying any lifelessness associated with its denotation as 'it', but registering in 'rather' a degree of uncertainty in the poet, so elusive is the experience.[29] The disinclination to express the presence in images has so far led to its emergence as 'silence', an 'invisible power', which yet 'catches me by the sleeve'. The language is suggestive rather than concrete, and when a concrete image does appear, it scarcely disturbs the notion of a being at once present and insubstantial. 'Sunlight quivering/ on a bare wall.' There is a move from the passive mode to the active, as the poet attempts to express the experience in a less esoteric manner. The questions are framed to focus reality. There is a nice play between 'Am I under regard' and 'It takes me seconds to focus', as watcher and watched interact.

This power, then, which is 'invisible' and is like 'sunlight quivering on a wall' can yet 'catch' and 'nudge', has 'consciousness' it seems, and can 'shift its gaze'. The images cannot escape their origin in the 'particularities of our physical make up'. Although the *via negativa* insists that God is 'not like' – represented here by silence and invisibility – the *via positiva* always intrudes into the equation, taking form here in the 'sunlight' and the anthropomorphic allusions. The poet's difficulty in describing the purely intuited experience is evident. The last stanza verges on the helpless:

> It has the universe
>   to be abroad in.
> There is nothing I can do

but the thought opens out again, generating Thomas's *tour de force*. Metaphors develop with astonishing rapidity, but they grow out of that reading of the presence which readers have constructed from the fragments of information implicit in the text. From the assembled properties there emerges a 'wild creature', creating a breath-holding suspense in the observer (and in the reader too), who hopes that though 'It has the universe/ to be abroad in' it will approach to drink. The introduction of the word 'drink' is enough to set up a whole new set of metaphors. 'Drink' generates the image of the silence as a pool, but it is 'my own silence', that is, the inner silence of the poet. The image of the wild creature, we need to remember, represents the presence of God, or the presence of God as intuited in the silence. It is then to the small pool of the poet's silence that the greater silence of God will come and drink. But Thomas must press the metaphor of the pool still further. The image of the creature drinking at a pool anticipates a reflection. The overtly framed image is the classical one of Narcissus, and implies self-love. Thomas, however, takes this negatively charged image and (as with 'incurred' earlier) daringly changes it into a positive one. It is a Miltonic device which effectively demonstrates the superiority of the Christian view over the classical. We are reminded that the image of God looking into the pool of one man's silence and loving his image there is also a Judaeo-Christian one, far removed from Narcissism. We might cite Moses, who 'wist not that the skin of his face shone while he talked with him' (Ex 34.29), or perhaps John, who says: 'it doth not yet appear what we shall be: but we know that, when he shall appear, we shall be like him; for we shall see him as he is' (1 John 3.2).

The final complication lies in 'its transparent face', for ambiguity lies in 'its'. 'Its' may refer to the pool or to the wild creature:

> or perhaps like Narcissus
> to linger a moment over its transparent face.

In the first case it becomes an image for the poet's silence, in which God sees his reflection. In the second, it emphasises the fact that God's face is transparent, that it has no adequate image or form, and so reaffirms the poet's faith in the *via negativa* as the only reliable form of expressing God.

In 'The Presence' the direct use of metaphor is delayed until the last paragraph where we have the introduction of the 'wild creature'. Up to this point the image has been created obliquely through the choice of verbs and adjectives. What is significant is that the creation

of an image is attempted at all, for Thomas is acutely aware of
the paradoxes and difficulties inherent in expressing the apprehension of God in figurative language. 'The Flower'[30] attempts to do so
in a rather different way from 'The Presence'. An obvious difference
between the two is that where 'The Presence' reads as a soliloquy,
'The Flower' is addressed directly to God, but more important differences remain. Thomas has often used landscape in the mode of
the *via positiva*. What he sees as the beauty of nature is allowed, on
these occasions, to speak of God and to stand as a metaphor for
God. But, as we have seen, he is also aware of the limitations of the
mode. In 'The Minister', for example, we noted that nature is not
always kind and, when it exacts so painful a way of life, it does not
produce a very satisfying image of God. In 'The Minister', therefore, landscape is eventually rejected as a means of mediating God,
because it is limited by the subjective reading which is inevitably
brought to it. In 'The Flower' nature is seen differently:

> I asked for riches
> You gave me the earth, the sea,
>   the immensity
> of the broad sky.

Nature is not at first identified with the 'riches' of the opening
line. This opening line is a surprise in itself, for the request for riches
does not seem appropriate to a religious text. Addressed to God,
the petition invites the reader to anticipate a request which reflects
the values inscribed in Scripture. Instead, we are given the general
term for material possessions. It is God who, as giver, turns the
request on its head by giving 'the earth, the sea, the immensity of
the broad sky'. This revision of the anticipated, literal meaning of
'riches' at the very outset is an endorsement of the positive qualities of landscape. The landscape is the riches. A measured pace is
imposed on the lines, which reinforces a sense of appreciation and
wonder, emphasised by the weight given – by placement – to the
phrase 'the immensity'. This is an unqualified acceptance not only
of the value of nature *per se*, but also of its value as a metaphor for
God. But the paragraph continues:

> I looked at them
> and learned I must withdraw

At this point we might suppose that Thomas is rejecting the idea of landscape as metaphor on similar grounds to those noted above. If so, we would be mistaken. To repeat ourselves briefly, nature here is not unkind, and its value is overtly endorsed. If Nature as metaphor is to be discarded once again, then it must be for some other reason. On this occasion it is not in the metaphor as vehicle that a weakness is perceived, but in the very concept of the *via positiva*. The image of nature which is presented is a very lovely one. However, there comes a point when, by the sheer force of its 'physicality' – the felt presence of the image – the *via positiva* becomes a barrier to a more perfect apprehension of God, who is essentially transcendent 'Other'. J.P. Ward comments:

'The Flower' and 'Sea-Watching' both present a scene or thing which stand in for God or some act of God. They are ambivalent however, for they both parallel the divine presence but also, by being so vividly present, stop the approach to the absent formless God himself.[31]

If the image of landscape is rejected at this point, it is not because of its limitations, but because of its substance. Because of the temptation to

rest in Nature, not the God of Nature.[32]

This is perhaps less of a problem for the mystic than for the poet. The mystic can avoid what Pseudo-Dionysius refers to as 'the mental or material images we form of God' by practising the *via negativa*. The most acute problem arises when the experience must be shared. For the poet what is required is a means of proceeding which will not create distracting or distorting images but which will still enable an apprehension of God to be expressed. It is in order to avoid that strong sense of the material which is conveyed by the *via positiva*, and to promote this deeper apprehension of God, that Thomas takes the way of the mystic and adjusts his position to that of the *via negativa*:

> I gave my eyes
> and my ears, and dwelt
> in a soundless darkness
>   in the shadow
> of your regard.

These lines are probably Thomas's most explicit expression of the *via negativa*, and echo the words of Pseudo-Dionysius:[33]

> Unto this darkness which is beyond Light we pray that we might come, and may attain unto vision *through the loss of sight and knowledge*, and that in ceasing thus to see or to know we may learn to know that which is beyond all perception and understanding (for this emptying of our faculties is true sight and knowledge) . . . (my italics)

As the poet-mystic waits on God, implied images pass fleetingly over the lines but fail to materialise. The archaism of 'dwelt/ in a soundless darkness' is suggestive of the anchorite and extends, rather than distracts, from our appreciation of the situation. But to express an apprehension of God in language which denies images is hardly possible. The entry into darkness is one – classic – approach. It might be objected that the use of 'darkness' is itself an image. The author of *The Cloud Of Unknowing*[34] counters this objection as follows:

> Now when I call this exercise a darkness or a cloud, do not think it is a cloud formed out of the vapours which float in the air, or a darkness such as you have in your house at night, when your candle is out. For such a darkness or such a cloud you can certainly imagine by subtle fancies. . . . But leave such falsehood alone. I mean nothing of the sort. When I say 'darkness' I mean a privation of knowing, just as whatever you do not know or have forgotten is dark to you, because you do not see it with your spiritual eyes. For this reason, that which is between you and your God is termed, not a cloud of the air, but a cloud of unknowing.

The 'Cloud' author is anxious to discriminate between things that are to be understood in a material way and things that are to be understood in a spiritual way. He makes this very clear in chapters LI and LVIII. So while the metaphor remains, the use of the image is discouraged. 'The darkness' itself is not something to be imagined, but is rather a condition of being, as Eliot has it in *Four Quartets*:[35]

> In order to arrive at what you do not know
> You must go by a way which is the *way of ignorance*.

In order to possess what you do not possess
You must go by the way of dispossession.

'In the shadow' appears at first to be no more than an extension
of the 'soundless darkness', but it has a significance of its own.
The shadow stands for God. It does not stand for the 'form' of
God; it is not 'God's shadow'. In fact, this image has no substance
because the shadow is itself not the shadow of a substantial object.
We are reminded of Donne's negative expression of himself in 'A
Nocturnall upon S. Lucies Day, Being the shortest day'. In describing his extremity he demonstrates perfectly, for our purpose, the
distinction Thomas wishes to convey, the profound absence of the
Deus Absconditus rather than the shadow of a presence. Donne's
poem[36] uses the *via negativa* to express how completely the loss of
his loved one has undone him:

Study me then, you who shall lovers bee
At the next world, that is, at the next Spring:
  For I am every dead thing,
  In whom love wrought new Alchimie.
   For his art did express
A quintessence even from nothingness,
From dull privations, and lean emptinesse:
He ruin'd mee, and I am re-begot
Of absence, darkness, death; things which are not.
But I am by her death, (which word wrongs her)
Of the first nothing, the Elixir grown;
  Were I a man, that I were one,
  I needs must know; I should preferre,
   If I were any beast,
Some ends, some means; Yea plants, yea stones detest
And love; All, all some properties invest;
If I an ordinary nothing were,
As shadow, 'a light, and body must be here.

While the shadow which concerns us is not, like Donne's, 're-
begot of death', neither is it an 'ordinary nothing' which presupposes a light and a body. There is nothing concrete behind the
shadow. Thomas presents us again with an image which refuses
to materialise, implied rather than present. It is rendered doubly
elusive by the play on 'regard', with its multiple meanings. We may

read it as meaning 'gaze', in which case the poet-mystic dwells with God's gaze upon him, or we might choose to read it as 'esteem' which suggests that the poet-mystic has God's full approval. Neither reading can be wholly satisfactory. Whichever reading we choose, the mystery remains, for it is not directly in God's 'regard' that the persona dwells, but in the *shadow* of that regard. Even though the metaphor must be anthropomorphic it has the curious effect of rendering peculiarly amorphous any figure we imagine. It is the shadow of an abstraction, a mystery reflecting an enigma. This is the technique Thomas uses to convey an impression of that which can be experienced but not expressed. Ricoeur, commenting on the necessity for technique of this kind says:

> So there is not a one-to-one relationship between word and meaning. [Here 'darkness', 'regard'.] And so it's a source of mis-understanding, but it's the source of all richness in language, because you play with this range of meanings which accompany one word. . . . But it is the task of poetry to make words mean as much as they can and not as little as they can.[37]

Ricoeur acknowledges the effectiveness of using such a technique when dealing with subjects that resist expression in more orthodox fashion:

> When some critics say, but in poetry language is not referential, maybe it is because they have a very narrow idea of what could be and what should be referential. They mean if it is referential, it has to do with the things of my life and the things of scientific thought.
> And therefore, we reinforce the prejudice that reality is only what is manipulatable. But if we have surmised that there is another layer of reality that only poetry may reach and express, then the suspension of referentiality is only one step and it is necessary that we must first lose contact with ordinary things in order maybe, thanks to this liberation of language, to redirect it once more towards some more deeply rooted forms of experience.

Thomas's approach to the numinous in this poem demonstrates what Ricoeur means by the 'liberation of language'.

Before examining the further development of the poem we should

now consider its form 'on the page', for it is characteristic of
Thomas to use space as well as text to create meaning.[38] We note
that the first paragraph appears to be densely packed (giving significance by placement to the phrase 'the immensity' as noted earlier),
then gives way to line spacing which isolates the pivotal phrase
of the poem:

> in a soundless darkness
>   in the shadow
>   of your regard.

Further careful placing of lines and spaces slows down the reading
of the central statement, and then the density of language returns,
pushing the reading forward and heightening the emotion of the
experience. Images, present in the first paragraph, and neutralised
in the central portion, proliferate in the final paragraph, and where
the first paragraph was carried forward swiftly by repetition (I asked,
I looked, I gazed) a similar effect is achieved in the last paragraph,
partly by repetition (not, nor, its own) and partly through the on-
ward movement created by the one very long sentence. I emphasise
this shaping of the poem because it seems to me to reflect the content; if not as architectural as Herbert's pattern poems, certainly in
the way it, so to speak, diminishes and swells. Not only does the
shape reflect the content, but it also helps to focus the meaning
more sharply. Thomas is, perhaps unusually, one of those poets
whose poems are not always best read aloud. It is in lingering over
phrases, observing line endings and noting the layout on the page
that we often gain the fullest meaning. This is true of 'The Flower',
in which much of the meaning is inscribed in the arrangement of
the words on the page.[39] Read aloud, a poem of fairly even tone and
speed is produced, appropriate perhaps to an act of meditation.
This is because of the difficulty of dramatising the spaces and com-
municating the effect of the distinctive shape. But read on the page,
our reading is influenced by the abrupt switches in layout which
effectively dramatise those shifts in the modes of consciousness
which are registered, and which interrupt the meditative process. It
seems, then, that the poem read aloud as an instrument of meditation, with its smooth, rhythmic flow, enacts a kind of *via positiva*,
while the disruptions of the poem on the page are more akin to a
via negativa, with the fullest meaning emerging from the tension
thus held.

The poem opens with the closely packed images of the first paragraph, but, according to the text, these must be discarded in order that a more satisfactory approach to God might be made. As imagery is left behind, so space and clarity focus the 'still centre' of the poem. We need to explain, then, the reburgeoning of images in the last paragraph. Ward sees the lines 'the soul/ grew in me, filling me/ with its fragrance', as an interruption which Thomas does not resist. He writes:

> yet what is beautiful irrepressibly returns. 'The soul/ grew in me, filling me/ with its fragrance'. The poet does not resist this interruption, and goes back finally to the sort of comparison we have long realized he finds irresistibly congenial.[40]

It is true that the poet-mystic does not resist expressing the beauty of this experience, but this is a justifiable moment of self-consciousness, the paradoxes of which we have discussed already. It is the moment of ecstasy, on the brink of evaporating by the very act of recognition.[41]

In the act of withdrawal into the soundless darkness the flower grows; but it is the soul that is filled with fragrance. Speaking of this fragrance Underhill writes:

> This fragrance, as St Augustine calls it, remains for ever with those who have thus been initiated, if only for a moment, into the presence of the Real: and this – the immortal and indescribable memory of their communion with That Which Is – gives to their work the perfume of the 'Inviolate Rose'.[42]

To return to the poem; this is an epiphany in the sense of a show-ing of God to the soul, an idea which is reinforced by:

> Men came
> to me from the four
> winds to hear me speak

which also reminds us of Epiphany,[43] and a note of joy mingled with awe is discernible. From this point the poem explodes into complicated syntax and a proliferation of images. In the context of the mystical tradition this has to represent more than that which the poet finds, in Ward's words 'irresistibly congenial'. Although it

appears at first to be a further shift from the *via negativa*, closer
reading reveals that this is another linguistic strategy for coping
with the difficulties of the mode. Complicated syntax is a way of
representing the *via negativa* (another is to use no syntax, or only
imperfect syntax).[44] While metaphors and images abound, they are
pressed into the service of the *via negativa*. The *via positiva* had
presented a metaphor for God in the riches of landscape; in the
earth, the sea, the immensity of the broad sky. Now out of the act
of withdrawal the flower grows – the thing unseen. But it is still
placed in a relationship with landscape and nature. The metaphors
and images take the substance of the *via positiva* and transform it by
expressing it in terms of the *via negativa*. The earth, the sea and the
sky of the first paragraph are all represented in the last paragraph,
but they have all been transformed. The idea that God both 'is and
is not like' which is at the heart of the *via positiva* is illuminated,
as positive and negative responses are registered in quick succes-
sion. The presence of God is imaged in the flower, an image drawn
from nature, but it is an unseen flower. Like a natural flower it has
roots, but the roots are not in the soil. 'The colour of the wide sea'
is presented as beautiful and positive, but the petals are not the
colour of the wide sea and the image is discarded as quickly as it is
grasped, but not before it has told us something about the flower.
Similarly, 'its own sky' is familiar and lovely for a moment, but the
staccato impact of 'shot' effects another revision, and we will return
to this shortly. The flower, then, is 'like' nature. But its roots are not
in the soil, and its colour is not that of the sea. It is like no other
species, it is not like nature. It is in fact the 'unseen' flower. Thus
'The Flower' validates nature, or landscape, as capable of mediating
God through the *via positiva*. But through the negative impulse of
the poem the image is refined and elevated. The reburgeoning of
images in this last paragraph is an integral part of both the thought
and form of the poem. The landscape of the first paragraph is not
only restated but transformed, from the substantial to the 'spiritual'
or transcendent of the last paragraph. It becomes the 'Other'. The
flower, we note, cannot be possessed. Again the experience of the
mystics is echoed:

> For there is no gift from God, nor has there ever been, which he
> gives in order that we might possess it and remain attached to it.
> Rather all his gifts in heaven and on earth were given solely in
> order that he could give the one gift, which is the gift of himself.[45]

So the ambiguous 'its own species with its own/ sky' suggests not only that the flower is unique but that it cannot be owned. Perhaps it is only in recognising this that the experience of landscape can be 'possessed'. This transformation of landscape is illustrated in the closing lines. The *via positiva* recognises that while material things can mediate God, the very fact of materiality is a limitation. Even

> the immensity
> of the broad sky

carries overtones of heaviness. It is interesting to note how these are countered in the closing lines:

> with its own
> sky over it, shot
> with the rainbow of your coming and going.

To appreciate the significance of this contrast we need to return to the beginning of the poem again and look more closely at the relationship which has been developed. The role of the poet-mystic is a passive one. Having 'asked' for riches the remaining verbs which apply to him are not generally energetic. Activity on the part of the poet-mystic consists of learning, growing, dwelling, sitting – barely perceived activity – and then speaking. God's activity is defined at the start as giving. He then disappears, reappearing very briefly in the 'shadow of your regard'. The activity of God seems to be limited to giving and looking, and as giving and looking are also attributed to the poet-mystic, these factors would seem to be the basis of the relationship. But when we encounter that explosive note in 'shot', it throws into relief all that has gone before. It shakes the reader out of that leisured manner of reading which the fairly loose structure has encouraged. It is startling in its suddenness, conveying a sky-piercing movement of force and vigour which is barely qualified by the image of the rainbow which follows. Instead of mediating God in a passive manner, this sky shimmers with the scintillating presence of God. It is reminiscent of Sartre's 'We see nothingness making the world irridescent, casting a shimmer over things'.[46] It is the innate glory perceived by Hopkins in 'God's Grandeur': 'it shines out like shook foil'. 'Shot' in this context is that of 'shot silk'. Here the presence dazzles, reflects, scintillates and shines; is constantly present but constantly changing.

This demonstrates vividly the activity which is going on. God reappears and instead of the fairly static presence, we see that God was on the move all the time. From the apparent blandness of 'the immensity/ of the broad sky', through the experience of darkness, we come to a sky which is shot with the rainbow of God's coming and going, and the two images conveyed by 'shot' combine to suggest that coming and going, presence and absence, are barely differentiated. The poem thus tries to reconcile stasis and withdrawal with engagement and action. Starting with the *via positiva*, it moves to the *via negativa*, then finds a way of demonstrating not only that both ways are valid, but also that they presuppose each other.

In this chapter we have considered the many ways in which the two *vias* manifest themselves. 'Via Negativa'[47] is a poem which addresses the negative way directly. Beginning as it does *in medias res* – and with a shocked exclamation – it is a corrective to a misunderstanding on the part of an implied, but unnamed, interrogator. It seeks to define more accurately the poet's perception of God. Thomas does this by playing on the tensions between exterior and interior, the distant and the near. If, as we may infer, the interrogator has supposed the poet's God to be substantial and domesticated, then an even greater sense of shock may lie in the first two lines:

> I never thought other than
> That God is that great absence

The sense of distance and exteriority is profound, but the rhythm and tone register confidence. An almost Hebraic balance of phrase and repetition is noted as the lines develop by way of re-emphasis and reiteration – the absence *is* the silence, the interstices the darkness and the echoes footprints. The great absence, the empty silence, the place where we go, all suggest images of a cosmic scale; they all indicate a movement outward on the part of the persona. And they are all images, or perhaps names, for God. All suggest the Other. At the same time they are all immanent: 'In our lives', 'Within' is the place where we 'go Seeking'. I have said that the great absence and the empty silence are 'images' of God, but we note that all the terms employed deny the imagination a point of focus; they all preserve the mystery. Even the idea of seeking, with its suggestion of eventual fulfilment in encounter, is deliberately undermined. The lines which follow suggest that God is himself the preserver of his own mystery, maintaining the 'interstices/ In our knowledge, the darkness/ Between stars'. Again, there is that sweeping movement between interior and exterior, the local and the cosmic. The gaps in our knowledge and the darkness between stars are all held in the same frame.[48] (The 'interstices in our knowledge' is not what Professor Charles Coulson called 'The God of the gaps'. God is never used by Thomas to 'explain' such things as escape our understanding. Rather, 'The interstices in our knowledge' refers to our knowledge of God.) And both are held in place by God. 'He keeps' can, of course, mean either that God maintains us in a state of not knowing, of spiritual and scientific ignorance in order to preserve his mystery,[49] or that our state of not knowing is acceptable because it is ultimately safeguarded by God. If we continue to read the poem as operating in the mode of Hebrew parallelism then 'the interstices/ In our knowledge,/ the darkness between stars' is restated in the continuing lines:

> His are the echoes
> We follow, the footprints he has just
> Left.

Images of absence proliferate, the interstices becoming 'echoes' and 'the darkness between stars' becoming God's 'footprints'. The whole is reminiscent of lines from the book of Job: 'These are but the outskirts of his ways: and how small a whisper we hear of him?'[50] But the placement of the line endings is significant. The momentary pause we are invited to make after 'just' gives added importance to 'Left', and links it to 'follow'. We can read not only 'the footprints he has *just* left' (a moment ago – we have only just missed him) but also 'the footprints he has just – *left*' (the signs he has deliberately placed for us to follow). With 'footprints' the scale is adjusted from the cosmic to the human, and after the images of absence and immensity the human perspective is touching and vulnerable:

> We put our hands in
> His side hoping to find
> It warm.

These lines are an amalgam of two allusions. The first, and most obvious, is the biblical one, in which the risen Christ invites Thomas to 'Reach hither thy finger, and behold my hands; and reach hither thy hand, and thrust *it* into my side; and be not faithless, but believing' (John 20:27). The second is personal to R.S. Thomas, and refers to his own practice, when out walking, of putting his hand in the place where a hare has recently lain, hoping to find it still warm.[51] The images fuse into a singularly appropriate representation of the two 'Ways'. God present and imaged in the flesh, available even to the exploratory touch of man, the *via positiva*, and the elusive God who has always 'just' left, is always on the move, but has left an indication of where he has been, his absence 'marked' as it were only by the warm place – the *via negativa*. The construction of the sentences in this poem encourages us to read them in pairs, or as I have suggested after the manner of Hebrew parallelisms. Thus we are invited to make connections between the two remaining sentences beginning 'We'.

Having reached out to touch the incarnated, resurrected Christ it should be possible to see him in people and places. People, and places, could be positive images of God. But the possibility is qualified by the ambiguities of 'miss', and it is not clear whether the fault lies in the people and places as mirrors of God or in the observers' inability to see what is there all the time. In keeping with the negative mode the poem ends on a falling cadence, a positive statement undermined by a wistful reflection. The poem is organised around the central lines:

> He keeps the interstices
> In our knowledge, the darkness
> Between stars.

Up to this point, as we have seen, we are presented with a cosmic scale, and the God who is indicated in abstract imagery is the ineffable, transcendent Godhead. After the pivotal point the reference is to the Christ, God incarnate. There is a marked shift in the relationship of the persona to these two images of God, the source of which lies in the degree of accessibility to God which is perceived. Of the transcendent God the persona has 'no hope to/ Arrive or find.' But of God incarnate we read: 'We put our hands in/ His side hoping to find . . .' Thomas rarely refers to the resurrected Christ in his poetry, and nowhere else is there such an expression of tenderness as here. The absent God may satisfy spiritual integrity, but there is a momentary wistfulness here, not only in hoping to find, but hoping to find it warm, with the warmth of human contact. These two images, so different from each other, yet both familiar representations of God, are linked by the placement of 'Between'. The suggestion is that God is absence and silence. God is presence and speaking (the allusion to touching the side of Christ is a response to a word: 'reach here thy finger'), and these are held in creative tension. There is 'no hope to arrive or find' and there is 'hoping to find'. Between these poles lies the 'darkness between stars', the cloud of unknowing, the refusal to claim understanding.

Having explored the many possible faces of God, in the end it seems Thomas is happiest with the veiled face and the cloud of unknowing. Ultimately, his is a God who is always on the move, and, in so far as we can ever see Thomas as content, he is content to follow after, never arriving.

6

Counterpoint

Counterpoint: 1. the technique involving the simultaneous sounding of two or more parts or melodies. 2. a melody or part combined with another melody or part. 3. the musical texture resulting from the simultaneous sounding of two or more melodies or parts. 4. to set in contrast.

(Collins English Dictionary)

The work of R.S. Thomas has, to the dismay of some orthodox readers, always comprised the 'simultaneous sounding of two or more melodies'. To expand the metaphor a little, we might say that anyone looking for unison, or for univocal expression, in his poetry is likely to be disappointed. His preferred mode of irony insists by its very nature on the 'simultaneous sounding' of two possible readings of the text. (There is therefore a perceived reader in the Thomas text, the reader who understands the irony, who recognises the tropes which are being undermined, and who cooperates with the author in producing meaning.)[1]

But it is his honesty in attempting to encompass all those features of life which least readily resonate with the notion of a loving God which many people find disturbing. While his style changes periodically, and certain preoccupations are foregrounded at various times, the pivotal concept is always the perceived gap between what I have called 'observation' and 'revelation', qualified only by the occasional positive poem which finds closure. Unison, therefore, is rarely his goal. He is, rather, content to point up the gaps and to challenge his readers to find a resolution.

To return to the 'musical' metaphor of our definition, we might say that the two melodies remain distinct but create a new 'musical texture'. The problem is demonstrated in *Counterpoint* [2] where it finds expression in the counterpoint between love and truth:

> The shivering of love's
> mirror as truth's frost
> begins mercilessly to take hold.

157

There is a paradoxical suggestion here that truth distorts. The 'shivering' mirror suggests that love is expressed through unstable and shifting images, or even that love is a delusion and itself unstable like water endorsing the premise of the Apostle Paul that we 'see through a glass, darkly'. He too, in his great hymn to love, was considering the gap between observation and revelation:

> For now we see through a glass, darkly; but then face to face: now I know in part; but then shall I know even as also I am known. (1 Cor 13. 12)

Paul recognises that what we observe is puzzling and confusing, but he avers that what we 'know' is partial. For Paul the resolution lies in the belief that truth will confirm revelation when we 'know' perfectly. The 'merciless' force of truth, represented in my argument by 'observation', is somewhat regretted by Thomas, who would like the 'warmer' concepts of love and beauty (revelation) to take priority, or at least have equal force:

> One thing I have asked
> Of the disposer of the issues
> Of life: that truth should defer
> To beauty. It was not granted.
> 'Petition'[3]

   The significance of this for our present exploration lies, of course, in the fact that the conventional image of God is constantly being challenged. (Thomas takes great delight in undermining what he calls the 'Father Christmas' image of God,[4] recognising that the image of God which we adopt has far-reaching effects on religious practice, especially that of prayer.)

   We have noticed how the perceived gap between observation and revelation produces the tensions which exist in each of the images of God which we have explored – art, landscape, myth, science and, in a slightly different way, the *via negativa* and *via positiva*.[5] All these both can and cannot function as images of God. We have considered the various positions which are elaborated in the typical Thomas text to be, by their nature, in opposition to one another; *Counterpoint* invites us to see them, rather, as different melodies which persist and create the distinctive texture of the work. In all Thomas's work there is what we might call a contrapuntal schema.[6] This schema is implicit in earlier volumes, but is fore-grounded in *Counterpoint*. It becomes not only the explicit object and method of the book, but is also represented in the choice of illustration for its cover. Because the book is, as I shall demonstrate, unified in form and content, I shall consider it separately from previous volumes while at the same time recognising that it underwrites all that has gone before, and, unconventionally perhaps, it is with the cover that we will begin our study.

The cover carries the reproduction of *A Lady Weighing Gold* by Jan Vermeer. The lady of the title, dressed in a velvet jacket trimmed with fur, holds a delicate balance in one hand. Her other hand rests lightly on the table, so that she in turn appears poised, balanced. (There are both pearls and coins on the table and it is not clear what is being weighed.) The form of the woman is framed by the large painting on the wall behind her. It appears to be a painting of Christ in Majesty, judging the world. The woman measures her material wealth and makes her judgment, set against the eschatological con-tent of the background painting, so illustrating the 'counterpoint' between temporal and eternal, material and spiritual.

I have said that observation and revelation are the two main 'melodies' of *Counterpoint*, but the volume is in fact more complex than that would suggest. In form the volume falls into four separate parts, unequal in length, and with each part having its own title. The first section is called *B.C.*, the second *Incarnation*, the third *Crucifixion* and the fourth *A.D.* Again, the temporal is set against the eternal. The referent for the passage of time as signified in the sub-titles is God. Thus God is, paradoxically, represented by time – time, in this context being that of salvation history. Within the poems and against this ordering structure, secular history is played out. As in the cover picture, the contrapuntal form enables each of these histories to illuminate the other. Within the poems themselves we will observe other juxtapositions of themes and ideas which operate similarly.

B.C. is concerned with the problem of language and of naming God. The counterpoint consists in overlaying images from pre-history with images from Scripture, with the result that new images, often surprising and almost surrealistic in style, emerge. Of the fif-teen poems in this section, eight are concerned with language or naming, three retell bible stories, and four present a mythical approach to the nature of God. The first and last poems are enough to enable us to see how Thomas images God in this section of the

book. (As none of the poems in this volume is named, I shall identify them where necessary by the first line and the page number.)
The first poem in the book (p. 8) generates images of primitive
'man' in the primaeval landscape. The opening line suggests a representational status for the blank page. The suggestion is the starting point for a series of allusions which, in dealing with abstractions,
create tantalising images which, in the mode of the *via negativa*,
negate substance and illuminate by what they do not say:

> This page should be left blank:
> snow where the abominable footprints
> have not yet appeared; sand
> for the pioneer to stare over
> in his questioning of the horizon.

Engaged with questions of pre-history, of the earth, of human
life and of language, the images are suitably elusive. The images
of snow and sand suggest a primitive, bare landscape, but it may
equally well be the landscape of pre-historic earth or the landscape
of the mind before language. The 'abominable footprints' may be
the prints of the pre-human or the prints of language on the page.
The juxtaposition of 'snow' with 'abominable' suggests the elusive,
supposedly primitive and semi-mythical 'abominable snowman'. In
each of these allusions a mark, a print, is registered, and so strong
is the image created that it takes careful reading to notice that in
fact, 'the abominable footprints/ have not yet appeared'. These five
lines emphasise the pristine blankness of the 'age'. 'Man' is both the
abominable snowman and the pioneer; the unmarked page suggests
a time before language has emerged and the staring pioneer anticipates the articulation of thought. Language then, it seems, is the
'abominable footprint(s)'. The second stanza reinforces the impression of language as something which mars and spoils:

> If you can imagine a brow puckered
> before thought, imagine this page
> immaculately conceived
> in the first tree, with man rising

The page is 'immaculately conceived'. Ignoring the religious associations for the moment, we might note that it is 'the page' which is
'immaculately conceived'; that is pure concept. Its representational

status here might be, as in the first stanza, the pristine emptiness of pre-history or of the mind before language developed.

The religious language, however, complicates the reading significantly, for the immaculate conception and the first tree both carry implications of the word/Word.[7] The page, or language, is implicit in the first tree. A parallel is drawn between the page and the first man. As the page is conceived in the tree so man is conceived in the mind of God; the 'immaculately conceived' is a reminder that the 'Word' is a fusion of concept and image, language and man. In this Edenic image God is present but unexpressed. This is the 'brow puckered/ before thought'. The advent of language is registered in 'man rising/ from on all fours' – speech being that faculty which most distinguishes humans from animals – but the arrival of language also brings the means to mis-express God. As the brow, perhaps in uncertainty, is puckered, so the page, immaculately conceived, is 'puckered', marred, by language; but we are left with the paradox that 'In the beginning was the Word',[8] and that it is through the metaphor of language that God has chosen to reveal himself.

The inadequacy of language, how to express God, and the persistent desire for an image are the problems that emerge in *B.C.*

The final poems in this section construct images of God in the manner of the mythic poems we have already considered. The last poem 'Bored with it' (p. 22) is in this mode.[9] The laconic tone produced by the syntax suggests a sophisticated and indolent god, one who is bored with the earth in its pristine state. There is only rock, rock eroding to sand. The earth is the 'dusty looking-glass for a god', glass produced perhaps from the sand, melting, in the process of erosion into a new thing. The leisurely tone obscures the implications of this phrase, which holds the key to the poem. God desires to see his image,[10] but a 'dusty looking-glass' cannot reflect God. If he wants to see his image in this particular looking-glass, he must disturb the dust. The boredom gives way to a lethargic act of creation:

> May as well . . . breathing,
> leading the dust
> a dance.

Thomas creates yet another version of that mythical god whose motives and intentions challenge the reader. Here the god, who might well be leaning on his elbow, idly surveying the earth, rouses himself just enough to disturb the dust. He breathes, 'leading the dust/ a dance'. A dilettante god relieving his boredom, being mischievous? Blowing the dust off a mirror? The conjunction of 'breathing' with 'dust' carries scriptural connotations:[11]

> And the Lord God formed man *of* the dust of the ground, and breathed into his nostrils the breath of life; and man became a living soul. (Gen. 2. 7)

By that sleight of hand we have noted before in Thomas, the dust is not blown away to reveal an image, but becomes in itself an image, as the god breathes life into the dust.

Consider the lines again – while the tone is laconic the implications are lively. This is achieved through the careful control of the line endings. We read 'leading the dust' and we might anticipate any number of possibilities. The god might be leading the dust into personhood, or into maturity or by the hand, but for Thomas, applying 'irony's inaudible laughter'[12] God is 'leading the dust/ a dance'. In this reading the metaphor suggests separation, a God who is in control but teasing his creation and keeping it at a distance. However, we are aware of other connotations which arise from the idea of the dance.

In Richard Rolle's *Incendium amoris* we find: 'But it is truly said that love goes first in the dance and leads the ring. It was nothing but love that put Christ thus low.'[13] Here the act of salvation is seen in terms of the dance. Again, we find Gerardus Van Der Leeuw[14] saying, 'Medieval mysticism takes up this theme and describes the whole life of the Lord in the form of a dance':

> Tomorrow shall be my dancing day;
> I would my true love did so chance
> To see the legend of my play,
> To call my true love to my dance.
> Sing, oh! my love, my love, my love,
> This have I done for my true love.
>
> Then I was born of a Virgin pure,
> Of her I took fleshly substance;
> Then I was knit to man's nature,
> To call my true love to my dance.

More familiar to the general reader, but illustrating the same theme, is Sidney Carter's modern hymn 'Lord of the Dance'. This modern ballad continues the tradition.[15] Here the whole of salvation history is seen as a dance: 'I danced in the morning when the world was begun/ And I danced in the moon and the stars and the sun . . .' So God is himself involved in this dance. The carol goes on to figure both the Incarnation and the Crucifixion as a dance: 'at Bethlehem I had my birth'; 'I danced on a Friday when the sun turned black; / It's hard to dance with the devil on your back.' We notice that the metaphor of the dance now registers not separation but involvement and engagement.

So humankind appears, born of God's boredom and his desire to see his own reflection. But that desire must not be underestimated. It suggests the possibility that 'man' can reflect God – as we noted in our reading of *via negativa* – and that this is satisfying to God. The metaphor of the dance, then, is part of the contrapuntal schema. It is a metaphor of separation, of dalliance and of distance, and also a metaphor of the most complete engagement. As a metaphor of separation it conforms to the mode of 'observation', reflecting life as we know it. As a metaphor of engagement it conforms to the mode of 'revelation', life as Scripture shows it to be.[16] The 'Lord of the Dance' may lead the dust a dance, but it is to his music that it dances.

But there is no room for complacency. With the act of creation questions arise and the laconic tone disappears:

> Where did the Furies
> come from, counterpointing
> his music?

Suddenly another melody has emerged, playing against God's tune, a melody apparently not of his making, a counterpoint which introduces the paradox of creation. We are reminded of the question in 'This page should be left blank' (p. 8) – 'where did the viruses come from?'

> The iron
> in his mind no antidote
> for anaemia of good
> will.

In true metaphysical mode, a curious new metaphor is created, disconcerting the reader with its scientific/medical imagery. It reinforces the theme of the volume in setting evolutionary history against the frame of salvation history. The timeless mode of the myth is sharply countered with this intrusion of the temporal. But the counter-image is not only a physical one. A condition of spiritual malaise is suggested, one which is echoed elsewhere in this volume:

> Beauty is ill
> and has a drawn
> face.[17]

The complexities of human life emerge, threatening to frustrate the divine intention. The emergence of the human voice implies a new relationship:

> Whose was the fadeless
> echo with its entreaty:
> Hold my hand?

The idea of the echo, which we noted in the mythic poems, returns. In 'Echoes' it was the echo of God's voice which carried the shapes towards him: 'Riding the echo the shapes came.' Here the echo is of the human voice which is trying to make contact and draw comfort from a God who is distant. The cry suggests loneliness, fear and vulnerability; it is the cry of a child in the night – 'Hold my hand.'

The god cannot escape the implications of his creation. Thomas reworks yet again the silence of God. Here the god tries to ignore the cries of humanity, but to no avail. There is a lovely paradox in the remaining lines: the god, like a tired parent disturbed by a crying child and longing for rest, withdraws into 'another sphere' as if to escape the demands of his creation. But the need of creation for its god is literally overwhelming. God is swallowed up by it and the incarnation is achieved.

The second section of this volume is called *Incarnation* and opens with a short sequence of three poems which are connected by theme. It considers the incarnation in the light of modern experience, reiterating the counterpoint of the main title. The remaining nine poems focus on the Nativity, but the opening sequence considers the whole life of the incarnate Christ. Here incarnation is given its fullest meaning, and it is with this short sequence of poems that we shall begin to look at this section.

The first poem in this sequence, then – in four stanzas of four lines each – looks at the Nativity. This is followed by a verse paragraph which considers the ministry and death of Christ. The final poem, which has four stanzas of three lines each, considers the resurrection. However, these observations fail to note the complex and radical treatment of the traditional theme. The reworking of myth as it appears in this sequence subverts the humanity which is the very essence of incarnation and suggests a counter-incarnation with all its attendant complications. The sequence opens on page 24 with 'Were you one of the three?' We notice that the three who 'came travelling' come not to the stable but to the workshop, a new destination for pilgrimage. Unwary as they, we accept this momentarily, remembering Nazareth. The gifts which are brought are not those of gold, frankincense and myrrh, but of heart, mind and soul. In view of the injunction that one should 'love the Lord your God with all your heart and with all your mind and with all your soul and with all your strength',[18] they seem appropriate gifts for the God-child. But there is something wrong with this Nativity:

> Was that a halo above it
> of molecules and electrons,
> with the metal gone hoarse trying
> to reiterate: Holy. Holy. Holy?

The halo of the Nativity is translated into the icons of modern 'other-worldliness' – molecules and electrons. Extending the analogy even further, 'the metal gone hoarse' indicates the difficulty these 'angels' have in crying 'Holy, holy, holy.' (The refrain comes from Isaiah 6.3, not the Gospel story, which has the angels singing 'Glory to God in the highest'). The unsuccessful attempt to reiterate is illuminated by the staccato effect achieved by tampering with the conventional punctuation – Isaiah, we note, has 'Holy, holy, holy, *is* the LORD of hosts' suggesting an ease and flow in the repetition which is not achieved here, where even the question mark is ambiguous. We have noted a similar attempt to engage science in an act of praise in the poem 'Reply':[19]

> Do the molecules
> bow down? Before what cradle
> do the travellers from afar,
> strontium and plutonium, hold out
> their thin gifts?

Again, the nature of the Incarnation is questioned, and as in the workshop image of our first stanza, the destination of the travellers is challenged. Are the modern representatives travelling to the same cradle? Exactly who, or what, is being worshipped?

The voice becomes cynical:

> You should have returned to your glass
> ball

The travellers to the workshop might have found a better vision than the one they honour; where the Magi returned home, these travellers are embroiled in the subsequent development of the incarnated:

> a listener

> to its sermons, participant
> in the miracles it performed.
> It was compliant, more than
> accessible to your request for a sign.

The last two lines of the stanza alert us to a serious disparity between the Christ of the Gospel, who resisted requests for a sign,[20] and the subject of this incarnation.

So, this incarnation is a counter-incarnation, an incarnation of something which speaks sermons and performs miracles and also complies with the wishes and desires of the 'listener'. What has taken form here is ungodly, but receives the gifts due to God. Science, figured in the electrons and molecules, tries to deify it. 'It' is, of course, the machine. Thomas, as we have already seen, sees the machine as subverting faith and practice, occupying in the human consciousness the place formerly occupied by God. By putting the machine in the manger, Thomas creates his most radical symbol for materialistic, secular 'man'. What is taking place here is a variation on the theme of *B.C.* There the counterpoint was between salvation history and evolutionary history. Here it is between salvation history and science. Pure science, of course, has Thomas's blessing, revealing as it does the complexity of the natural world; hence the potential for the electrons and molecules to praise God. But the exploitation of science to material ends is anathema to him.[21]

In the light of this reading the remaining stanzas become more accessible. The second poem in the sequence moves on to the ministry of Christ. The voice has been addressing a second person – the reader? A perceived 'you' who has subscribed to the veneration of the machine? 'Were you one of the three . . . ?' 'You should have returned to your glass . . .' There might have been a different, better future if an alternative route had been chosen. But once invented the machine cannot be uninvented. Now the verse paragraph reviews the results, apostrophising the perceived listener: 'you made sacrifice/of your fellows'. In setting the machine in the place of Christ the drama of the Gospel is set in reverse. In the world in which the machine is god, his kingdom is 'all of this world'. Christ asserted that his kingdom was not of this world.[22] Then, whereas Christ was sacrificed for his fellows, here, in the world where the machine is god, men sacrifice each other on its altars. Where they should have been saved from the tyranny of the clock, they become its victims.

> And the cross
> that was set up was the rod
> and the crankshaft man's body
> was nailed to with no power

In a complex parody of the Crucifixion, the machine becomes the cross on which men suffer to no end. There is a curious reversal of figures, for where the machine is received like the child in the manger, it does not become the saviour but the instrument on which men are sacrificed. The parody is pressed further as the machine taunts the victim. As the drama of the Gospel is reversed, the complications proliferate. The 'child' in the manger – that is, the machine – has become not the figure on the cross, but the cross itself. If there is to be a resurrection, it will not be of the machine but of the human figure which is nailed to it.

So the Christ figure in this poem associates profoundly with the human figure. The image of the Resurrection in the final poem in this sequence symbolises the potential reinstatement of 'man' to his position of authority over the machine.

As the sequence develops, the poem becomes increasingly surrealistic as human qualities are attributed to the machine in a grotesque parody of the Resurrection story (p. 25). The time sequence shifts, embracing the present and mythologising it. Looking back, as it were, on the 'machine age' – and having given new significance to that commonplace – Thomas, in the role of seer, provides us with the answers to his questions. The outcome is chilling. There is to be no Resurrection. The machine will not 'acknowledge lordship'. The body is not raised after three days – nor after three years. The sepulchre fills up with humanity's bones:

> Was this where a god died?

The ambiguity of the line sums up the religious and ethical implications of the poem. The 'advent' of the machine – and one can use the word in both its meanings – has perhaps been the death of God. Humanity has worshipped at the shrine of the workshop, choosing the machine as saviour. Does a god live if no one believes in him, or must he, like Barrie's fairies,[23] die? But the 'god' of this line can, of course, also mean man. While the machine seemed, like Satan, to be able to promise all the kingdoms of this world,[24] the worship of the machine and of the materialism it represents destroys the worshipper:

> On the skyline I have seen gantries
> with their arms out awkwardly
> as love and money trying to be reconciled.

The gantries are like crosses on the skyline. They become icons of the modern era, a fusion of possibilities. Where the cross symbolises love the gantries symbolise money. The stanza is curiously moving, and this effect is the result of the personification of the gantries; the 'arms out awkwardly' suggests an attempted embrace, a not quite achieved reconciliation.[25] The awkwardness reflects the attempt of the modern era to reconcile religion with the materialism of the society in which we live.

The effect of symbolising the materialism of the age by inserting the machine into the place formerly occupied by God is that the image of Christ becomes dislocated, free-floating. It is and is not present. We notice how the life and ministry of Jesus form the frame, but because there is a profound split between the function of 'god' and that of 'saviour' there is no continuity. There is no atonement. So the imagery associated with the gospel story is distorted and fractured, and although the Christ-figure is signified, he cannot be accommodated in the text.[26]

In contrast to this comment on a materialistic society, the poem which follows, 'Top left an angel' (p. 26), turns to art for an alternative view of the Nativity.

The immediate counterpoint to the theme of 'science as religion' emerges.[27] The poet here appears to stand in contemplation of a painting. The images which are generated belong to a traditional form of art and are far removed from those surrealistic ones we have just considered. This is an 'Old Master', a repository of received tradition; it stands in that position of 'between here and now' which we noted earlier. That is to say, it represents a caught moment in time, pinned down and framed, but read by a continuously contemporary eye. A painting of the Nativity is described with an economy which is only complicated by the carefully curtailed line endings. Where the previous poem presented an ambiguous and radical version of the Nativity, here an almost reductive accuracy is employed. It records a world in which 'good' and 'bad', 'heaven' and 'hell', are clearly defined: 'Top left an angel'; 'Top right . . . a star'; 'From both/ bottom corners devils'. Each is allocated its own space and function. There is none of that dislocation we observed in the previous poem. Here the child is firmly 'at the centre'. What response can be made 'now' to so confident an image? The source of doubt is not in the images presented but in the observer, and the problem is reflected in the complicated syntax of the single sentence, which forms the response to the painting. The syntactical problem lies in the question mark at the end of the sentence, and the qualifying term 'like':

> How old at the centre
> the child's face gazing
> into love's too human
> face, like one prepared
> for it to have its way
> and continue smiling?

How do we read this sentence? It appears to be an exclamation remarking how old the child's face looks, until the sentence is extended by that complicating 'like' and the unexpected question mark. Are we being invited to share the impression that the child's face at the centre looks old, or to agree that it is 'like one prepared'? Whose is the 'too human face' and who is the 'one prepared'? Who is to have its way and who will continue smiling? The child's face gazing into love's too human face is a relationship of mutuality in which one smiles even as it suffers, and the other has its way. It is not clear who is doing which of these actions. Both figures might be doing both actions. The complication of the relationship and the difficulty in attributing the actions parallels that blurring of roles which we noted in the mythic poems. There it was often difficult to decide whether the sentiments expressed were those of God or of a human figure. Only the child is identified in this picture, but we assume that the other figure is the Virgin Mary. However, the human figure can also be inserted into the text as the 'too human face'. Thus we might produce a reading in which the Virgin Mary is prepared for Christ to have his way and to continue smiling – which implies *her* assent to the Crucifixion. Or we might produce the reading that Christ is prepared for us to have our way and to continue smiling – which implies *his* assent to the Crucifixion. Whichever reading we choose, there is an acceptance of a future horror which presumably is transcended. The difficulty of deciding who is performing which part of the action is central to the way the poem works as it is precisely engaged with the interconnection of the various principles which between them make up the 'dance' of salvation which we noted in 'Bored with it'.[28] The notion of the dance as a 'ring' is a significant comment on the intensity of the engagement of the principles. The difficulty in discrimination also has a bearing on the image of God and our understanding of the nature of God. The foregrounding of the problem of knowing who is suffering, who is allowing suffering and who is smiling, is one of the strategies Thomas adopts in order to undermine any simplistic notion of God. The situation is further complicated by the insinuation of the 'devils' into the corners.

The Incarnation is represented in a painting again on page 28: 'No clouds overhead.' It seems that the Crucifixion is unavoidably present in the Nativity. The opening stanza has a clarity of detail that appeals to the imagination. It presents an idyllic, untroubled scene where even the shadows are integrated into the experience of well-being. The positive of the Nativity defines the negative of the Crucifixion:

> The shadows
> are immediate and are thrown
>
> by upholstered branches,
> not by that angled
> event that from beyond

The solidity and presence suggested by the 'upholstered branches' contrasts strongly with the abstract terms of the 'angled event'. But the 'angled event', in defiance of the statement, insinuates its presence into the text if not into the picture. Then begins that interbreeding of image with image which Thomas executes so well. The comfortable, unthreatening branches of the tree in the painting generate the 'angled event' which can barely be named, in a merging of images which is reminiscent of the merging of the Nativity with the Passion in the medieval lyric.[29] It puts its roots down 'from beyond the horizon'. This enforces the idea of the Crucifixion lying in the future. But 'from beyond the horizon' might equally well be looking back. The roots were put down in ages past:

> This is Eden
> over again.

The principal events of salvation history are focused in the tree. In the painting an imaginary tree casts comfortable shadows. But the shadows might be the shadows of Calvary or of Eden. The influence of medieval imagery and thought persists.[30] The tree of the painting, the tree which is the cross, and the tree of the knowledge of good and evil all stand in one place.[31] The painting has been read as a record of salvation history, a counterpoint to the radical presentation with which we began. But the radical is implied in the conventional. The caught moment is presented to the eye, but the observation is made that 'The snake sleeps'.

The section *Crucifixion* has only five poems and, like *Incarnation*, opens with a longer poem of irregular stanzas.[32] The opening image picks up the image of dance which we noted in *B.C.* and *Incarnation*. In *B.C.* we read:

> breathing
> leading the dust a dance . . .

The dust, we remember, was a 'dusty/ looking-glass for a god'. Teasing out the implications we find that the dusty looking-glass is to provide an image for the god, who, breathing life into it, will 'lead the dust a dance'. That image now dances or 'capers' at God's right hand:

> God's fool, God's jester
> capering at his right hand

Again, the image is a medieval one, drawing here on the medieval trope of Christ 'dancing' on the cross. The lines are grimly under-cut: 'in torment . . .' This is a Good Friday poem and the darkness and negation which are present are justified. It is as if the world endures one long Good Friday, the Saviour-fool still suffering in the human frame. The poem continues:

> A god has no alternative
> but himself. With what crown
> plurality but with thorns?
> Whose is the mirthless laughter
> at the beloved irony
> at his side?

The inability to distinguish the figures prevails. The Christ figure is identified as the – 'beloved irony' – the irony presumably lying in the mystery of the unity of the Godhead; the source of the laughter is not identified, but we are reminded of the 'loud, uncontrollable, laughter of God' in the earlier poem 'Rough',[33] and 'in his side like an incurred stitch, Jesus':

> The universe over,
> omniscience warns, the crosses
> are being erected from such
> material as is available
> to remorse.

The deeply ambiguous phrase which opens this sentence creates a dark and disturbing picture. We can choose to read it as 'all over the universe' or 'the universe being over'. Either reading is disturb-ing. Remembering the gantries which were like crosses,[34] we can produce the meaning that all over the world sacrifices are being made to materialism, and that something or someone is suffering. Or the omniscient voice warns of a cataclysmic event which will leave us to mark the graves with 'such/ material as is available/ to remorse'.

The image of Good Friday is extended to embrace the condi-tion of the whole world, where the whole world becomes a Good Friday; God remains crucified and darkness has not been relieved. What possible counterpoint can there be to so bleak a vision? There is only one 'option':

> Remembering,
> as one goes out into space,
> on the way to the sun,
> how dark it will grow,
> I stare up into the darkness

Again, image develops into image. The resolution, itself an unusual phenomenon in Thomas, is found in analogy. The darkness
is part of the movement towards light, and is a promise of the light
to come. The darkness of space becomes a metaphor for the darkness of God's face. The biblical term 'countenance' brings the response into the orbit of faith, a response which grows stronger as
it develops:

> knowing it
> a reflection.

We are introduced to the paradoxical notion that darkness is a
reflection. The image is extended, bringing back the ideas of reflection and mirrors. The final image of the mirror has been prepared
for. In the section entitled B.C.,[35] Thomas uses the mirror as a way
of considering the mind of God and the mystery of the Godhead:

> Who can read God's mind?
> Was it two mirrors echoing
> one another? And was the Holy
> Spirit the breath clouding them
> unable to discover
> precedence in derivation
> from the origin and the image,
> perplexities of Nicaea?

The difficulties of identification which we have considered are
foregrounded in the reference to Nicaea.[36] Christ is not just the
'image' of God, but the 'mirror image'. This idea was reinforced[37] in
the 'dusty looking-glass'. There we noted the similarity of purpose
in Paul's 'through a glass darkly'. Now the persona gazes into
darkness as into the 'back of love's looking-glass'. He identifies
with the crucified Christ in enduring the darkness, recognising it
as the darkness of God's countenance, and engaging in the dance.
The present darkness is a reflection – a paradox in itself – of the three

days which Christ spent in the tomb. There is no surprise at the darkness any more, no wrestling with God. There is no alternative, only 'this one option'. But it is received with equanimity. The darkness which descended at Calvary and the darkness of unknowing become one, but they are not without hope.

The poem which faces 'God's Fool', however, 'Not the Empty tomb' (p. 37), sees not the empty tomb but the empty cross as the symbol of hope. This is a personal commitment of Thomas to what he sees as a very modern symbol. Its shape – spare, geometric – appeals to his asceticism. Resurrection in this poem is symbolised in the cross burgeoning, becoming perhaps, the tree of life, the tree that was at the beginning, in another of its incarnations:

> you will see the arms
> put on leaves. Not a crown
> of thorns, but a crown of flowers
> haloing it, with a bird singing
> as though perched on paradise's threshold.

Crowned now with flowers it becomes the doorway to paradise. But the injunction is to 'Look long enough'. The cross is the icon of faith and if Thomas finds any respite from his wrestling, it is, even if only momentarily and after long looking, here.[38] (That the respite is short-lived is demonstrated in the close proximity of the poem 'Silent, Lord' (p. 39).)

After a short pause between stanzas there is a sudden change of tone. The affirmative, almost romantic language of the first stanza is jettisoned and there is a sudden change of key. The counterpoint is registered in the single poem. Pleasant though the vision is, the modern world presses in, its problems registered in the altered tone: 'Our churches/ are as limousines in the procession . . .' It is an uncomfortable, disconcerting transition, using, as the stanza proceeds, a vocabulary drawn from a number of different language sets – modern, scientific, classical and ecclesiastical. The modern mode of adherence is castigated and there is an inference of the 'one thing needful': the cross, as symbolised in the Eucharist, seems to be the needful thing. The poem closes by picking up the bird-image from the first stanza:

> one crumb of bread
> on the tongue for the bird-like
> intelligence to be made tame by.

The intelligence needs to be convinced that it is safe to approach
the cross in an act of faith, to become the

> bird singing
> as though perched on paradise's threshold.

This vision, which is achieved in the first stanza, lies in contrast
to the clumsy attempts at faith in the second. But there is still hope.
The problems of science and materialism are neutralised in the cross
which is 'de-nuclearised' and 'uncontaminated'. It is in the shared
bread and wine that confidence is nurtured, and the 'one crumb of
bread' suggests that a mustard seed faith is enough.

B.C. opened with the image of a man staring into the future:
'sand/ for the pioneer to stare over/ in his questioning of the
horizon'. *Crucifixion* closes with the image of a face staring 'as over
twenty centuries / it has stared, from unfathomable/ darkness into
unfathomable light'.[39] The darkness there might be read as the
darkness of the Crucifixion and of isolation from God, and the
light might represent eternity. Again, there is the suggestion that,
in the mode of the 'counterpoint', humanity is moving from the
darkness of the past into the brightness of the future. However, as
we have already seen, darkness is also the reflection of God, and
the emphasis might rather be on the 'unfathomable' nature of both
darkness and light. As we move on to the section *A.D.*[40] we find
that this is supported by the opening poem, where there is very
little encouragement to suppose the future, or even the present, is
particularly bright. Beginning 'We must reverse our lenses', the poem
suggests that in the modern era we have imagined that we too have
left some kind of darkness behind us and are progressing towards
the light. We have habitually represented our history as darkness,
and have assumed that we are moving, by means of the developing
intellect and the acquisition of knowledge, towards the light. This
is the positivist view of knowledge as, essentially, progress. It is
not a theory which Thomas subscribes to,[41] and he expresses his
demurral by setting particular value on two distinct periods which
pre-date the positivists. The first is pre-history and the second is
medieval history. Thomas's interest in pre-history is registered in
his preoccupation with the great age of Precambrian rocks, and in
references to cave-dwellers and to primitive societies.[42] The pre-
dilection for medieval culture is manifest in the theology which
permeates the work, and in frequent references to paintings and

religious images of the period. These two periods are referred to over and over again in Thomas's poetry, occasionally finding a place in the same poem. 'Forest Dwellers',[43] for example, effectively links the two periods to make its point, and it is worth looking at it in some detail as a preface to reading 'We must reverse our lenses'. Two stanzas are of particular interest:

> Who called them forth to walk
> in the green light, their thoughts
> on darkness? Their women,
> who are not Madonnas, have babes
> at the breast with the wise,
> time-ridden faces of the Christ
> child in a painting by a Florentine

> master. The warriors prepare poison
> with love's care for the Sebastians
> of their arrows. They have no
> God, but follow the contradictions
> of a ritual that says
> life must die that life
> may go on. They wear flowers in their hair.

We can see how some of the lines from this poem were reworked in 'Top Left an Angel'.[44] 'Forest Dwellers' provides a gloss on the difficulties of that poem, suggesting, perhaps, that the child is all children and the mother all mothers. That the moment itself is, perhaps, timeless. But, in 'Forest Dwellers' it is the innocence of the race that Thomas finds endearing. Where he, and we, labour to make sense of the contradictions he perceives in life, they 'follow the contradictions'. (The line break is crucial to the point.) The paradox of the ritual is performed because it is performed. They have no God. The juxtaposition of poison with love gives them no problems; love, it seems, is the condition of life. Untrammelled by the burden of enquiry, they 'wear flowers in their hair'.

But the medieval world, too, is inscribed in 'Forest Dwellers'. It is with the medieval world that these primitive people are associated, not with the modern world. The same acknowledgement of 'the verities' is represented in the Florentine master as Thomas recognises in the forest dwellers ('time-ridden' functions rather as 'How old at the centre' in 'Top Left an Angel'). In the industrial-technological era[45] we, it seems, are more in the dark than they.

So, to return to the poem with which *A.D.* begins: 'We must reverse our lenses'. The trope of the 'wrong end of the lens' is one which Thomas favours.[46] We notice how the poem is illuminated by the images of flowers and painting which we observed in 'Forest Dwellers'. That time, which we have labelled 'dark', was actually a dawn that 'had the brightness of flowers'. Post-lapsarian human history, St Jerome suggests, is a process of decline.[47] Thomas seems to concur:

> It is the future is dark
> because one by one
> we are removing these paintings
> from our exhibition. We walk
> between blank walls, scrawled
> over with the graffiti
> of a species . . .

We are not moving into the light but into the dark, because we have left behind those means of mediating God which previous periods of history valued. Referring to the cave-dwellers, an earlier poem, 'The Gap',[48] says:

> Their hand moved in the dark
> like a priest's, giving its blessing
> to a bare wall.
> . . . This was before
> the fall.

Here, art is a sacrament, a state of innocence which is violated by intellect:

> Somewhere between them and us
> the mind climbed up into the tree
> of knowledge, and saw the forbidden subjects . . .

Where the cave-dwellers have a hand moving 'like a priest's, giving its/ blessing to a bare wall' we only have walls which are blank, scrawled over with graffiti. The 'bare' walls and the 'blank' walls take on a certain significance. The drawings of the cave-dwellers were both a celebration and an invocation. Their religion naturally sought expression; the religion and the life were inseparable.

It seems that for Thomas this period is analogous to the pre-fall state, and that many of its virtues he sees preserved in the medieval period. (It is perhaps this ability to express faith in images which, for Thomas, relates them to the Middle Ages.)[49] The counterpoint of the secular, modern age is figured in the graffiti on the blank wall. The 'blank wall' suggests that there is no 'given' to generate a unified response; meaning must be constructed by the individual consciousness, but what is in fact constructed is only 'graffiti', a fragmented discourse which fails to create either order or beauty. We have removed 'these paintings/ from our exhibition'. The paintings in this poem might be the paintings of 'The Gap' which 'bless the bare wall', or the paintings of the 'Florentine'. They are both an effective, non-verbal means of expressing the unity of faith and life. For us, the attempts of language to follow suit succeed in producing only 'graffiti'. In *Mass for Hard Times*[50] the opposition of art/language takes the form of altar/pulpit, and this is another way of expressing the opposition, or even the perceived superiority, of the visual to the verbal. Gerald Hammond makes some interesting points on this same opposition in *Fleeting Things*. There he sees it as the 'Puritan emphasis upon the spoken word confronting Anglican values of ceremony and ritual designed to work principally in images'.[51]

We see ourselves, then, says Thomas, as moving either into the light or into the dark. The counterpoint is underlined in the closing lines:

> not to discover
> its incipient wings, but the slime
> rather and the quagmire from which
> it believes itself to have emerged.

The way we see ourselves has far-reaching effects on how we see God. We can see ourselves, as the psalmist does, as made by God 'a little lower than the angels',[52] in other words, having 'incipient wings'; or we can see ourselves in the evolutionary mode as having emerged from the 'slime and the quagmire'. We note how the main theme of *Counterpoint* as evolutionary history set against salvation history is being played out.

The problems of using language to express mystical experience is a recurring and, for Thomas, a worrying theme.[53] Its weaknesses, suggested by the 'graffiti' of 'We must reverse our lenses'– which

initiates a small sequence of four, linked poems – are further emphasised in the next poem in the sequence, 'The way the tree's
boughs' (p. 43). The imagery in this poem is as dense as in the poem
that opened B.C. It is difficult to hold on to the shifting perspectives
and even more difficult to express them – an apt illustration of
the very point Thomas is hoping to make. The tone is meditative,
opening *in medias res*, creating the impression that we are eaves-
dropping on the thoughts of the speaker, a notion that is emphasised
by the absence of syntax.[54] The unexpected juxtaposition of images
is worthy of the metaphysicals, and this observation is validated
when we note how the argument moves in a circular motion not
unlike a Herbert poem.[55] In the first stanza the natural image dominates. We are aware of the tree, the boughs, the leaves, all enhanced
and quickened by the suggestion of the April day. The intertwining
of the boughs of the tree reminds the speaker of the pattern of a
brain, whose thoughts become the leaves on the tree. So thought, it
is implied, should relate to language.

The poem continues in the 'stream of consciousness' mode, developing by association. The images double back on themselves,
the brain now in turn resembling a wood. But thought does not
find expression in an adequate form. Thought is held fast in the
'impenetrable thicket' of the brain. The analogy is drawn from the
Old Testament story of Abraham and Isaac.[56] About to sacrifice
his son to God, Abraham's hand is stayed and he is shown a sub-
stitute sacrifice, a ram caught in a thicket by the horns. Interestingly, Thomas seems to suggest here – flying in the face of
modern linguistics – that thought precedes language. That the idea
is held in the brain but cannot be effectively transmitted through
speech.

The implications of the second stanza affect our reading of the
first and we must retrace our steps. Tenor and vehicle have been
reversed between the stanzas. The tree which was like a brain has
become the brain which is like a 'tree', here the thicket. The brain
in each of these images, however, expresses thoughts. Having seen
the necessary compromise in the second image, where thought is a
sacrifice to language, we should consider the manner of expression
found in the first:

> pattern of an immense
> brain whose thoughts are the leaves
> proliferating in April.

This is how thought should relate to language. As the leaves naturally and spontaneously, and with great beauty, express the 'inner'
life of the tree, so language, ideally, should express thought. The
leaves do not mis-express the tree. We are reminded of Yeats's lines
in 'Among School Children':[57]

> O chestnut-tree, great-rooted blossomer,
> Are you the leaf, the blossom or the bole?
> O body swayed to music, O brightening glance,
> How can we know the dancer from the dance?

There is a further dimension which must be noted, and that is the
interplay between the religious images. We can produce the reading that the 'immense brain' is God's brain:

> whose thoughts are the leaves
> proliferating in April.

The tree burgeoning in April reiterates the other trees which appear
in this volume and which represent the crucifixion. We have said
that in the tree the leaves are an expression of the 'life', or nature,
of the tree. The leaves express in concrete form what the tree 'is'. So
God's thoughts find direct expression in creation. His word will
take on a positive form, which will adequately express his nature.
For the Christian the 'Word' of God, the Logos, is the Christ. As the
tree, in expressing itself does so by producing, or reproducing itself,
so the Father, in speaking, produces an adequate signifier. God's
Word, his self-expression, is the Christ. We might say that the Son
reveals the nature of the Father, or 'speaks' the Father. In our discussion of the first poem in *B.C.* we noted that 'the Word is a fusion
of concept and image, language and man'. In the language of God
there is no gap between signifier and signified – the Word was
made flesh.[58]

It is the gap between the signifier and the signified that Thomas
finds frustrating. Language, we have noted, brings with it the means
to mis-express God. The twist in the tail is, of course, that in salvation history it is the Word which is sacrificed. In this poem it is
the thought that is sacrificed to the word. Unable to find words
adequate to the quality of the thought, inadequate expression, it
seems, is preferable to no expression at all. It is as if the gap between
signifier and signified is a product of the fall itself.[59] Thomas is well
aware of the irony of marking the inadequacy of language in speech:

> In the silence
> that is his chosen medium
> of communication and telling
> others about it
> in words. Is there no way
> not to be the sport
> of reason?[60]

It comes as no surprise, then, that many of the poems in *A.D.* recognise the only appropriate means of communication to be silence. In
a world in which prayer seems to be impossible, and in which faith
has been undermined by philosophy and science[61] how is faith to
be practised or spiritual experience expressed?

Thomas has developed a delicate approach to describing spiritual
encounter which has become the hallmark of his art. Drawing on
abstracts, and images which are often translucent or fluid, he conveys
a rare sense of other-worldliness. The poem 'The withholding',[62]
to anticipate, is typical of the style. Silence, anonymity and absence
denude the imagination of form, and the qualities associated with
those images which do appear, the mirror and the spring-tide, are
themselves shifting and unstable, registering themselves in the
mind as a metallic sheen. Thomas says he 'plays a small pipe a little
to the side of the main road'.[63] Thinking of his approach to the mystical poems we might also say that he is an artist who paints from
a limited palette. The colours and the spaces which infuse the poems
are those of the seascape, but the limited palette applies also to the
texture of the language he chooses, the gentleness of the assonance,
the carefully selected consonants and the delicate precision of the
rhythms. It is tempting to think that the language and images find
their origin in the landscape he inhabits. Derek Walcott, responding
to a remark about the richness of his own language, readily supposes
that it emerges from the landscape in which he lives:

> I don't think you can separate language from geography . . . I
> come from a very luxuriant vegetation and what may appear to
> be lush is normal for us. So I think that if there is either an
> exuberance of language or richness, then I think it's because I
> come out of a landscape that has these qualities.[64]

This being so, it is not surprising that Thomas's poetry shimmers
with light and mist and water.

Those poems in *A.D.* which underwrite the spiritual aspect of *Counterpoint*, projecting a positive image of God, rely on the techniques I have observed. The place of silence is crucial. In 'The withholding' (p. 45) the silence *is* the prayer; God is not even requested to note the silence:

> I waited upon
> him as a mirror . . .

The idea of waiting like a mirror waiting upon absence is profound.

Waiting like a mirror would be to wait without fret or hurry, hoping for nothing. As it waits upon absence, so the persona too waits upon absence, for absence is an important mode by which God can be known. But a mirror only exists to reflect the user, a complication which is implied by the careful line endings. 'Man' is the mirror of God; the image of God is reiterated, but as always with Thomas the meaning is in excess of the language, for God, in turn, is the mirror of man. We are reminded of 'The Presence' where the images are equally interchangeable:

> There is nothing I can do
> but fill myself with my own
>   silence, hoping it will approach
>   like a wild creature to drink
> there, or perhaps like Narcissus
> to linger a moment over its transparent face.

The necessity of patient waiting on God is reiterated:

> Time passed. Once
> from the closeness
> of the invisible,
> or in the after-draught
>
> of the far off, hurrying
> about the immensity
> of his being, I rose brimming
> towards him like the spring-tide

The lengthy passage of time counterpoints that 'Once', emphasising the degree of self-giving necessary for receiving the brief moment of epiphany. Immediately image and syntax disintegrate, leaving only an impression of an experience, of a God who moves in the whirlwind, the God of Moses and Elijah:[65]

> I rose brimming
> towards him like the spring-tide.

That 'Once' is enough. The fulfilment is expressed in the word 'brimming'. The response is emotional and spontaneous not intellectual and measured; it is the flower which opens on 'the mind's tree of thorns'.[66] This tension between the mind and the emotions is the fundamental 'counterpoint' in the whole of Thomas's oeuvre. It is registered in the poem which precedes this in *A.D.*[67] The second stanza there reads:

> The philosophers had done
> their work well, demolishing
> proofs we never believed in.

It will be reiterated movingly in 'Sonata in X', *Mass for Hard Times*:

> The evolutionists told
> me I was wrong. My premises,
> the philosophers assured me,
> were incorrect. Perpendicular
> I agreed, but on my knees
> looking up, cap in hand,
> at the night sky I laid astronomy
> on one side . . .

A 'counterpoint', we have said, 'is the simultaneous sounding of two different melodies'. On page 54 a poem appears which uses the 'melodies' in a subtle way; a mystery of the natural world becomes an image for the mystery of the spiritual.[68] The deep-seated, but irrational response to God which Thomas confesses in 'Sonata in X' finds its paradigm here in the instinctive behaviour of the migrant bird. The passage of the bird into the wide tracts of sky is a purely natural instinctive action. The bird does not fret about whether it will arrive in the gentler 'climate of its conception'. It merely responds to the urgency within and the position of the sun. From this natural phenomenon Thomas creates a most beautiful metaphor for the aspiration of the soul towards God. Again, we see that what matters is the one moment of achievement. The image of God is not one of form but of void. He is like the weather through which we travel; or the wind – the Holy Spirit – which 'bloweth where it listeth';[69] we don't know where it comes from or where it goes to, but it is the journey which is important. 'The climate of our conception' might be the place to which we aspire, the perceived journey's end; it reminds us of 'Intimations of Immortality'[70] with its suggestion that we come from 'heaven which is our home'. But the 'climate of our conception' might mean an illusion, something we have imagined for ourselves. Does it matter which? Apparently not. It is enough that we have been given the facility to respond to his prompting:

> Enough if we have been given wings
> and a needle in the mind
> to respond to his bleak north.

The spiritual climate is austere. There is little for our comfort. But however bleak 'his north' might be, there are still those rare moments of presence:

> There are times even at the Pole
> when he, too, pauses in his withdrawal
> so that it is light there all night long.

The use of a negative means of representing God persists. It seems that the norm in spiritual experience is one in which the period of darkness habitually exceeds that of light, but pursuing the metaphor of the compass (the needle in the mind) and the migratory birds, even at the Pole – at the bleakest times in our experience – he, like the sun, pauses in his withdrawal. The metaphor precludes anything as positive as God drawing near. But he

> pauses in his withdrawal
> so that it is light there all night long.

This is not as bleak a poem as some have thought. It is a demonstration of negative capability achieving a positive resolution.

What, then, might we expect as we draw to the close of the volume? To anticipate any resolution more positive than the one above would not be realistic. There are however, rare occasions

when R.S. Thomas feels justified in resting his case and he does
so here by drawing entirely on the resources of Scripture. The
penultimate poem in *A.D.* (p. 62) is a careful fusing of religious
images:

> When we are weak, we are
> strong. When our eyes close
> on the world, then somewhere
> within us the bush
> burns. When we are poor
> and aware of the inadequacy
> of our table, it is to that
> uninvited the guest comes.

We hear many voices in these few lines: the Apostle Paul, the Old
Testament, St John, even George Herbert.[71] They serve to strengthen
by association the mood of the poem. But more important than the
recognition of the sources is the way in which they are used to
create a restful response to the incessant wrestling which Thomas is
engaged in. It is, he says, when we acknowledge that we don't know
the answers, and we stop striving, that the moment of Epiphany
is granted. Thomas himself sums up the result of his efforts in the
last poem:

> I think that maybe
> I will be a little surer
> of being a little nearer
> That's all. Eternity
> is in the understanding
> that that little is more than enough.

7

Conclusion

The aim of this study has been to determine that for Thomas the task of the religious poet – to remind ourselves of the place from which we started – is not to preach certainty but to explore doubt and other negative feelings and, finally, to wait in darkness; a darkness which may on occasion (as the author of *The Cloud of Unknowing* well knew) flame with love.

This project is as present in Thomas's 'non-religious' poems as in the more obviously religious ones. Our reading of images of women adumbrated the problematics of reading images of God. We were alerted to the possibility of multiple readings; to the problem of identifying the nature of selfhood; to the inevitability of the gap between observation and reality.

Through the poems which dealt more generally with art, we were prepared for the variety of approaches which Thomas is likely to take towards his subject; the creativity of his sliding perspectives which enlarge our perception of the subject; his habit of often engaging the reader in the poem as closely as a 'donor' in a painting; and most of all perhaps, the tendency of the subject suddenly to transcend itself in a moment of vision. All these features serve as metaphors for our reading of images of God. Our reading of landscape demonstrates that the *via negativa* has been present from the earliest work, challenging our assumptions about nature and pointing up the tension between ideal and actual experience, a tension which often found expression in the problematics of language.

Those poems which we designated 'mythic', together with the 'science' poems, demanded that readers should actually experience the two *vias* in their response to the poems – readers have to decide for themselves whether God 'is' or 'is not' like this. Where, in reading landscape as a metaphor for God, there was a conflict, or gap, between the ideal and the actual, in these poems the conflict, the perceived gap, is between observation and vision. The mythic poems actually operate in the gap between lived experience and spiritual perception. While the notion of 'Otherness' is strongly focused in these poems it is significant that we find here a blurring of subject and object.

This blurring of subject and object is particularly noticeable where God is imaged as personal. The need to obscure difference is focused and the negation of representation is demonstrated in the attempt to escape from concrete images. Indeed, some of the most successful poems are those in which God is represented by the non-tangible – absence, light or intimations of movement. These poems particularly address the same problem as that encountered by Nicholas of Cusa and the author of *The Cloud of Unknowing*: how to speak of the ineffable. A solution is found in the gap between the *via negativa* and the *via positiva*. All these tensions and oppositions are reinforced in *Counterpoint*, where they are imaged in the opposition between sacred and secular history. While all the major themes we have considered see language, and our use of language, as an important factor in imaging God, *Counterpoint* focuses the problem of language more acutely and consistently. Attention is drawn to the fragmentary nature of discourse, and the 'gaps' which we have noted in the texts are now foregrounded and dramatised more often.

We have already noted that Thomas often uses a single image in a number of ways, often contradictory. In keeping with this, the notion of 'the gap', when foregrounded in the poetry, can be either positive or negative. When it represents the gap between the actual and the ideal, as we find, for instance, in 'Forest Dwellers' it is a negative thing, a symbol of a lost unity with nature and with God. When it is the gap which represents 'between' – as in 'Via Negativa' where God is both found and not found – it is positive, the space in which God operates. The ideal, however, would seem to be no gap at all, and this brings us back to the problem of language, to the perceived gap between signified and signifier.

While I am not a fully committed critical theorist, I must admit that I find the language set used by theorists, with its religious overtones, quite fascinating. In this study we have been interested in what Thomas, and we as readers, recognise as a fundamental gap at the heart of all our religious experience. The desire to image God as presence can never be fulfilled. Critical theorists, referring to language, also recognise a desire for presence which cannot be achieved. The project of the modern critical theorist and of the mystic seem to stand as metaphors for one another. For the mystic, however, the accomplishment of presence can be achieved in the 'moment of passive union'. This is possible because whereas speech is linear, a series of consecutive moments articulated in time, the moment of passive union is not consecutive. It refuses fragmentation.

Meister Eckhart tells us:

> The union of God with the soul is so great that it is scarcely to be believed. And God is in himself so far above that no form of knowledge or desire can ever reach him. The desire for God reaches further than anything which can be comprehended by the intellect . . . But nothing that the intellect can grasp and nothing that desire can desire is God. Where understanding and desire end, there is darkness and there God's radiance begins.[1]

In the course of this exploration I have sometimes used the phrase 'inadequacy of language'. To speak of 'inadequacy of language', however, might suggest that we know what we wish to say and that if we had the 'right' words, or if words were 'fixed' to a precise meaning, then we could say it. In the context of imaging God, of expressing the 'Other', this is not the case. The moment of passive union is pure and simple Presence, when we 'know'. But what we know we do not know.[2] Therefore, perhaps we ought not to refer to the inadequacy of language to express the mystical experience of Presence; rather, we may acknowledge the perfection of presence which refuses articulation because articulation is linear, fragmented and most of all unnecessary.

The words of Ricoeur return with increased potency:[3]

> we reinforce the prejudice that reality is only what is manipulatable. But if we have surmised that there is another layer of reality that only poetry may reach and express, then the suspension of referentiality is only one step and it is necessary that we must first lose contact with ordinary things in order, maybe, thanks to this liberation of language, to redirect it once more towards some more deeply rooted forms of experience.

We can only approximate the experience of Presence if we wish to share that experience. To do this we must allow language to play in the Presence, to find its exuberant expression of the 'almost' and the 'nearly' and the 'like', and we can delight in this play.

Hence the need for metaphor and other poetic devices, such as Thomas's playful use of line endings which suggest links which the formal syntax does not, which can both affirm and deny likeness.

Metaphor is an indispensable part of our language, so much so that it has become 'natural'. It seems 'natural' to say that we do not know what God is 'like'. What we probably mean is that we do not know what God is. This does not mean that we cannot know that he is.

The author of *The Cloud of Unknowing* says: 'God cannot be thought but he may well be loved.'[4] It is, then, a paradox that in Thomas's work there is a sense of almost agonizing thought, but not a very great sense of love. Yet, significantly I think, one of the few moments where we feel love is at the heart of the experience is in the poem which is called 'The Presence'. When this most private of men speaks in tones such as these, we become eavesdroppers on a tender moment in a stormy love-affair, and can allow ourselves to think for a moment that the desire for Presence and for Love are one and the same thing.

We may do no better, in conclusion, than to give Thomas the last word, which could be taken as a summary:[5]

> There is a language
> beyond speech we are given to learn
> by a suspension of the categories
> of the present. Hurrying to and fro
> in the imagination, we find its furniture
> is of no period, yet all its rooms
> blend to accommodate the restlessness
> of the spirit. So in the huge night,
> awakening, I have re-interpreted
> the stars signals and seen the reflection
> in an eternal mirror of the mystery
> terrifying enough to be named Love.

Notes

Chapter 1 Introduction

1. Joseph Flavius, *Jewish War*, l. 152f; and *Antiquities of the Jews*, 14. 71f. See also Cecil Roth, *A Short History of the Jewish People* (Macmillan, London, 1936).
2. Nicholas of Cusa, *Of Learned Ignorance*, chapter XIII, cited in F.C. Happold, *Mysticism: A Study and an Anthology* (Penguin, Harmondsworth, 1990), p. 339.
3. Meister Eckhart, sermon LXXXIII, cited in Happold, p. 177. See also sermon XC1X in ibid., p. 274.
4. W.R. Inge, *Personal Religion and The Life of Devotion* (Longmans and Co., London, 1924), p. 22.
5. I have not been able to confirm the pronominal referent of Nicholas's original, but the distinction between singular and plural pronoun does not materially affect my argument.
6. David Goldberg and John Rayner, *The Jewish People: Their History and Religion* (Penguin, Harmondsworth, 1989), p. 242.
7. Happold, p. 64.
8. For discussion of this point, see Brant Pelphrey, *Christ our Mother: Julian of Norwich* (Darton, Longman and Todd, London, 1989); Caroline Walker Bynum, *Jesus as Mother: Studies in the Spirituality of the High Middle Ages* (University of California Press, London, 1982). See also Happold, p. 65. Here Happold seems to accept Dr Martin Johnson's premise that the word Father 'is a symbol which is not misleading'. I would wish to demur.
9. Mary Daly says: 'In 1972, Episcopal Bishop C. Kilmer Myers asserted that since Jesus was male, women cannot be ordained.' This is an argument which has resurfaced in the current debate in England. Mary Daly, *Beyond God the Father: Towards a Philosophy of Women's Liberation* (The Women's Press, London, 1986).
10. Helen Gardner, *The Art of T. S. Eliot* (Cresset Press, London, 1949).
11. *Song at the Year's Turning* (Rupert Hart-Davis, London, 1955); see also Ezekiel 22. 30.
12. *H'm* (Macmillan, London, 1972), p. 33.
13. *Laboratories of the Spirit* (Macmillan, London, 1975), p. 36.
14. *Frequencies* (Macmillan, London, 1978), p. 14.
15. *The Penguin Book of Religious Verse* (Penguin, Harmondsworth, 1963).
16. Dame Helen Gardner, in *Religion and Literature* (Faber and Faber, London, 1971).
17. A point made earlier in my unpublished undergraduate dissertation, 'The Religious Poet in a Secular Age'.
18. 'The Minister', R.S. Thomas's play for voices first broadcast as part of Aneurin Talfan's BBC Series 'Radio Poems', 1952, and published

in *Selected Poems* 1946–1968 (Bloodaxe Books, Newcastle upon Tyne, 1986).

19. *Mass for Hard Times* (Bloodaxe Books, Newcastle upon Tyne, 1992) appeared shortly before the completion of this work and could not appear prominently. In my judgement, while introducing further, very interesting, experimental forms, it provides an interesting gloss on the more difficult *Counterpoint*.

20. A practice I had not adopted at the time of writing the article referred to in note 17.

21. These readers would find, if not support, then certainly sympathy, from the following, for example: Roland Mathias, *The Anglo-Welsh Review*, vol. 21–2 (1972–3), pp. 201–3: 'For *H'm* as its title may infer, is scarcely a volume of faith.' Or Robert Nisbet, who called his article for *Planet* (vol. 35 (1976), pp. 26–30): 'R.S. Thomas: The Landscape of Near-despair'. Lethbridge also asks: 'I wonder if I detect some despair, discouragement? Or are these just moments of lowering weather?' 'R.S. Thomas talks to J.B. Lethbridge', *Anglo-Welsh Review* No. 74 (1983), pp. 36–56.

Chapter 2   Reading the Image

1. Ezra Pound, in *Poets on Painters: Essays in the Art of Painting by Twentieth Century Poets*, ed. J.D. McClatchy (University of California Press, Berkeley, 1988).

2. Germain Bazin, *Impressionist Paintings in the Louvre* (Thames and Hudson, London, 1958).

3. See John Berger, *Ways of Seeing* (BBC and Penguin, London, 1972), p. 56.

4. This painting appears in Bazin only in monochrome, but Thomas is clearly working from a knowledge of the colour plate.

5. Michael Levey, *From Giotto To Cézanne: A Concise History of Painting* (Thames and Hudson, London, 1962), p. 290.

6. From an altarpiece in Aix-en-Provence, dated 1465.

7. An interesting article which makes a similar point but develops differently is James Davies, 'Attempts to Evade: R. S. Thomas's "Impressions"', *Anglo-Welsh Review*, No. 79 (1985), pp. 70–83.

8. '. . . women were expected to be frail, it was thought ladylike' (*c.* 1900). Unlike their Edwardian mothers, modern girls were not afraid of the sun. Coco Chanel set a trend in cultivating a tan after she bought herself a house in the South of France and allowed her skin to darken. A healthy outdoor look was becoming a sign of affluence, suggesting sunbathing in the Riviera rather than potato picking in Essex. (*c.* 1930). (Angela Holdsworth, *Out of the Doll's House. The Story of Women in the 20th Century* (BBC Books, London, 1988), pp. 86, 16)

9. Andrew Marvell, *The Poems of Andrew Marvell*, ed. Hugh Macdonald (Routledge and Kegan Paul, London, 1952).

10. Luke 1. 35.

11. I have benefited from discussing this stanza with Helen Wilcox.

12. Simone de Beauvoir, *The Second Sex* (Penguin, Harmondsworth, 1972).

13. The forename 'Angèle' comes from 'Angela' and means 'the angelic girl or woman'. Eric Partridge, *Name This Child: A Dictionary of Modern British and American Given or Christian Names* (Hamish Hamilton, London, 1936).

14. Bazin, p. 226.

15. ' "Probings": An Interview with R.S. Thomas' [with Ned Thomas], *Planet*, No. 80 (1990), pp. 28–52.

16. *The Concise Mythological Dictionary* (G.P. Putnam's Sons, London, 1963).

17. An added complication to the woman-as-tree image is expressed in these lines from a Rilke poem:

> From women's sleeves none ever grew
> so ripe, so shimmeringly:
> I am the day, I am the dew,
> you, Lady, are the tree.

These are the words of the angel to the Virgin. The title of the poem is 'The Annunciation', *Selected Poems: Rilke*, trans. J.B. Leishman (Penguin, Harmondsworth, 1964).

18. Thomas has complained about this: 'Through publishing the illustrations in monochrome the publishers lessened the impact of some of the poems.' *Planet*, No. 80 (April/May 1990), p. 51.

19. Mullins points out how often women in paintings have been likened to fruit and food, with all its association of desire and consumption (Edwin Mullins, *The Painted Witch: FEMALE BODY: MALE ART*, Martin Secker & Warburg, London, 1985, p. 86). Kenneth Clark, in his *The Nude: A Study of Ideal Art* (John Murray, London, 1956), refers to the nude variously as follows: 'sensuous as strawberries' (p. 103); 'painted with as unprejudiced sensuality as if she were a peach or a pear' (p. 116); 'they are placed before us with the same unselfconscious piety as the sheaves of corn and piled up pumpkins which decorate a village church at harvest festival.' (p. 133); The face of Boticelli's Venus is a 'fruit among fruits' (p. 94). Venus de Milo makes us think of 'an elm tree in a field of corn' (p. 83).

20. In Herbert's 'Paradise', for example, God and the soul are presented as fruit to one another:

> Inclose me still for fear I START.
> Be to me rather sharp and TART,
> Than let me want thy hand and ART.

God is enjoined to be 'tart' to the soul rather than let it 'want his hand and art', i.e. as in pruning, which is patterned in the poem (*The Temple: The English Poems of George Herbert*, ed. C.A. Patrides, Dent, London, 1974).

21. Bazin, p. 112.

22. This was to protect them from the sound of the sirens' music. The sirens were ancient Greek sea-nymphs who by the irresistible charm of their song lured mariners to their destruction on the rocks surrounding their island. Odysseus escaped them by stuffing his companions'

ears with wax and having himself lashed to the mast of his ship. (*Concise Mythological Dictionary*, p. 154)

23. Circe was famed for her magic arts and potions, and changed all men who visited the island where she dwelt into swine by having them taste of the contents of her magic cup. When Odysseus and his companions were cast upon her island, she transformed Odysseus's men into swine (ibid., p. 41).

24. Compared to much of the dancing of the day, Jane Avril's dance is modest. According to Bazin (p. 246): 'her orange, black or lilac dresses were famous for their refined elegance. Her grace and distinction, poles apart from the vulgarity of La Goulue, fascinated Lautrec. He was even more attracted by her face "pale nervous ailing", her intelligence, and also by a quality of bitter sadness. Endowed with some degree of culture she was worthy of a better setting. Like him she seemed abandoned'.

25. Edwin Mullins, *The Painted Witch. FEMALE BODY: MALE ART* (Secker & Warburg, London, 1985).

26. John Rewald, *The History of Impressionism* (The Museum of Modern Art, New York, 1946), p. 584.

27. William Gaunt (notes by Kathleen Adler), *Renoir* (Phaidon Press, London, 1962), p. 46.

28. Bazin, p. 270.

29. 'Degas: *Portrait of a Young Woman*', *Between Here and Now* (Macmillan, London, 1975), p. 21.

30. *Poets on Painters: Essays on the Art of Painting by Twentieth-Century Poets*, ed. J.D. McClatchy (University of California Press, Berkeley, 1988), p. 55.

31. Ibid.

32. Ibid.

33. Ibid.

34. Clark, p. 159.

35. Ibid., p. 6.

36. Ibid.

37. Gaunt, *Renoir*.

38. Rewald, p. 582; see also 'Harbour', *Young and Old: R. S. Thomas* (Chatto and Windus, London, 1972), p. 10.

39. Walter Pater, 'All arts aspire to the condition of music', *The Renaissance: Studies in Art and Poetry*, ed. Donald Hill (University of California, Berkeley, 1980), p. 106.

40. 'R. S. Thomas talks to J. B. Lethbridge', *Anglo-Welsh Review*. No. 74 (1983), pp. 36–56.

41. See 1 Corinthians 15. 22; 2 Corinthians 5. 17; Romans 5. 14. Warner says: 'The economy and proportion of this Pauline idea gave it great power and appeal. To this day it is a specially graceful analogue, thrown over the history of western attitudes to women, the whole mighty span resting on Eve the temptress on one side and Mary the paragon on the other' (Marina Warner, *Alone of all Her Sex: The Myth and Cult of the Virgin*, Weidenfeld and Nicolson, London, 1976), pp. 59–60.

42. *Poetry for Supper* (Rupert Hart-Davis, London, 1958), p. 27.
43. S.T. Coleridge, *Biographia Literaria XIII* (Dent, London, 1956).
44. Introduction to *The Penguin Book of Religious Verse* (Penguin, Harmondsworth, 1963), p. 8.
45. *Laboratories of the Spirit* (Macmillan, London, 1975), p. 38; renamed 'Veneziano: The Annunciation', in *Later Poems 1972–1982* (Macmillan, London, 1983), p. 69.
46. T.S. Eliot, *Four Quartets;* 'Burnt Norton', *Collected Poems 1909–1962* (Faber and Faber, London, 1963).
47. Yrjo Hirn, *The Sacred Shrine* (Macmillan, London, 1912), p. 293.
48. Ibid., p. 335; see also Ez. 44. 2.
49. Ibid., pp. 438–9; also: the lily as symbol of the Virgin in Chaucer:

> Wherefore in laude, as I best ken or may,
> Of thee and of the white lylye flour,
> Which that the bar, and is a mayde alway
> The Prioress's Tale, VII. 460–2

50. See Chaucer: *Complete Works,* ed. F.N. Robinson (Oxford University Press, London, 1957). Variants of this pattern are also used in The Shipman's and Nun's Priest's tales.
51. See note 38.
52. This poem appears as 'Degas: Woman Combing', in *Later Poems,* p. 58.
53. Nemerov, *Poets on Painters,* ed. J.D. McClatchy, p. 184.
54. D.H. Lawrence, ibid., p. 51.
55. See Introduction, p. 1.
56. Bazin, p. 260.
57. G. Van der Leeuw, *Sacred and Profane Beauty: The Holy in Art* (Weidenfeld and Nicolson, London, 1963), p. 210.
58. J. Pissarro, *Monet's Cathedral* (Pavilion Books, London, 1990), pp. 23–7.
59. 'Sea-Watching', *Laboratories of the Spirit,* p. 64.
60. 'Monet: *Rouen Cathedral, Full Sunshine*' is one of only two poems from *Between Here and Now* which Thomas selected for *Later Poems,* where it does not have the accompanying picture. The other is 'Renoir: *The Bathers*'. This would suggest that Thomas believes they can stand alone.
61. Bazin, p. 222.
62. Wallace Stevens, *Poets on Painters,* p. 120.

Chapter 3   Landscape as Image

1. William Wordsworth, 'Lines Written a Few Miles above Tintern Abbey', in Stephen Gill, ed., *William Wordsworth* (Oxford University Press, Oxford, 1984), p. 131.
2. Alfred Lord Tennyson, 'In Memoriam', *Tennyson: In Memoriam, Maud and other poems,* ed. John Jump (Dent, London, 1974), p. 105.
3. *Laboratories of the Spirit* (Macmillan, London, 1975), p. 60.
4. Ibid., p. 36.

5. 'The Minister' was broadcast on the Welsh Regional programme of the BBC in 1952. Thomas remembers 'The Minister' as 'part of Aneirin Talfan's BBC series *Radio Poems*'; see 'R.S. Thomas Interview', *Planet*, No. 80 (April/May 1990), p. 33. It is reproduced in *Song at the Year's Turning* (Rupert Hart-Davis, London, 1955) and also in *Selected Poems 1946–1968* (MacGibbon/Hart-Davis, London, 1973) and *Selected Poems 1946–1968* (Bloodaxe Books, Newcastle upon Tyne, 1986).

6. 'Servant', *The Bread of Truth* (Rupert Hart-Davis, London, 1963), p. 41.

7. William Shakespeare, *A Midsummer Night's Dream*, II(i).

8. 'Green' seems to signify Welshness in Thomas's imagery. Cf. 'Strangers', *The Bread of Truth* p. 32: 'the folk with the green blouses which you displace'.

9. Cf. Graham Greene's religious novels, where at the climax the realist mode is often abandoned in favour of a quasi-mystical awareness.

10. To anticipate, the narrator refers us to a passage from *The Mabinogion* where we find the yellow broom, the white shoots of the marsh trefoil 'from amidst the fine gravel of a welling spring'; the reddest foxgloves; the 'four white trefoils'; the mewed hawk and the thrice-mewed falcon and the white swan. *The Mabinogion*, trans. Gwyn Jones and Thomas Jones (Dent, London and Melbourne, 1949), pp. 110–11.

11. See 'The Untamed', *The Bread of Truth*, p. 33; 'A Welshman at St James' Park', *Pietà* (Rupert Hart-Davis, London, 1966), p. 23; 'Bleak Liturgies', *Mass for Hard Times* (Bloodaxe Books, Newcastle upon Tyne, 1992), p. 60.

12. Cf. Wordsworth 'To a Skylark' (*William Wordsworth*, p. 238):

Pouring out praise to the Almighty Giver,
Joy and jollity be with us both!

13. T.S. Eliot, 'The Dry Salvages', *Four Quartets: Collected Poems 1909–1962* (Faber and Faber, London, 1963), p. 208.

14. William Barrett, *Irrational Man: A Study in Existential Philosophy* (Greenwood Press, Westport, CT, 1977), pp. 25–7.

15. 'Black letter' also refers to Gothic script.

16.   History showed us
He was too big to be nailed to the wall
Of a stone chapel, yet still we crammed him
Between the boards of a black book
            'A Welsh Testament', *Tares* (Rupert
                    Hart-Davis, London, 1961), p. 39

17. Barrett, pp. 27ff.

18. Isaiah 61.3.

19. As note 1 above.

20. S.T. Coleridge, 'Frost at Midnight', *Poems of Coleridge*, ed. John Lane (The Bodley Head, London, 1909), p. 206.

21. Wordsworth, 'Lines Written a Few Miles above Tintern Abbey'.

22. T.S. Eliot, 'The Waste Land', p. 61.

23. Ecclesiastes 12.6.

24. George Eliot, *Adam Bede*, ch. 5: 'Let me take you into that dining room. . . . We will enter very softly . . .' (Penguin Classics, Harmondsworth, 1985), p. 98.

25. Isaiah 60.2.

26. W.B. Yeats, 'The Second Coming', *Collected Poems* (Macmillan, London, 1982), p. 210.

27. 'The significance of the creation of the first actor cannot be overestimated. It was now possible not only for the actor but for the chorus also to take parts. The actor could play the god or hero, the chorus worshippers, subjects, soldiers, or whatever the story required. It was now also possible to introduce dialogue between actor and chorus. The chorus as well as retaining their original function as narrator, could also address the actor in character. This dual function of the chorus . . . is the distinctive feature of the Greek drama' (Peter Arnott, *An Introduction to the Greek Theatre* (Macmillan, London, 1961)).

28. Even God had a Welsh name:

> We spoke to him in the old language;
> He was to have a peculiar care
> For the Welsh people.
>   'A Welsh Testament'

According to Ward the idea of the chosen people has a place in the Welsh tradition of preaching. He says: 'The parallels with Moses and the Israelites enslaved by the Egyptians but determined by history, and God, to move to freedom by spreading God's word, were not uncommonly cited during the high moments of Welsh nonconformity' (J.P. Ward, *The Poetry of R.S. Thomas* (Poetry Wales Press, Bridgend, 1987), p. 31).

29.
> Phrase by phrase there formed
> The old reply to the earth's
> Question; the lips affirmed
>
> With tired patience the worth
> Of bird and flower, appealed
> To vows made at his birth.
>   'So', *Bread of Truth*, p. 22

30. A.M. Allchin, *Ann Griffiths: The Furnace and the Fountain* (University of Wales Press, Cardiff, 1987).

31. Glyn Tegai Hughes, *Williams Pantecelyn* (University of Wales Press, Cardiff, 1983), p. 108.

32. 'The Healing Herb and the Rose of Love: The Piety of Two Welsh Puritans', *Reformation Conformity and Dissent: Essays in Honour of Geoffrey Nuttall*, ed. R. Buick Knox (Epworth Press, London, 1977).

33. Idris H. Bell, *Welsh Poetry* (Clarendon Press, Oxford, 1936).

34. Translation from Bell, ibid.

35. Translation from *The Furnace and the Fountain*. Verse translations of this hymn do not demonstrate the point as strongly as the paraphrase.

36. For a detailed consideration of the place of nature in the work of Pantecelyn, see Hughes, *Williams Pantecelyn*.

37. W. Meredith Morris, *The Renaissance and Welsh Literature* (James James, Maesteg, 1908).
38. 'The Healing Herb and the Rose of Love: The Piety of Two Welsh Puritans'.
39. According to Tudor Jones this is from Llwyd's last book: 'Gair o'r Gair: Neu Son am Swn (1656), *Gweithiau Morgan Llwyd* II, pp. 189–92.
40. In *The Mabinogion*, Olwen is the beautiful daughter of Ysbaddaden Chief Giant.
41. Song of Songs, 4.12ff.
42. 'Olwen', literally 'white-path' – perhaps from the 'four white trefoils' which 'sprang up behind her wherever she went'.
43. The story of Melangell dates from the 6th–8th centuries: traditionally, she was a princess who fled to Wales from Ireland to avoid an arranged marriage. She founded a community of nuns on land given her by the prince, where the church, built in the twelfth century, stands today (*Companion to Welsh Literature*, p. 394).
44. *Song At The Year's Turning, 1942–1954* (Rupert Hart-Davis, London, 1955), p. 64.
45. There are exceptions: 'Invasion on the Farm', *Song at the Year's Turning*, p. 102.
46. 'Resolution and Independence', *William Wordsworth*, p. 260.
47. 'Valediction', *Song at the Year's Turning, 1942–1954*, p. 65.
48. 'Autumn On The Land', *Song at the Year's Turning*, p. 106.
49. *Poetry For Supper*, p. 28.
50. 'Which', *Tares*, p. 42.
51. *An Acre of Land*, p. 15.
52. 'Absolution', *Poetry for Supper*, p. 44.
53. 'The Parish', *Tares*, p. 15.
54. Matthew 7.13–14. Thomas refers to himself as 'playing a small pipe a little apart from the main road' (R.G. Thomas, 'Humanus Sum: A second look at R.S. Thomas', in *The Anglo-Welsh Review*, Vol. XVIII, No. 42 (1970), pp. 55–62).
55. *Pieta*, p. 24.
56. *Laboratories of the Spirit*, p. 19.
57. Marion Glasscoe, ed., *Julian of Norwich: A Revelation of Love* (University of Exeter, Exeter, 1976), p. 5.
58. *Song at the Year's Turning*, p. 115.
59.

> Their horizon contracted
> to the one small, stone-riddled field
> with its tree, where the weather was nailing
> the appalled body that had asked to be born.
> 'Hill Christmas',
> *Laboratories of the Spirit*, p. 42

60. *Laboratories of the Spirit*, p. 20.
61. See 'The Minister': 'This is the land where men labour/ In silence, and the rusted harrow/ Breaks its teeth on the grey stones'.
62. Glasscoe, ed., *Julian of Norwich: A Revelation of Love*, p. 19.

63.   Acts 2.1–4.
64.   Psalm 132.
65.   'The Moor', *Pietà*, p. 24; 'Alive', *Laboratories of the Spirit*, p. 51.
66.   Glasscoe, ed., *Julian of Norwich: A Revelation of Love*, p. 35.
67.   Brian Wren, *What Language Shall I Borrow? God-Talk in Worship: A Male Response to Feminist Theology* (SCM, London, 1989), p. 132.

Chapter 4   Myth and Science as Images of God

1.   'R.S. Thomas talks to J.B. Lethbridge', *Anglo-Welsh Review*, No. 74 (1983), p. 40.

2.   'an often-ancient concept pointing at some phenomena of nature, the origin of man, or the costumes and rites of people, mostly involving the exploits of gods and heroes' (*Literary Criticism and Myth*, ed. J.P. Strelka (The Pennsylvania State University Press, University Park and London, 1973), p. vii); 'any anonymously composed story telling of origins and destinies: the explanations a society offers its young of why the world is and why we do as we do, its pedagogic images of the nature and destiny of men' (Wellek and Warren, ibid., p. viii); the 'union of ritual and dream in a form of verbal communication' (Northrop Frye, ibid., p. vii).

3.   'Pisces', *Song At The Year's Turning*, p. 110.

4.   This poem finds its form in the nursery rhyme 'Who killed Cock Robin?'.

5.   From early times fish, especially dried fish, has taken the place of meat on days of fasting and abstinence. *Oxford Dictionary of the Christian Church*, sv.fish.

6.   Mark 14.22, Luke 22.19, Matt. 26.26.

7.   'Icthus': see *Oxford Dictionary of the Christian Church*, sv. fish.

8.   'Corpus Christi Carol' (Anon.), *The New Oxford Book Of English Verse*, ed. Helen Gardner (Oxford University Press, Oxford, 1972), p. 17.

9.   'Song for Gwydion', *Song At The Year's Turning*, p. 48.

10.   J.P. Ward, *The Poetry of R.S. Thomas* (Poetry Wales Press, Bridgend, 1978), p. 77.

11.   'January', *Song At The Year's Turning*, p. 107.

12.   One obvious exception is 'Ah', *Pietà*, p. 45.

13.   *Laboratories of The Spirit*, p. 36.

14.   Ibid., p. 11.

15.   *Frequencies*, p. 15.

16.   Rewald, p. 430.

17.   Cf. Walt Whitman, 'Song of Myself', *A Choice of Whitman's Verse* (Faber and Faber, London, 1968), p. 28:

      Tenderly will I use you curling grass,
      It may be you transpire from the breasts of young men . . .
      this grass is very dark . . . Darker than the colorless beards of old men.

18.   'Although there is competition, it usually takes place within a wider system of cooperation, so that the larger system is kept in balance.

Even predator – prey relationships that are destructive for the imme-
diate prey are generally beneficient for both species' (Capra Fritjof,
The Turning Point: Science, Society, and the Rising Culture (Fontana,
London, 1983), p. 302).

19. What adds significance to the reading of the hierarchy as the *scala
naturae* is that it is an order that has failed. According to Isobel
Rivers: 'Man's position at the centre of the universe was paradoxical; imperfect and earthbound, he was unhappily aware of the difference between the earthly and the heavenly spheres of existence,
yet he also knew that the cosmos has been created for him, and that
through a proper exercise of the celestial faculties with which he was
endowed he could aspire to the heavens. This religious and moral
significance supported the long belief in the traditional cosmology.
Yet this cosmology failed because *it did not fit the observed facts*: by the
end of the 17th century it no longer survived as science, but only
as poetic myth' (Isobel Rivers, *Classical and Christian Ideas in English
Renaissance Poetry* (George Allen and Unwin, London, 1979), p. 75,
emphasis added).

20. The Aristotelian Unmoved Mover, who moves the cosmos because
he is an object of love, becomes the Christian God who moves the
cosmos through his active love of his creation (ibid., p. 74).

21. Sheena Pugh makes a similar point in her review of *Counterpoint
Poetry Wales* '91 26. 4, but does not proceed beyond the notion of
indifference.

22. *Concise Mythological Dictionary*, p. 24.

23. The name 'Isaac' (Isaac is a type of Christ) means 'laughter'.

24. Poems are selected to clarify my point rather than in chronological
order.

25. see 1 Peter 2.9: 'But ye are a royal priesthood, an holy nation, a
people of his own, that ye should show forth the praises of him
who hath called you out of darkness into his marvellous light'.

26. God says: '*It is* not good that the man should be alone' (Gen 2.18).

27. *A Dance to the Music of Time* is the title of a series of volumes by
Anthony Powell. The following lines, which seem particularly relevant to my point, appear in the early pages of the first book in the
series: 'These classical projections, and something in the physical
attitudes of the men themselves as they turned from the fire, suddenly suggested Poussin's scene in which the Seasons, hand in hand
and facing outward, tread in rhythm to the notes of the lyre that the
winged and naked greybeard plays. The image of Time brought
thoughts of mortality: of human beings, facing outward like the
Seasons, moving hand in hand in intricate measure: stepping slowly,
methodically, sometimes a trifle awkwardly, in evolutions that take
recognisable shape: or breaking into seemingly meaningless gyra-
tions, while partners disappear only to reappear again, once more
giving pattern to the spectacle: unable to control the melody, unable,
perhaps, to control the steps of the dance' (Anthony Powell, *A Dance
to the Music of Time: A Question of Upbringing* (Collins/Fontana,
London and Glasgow, 1967), p. 6).

28. See 'Other', *H'm*, p. 36.
29. See 'Fugue for Ann Griffiths', *Welsh Airs* (Poetry Wales Press, Bridgend, 1987), p. 50.
30. 'Petition', *H'm*, p. 2.
31. Ward, pp. 79–80.
32. These voices may be read as a young person in dialogue with an older one; this reflects our definition of myth as 'the explanations a society offers its young of why we do as we do' (Wellek and Warren), in Stelka, ed., *Literary Criticism and Myth*).
33. Coleridge, 'Frost at Midnight', *The Poems of Coleridge* (The Bodley Hend, London, 1909), p. 206.
34. T.S. Eliot, 'Gerontian', 'Swaddled with darkness', p. 39.
35. 'The Gap', *Frequencies*, p. 7.
36. Gen. 3. 8ff.
37. 'Ash Wednesday', IV; T.S. Eliot, 'White light folded', p. 100.
38. 'Man has developed consciousness slowly and laboriously, in a process that took untold ages to reach the civilised state (which is arbitrarily dated from the invention of script in 4000BC). And this evolution is far from complete, for large areas of the human mind are still shrouded in darkness' (Carl Jung, *Man and his Symbols* (Aldus in association with W.H. Allan, London, 1964), p. 23).
39. J.P. Ward, *The Poetry of R. S. Thomas* (Poetry Wales, Bridgend, 1978); the phrase ultimately derives from Kierkegaard.
40. Gen 3.6.
41. See 'Amen', *Laboratories of the Spirit*, p. 5.
42. Gen 3.10.
43. Luke 23.34.
44. *Between Here and Now*, p. 82.
45. Simone de Beauvoir sees a similar development and separation in primitive man. She says: 'The great god Pan begins to fade when the first hammer blow resounds and the reign of man begins' (*The Second Sex*, p. 100).
46. The difficulty of accommodating the problem of pain is recognised by John Rodwell. He suggests that if there is a God, God must be seen as a God who is sensitive to the pain of creation. There is a seamless continuity between the complexity of the created order, the pain of human beings and God's intimate knowledge of all that is (Angela Tilby, *Soul* (BBC, London, 1992), p. 37).
47.   we die
                    with the knowledge that your resistance
                    is endless at the frontier of the great poem.
                    'The Combat', *Laboratories of the Spirit*, p. 43

48. 'The Tree', *Later Poems*, p. 187.
49. *Soul*, p. 48.
50. 'Other', *H'm*, p. 36. (There is also a poem called 'The Other' which refers directly to the machine. See *New Poems*, p. 180.)
51. Exodus 20.
52. Robert Herrick, 'Corinna is going a-Maying', *'The Poetical Works of*

Robert Herrick, ed. F.W. Moorman and Humphrey Milford (Oxford University Press, London, 1921), p. 68.
53. 'Daunced ful ofte in many a grene mede', 'The Canterbury Tales', *The Complete Works of Chaucer*, p. 85, l. 905.
54. 'The Provincial', *Pietà*, p. 16.
55. 'The Hand', *Laboratories of the Spirit*, p. 2.
56. 'Earth', *H'm*, p. 28.
57. 'God's Story', *Laboratories of the Spirit*, p. 7.
58. The definitive expression of these 'mixed things' is to be found in *The Epistle of Discretion of Stirrings: The Cloud of Unknowing and related treatises*, ed. Phyllis Hodgson (University of Exeter, Exeter, 1982), p. 114.
59. 'That Day', *H'm*, p. 31.
60. 'Emerging', *Laboratories of the Spirit*, p. 1.
61. *Planet*, Nos 28–32, 1975–6, p. 51.
62. This is an extract from an interview given by R.S. Thomas to the author. It is included as Appendix II in the thesis 'Images of God in the poetry of R.S. Thomas', at the University of Wales, Cardiff.
63. 'The Other', *Later Poems*.
64. Introduction to *The Penguin Book of Religious Verse*, p. 9.
65. Cf. Ted Hughes, *The Iron Man* (Faber and Faber, London, 1968).
66. Gerard Manley Hopkins, 'God's Grandeur', *Gerard Manley Hopkins: Poems and Prose*, sel. W.H. Gardner (Penguin, Harmondsworth, 1953), p. 27.
67. 'Postscript', *H'm*, p. 22.
68. *Anglo-Welsh Review*, No. 74, p. 43.
69. 'Reply', *Experimenting With An Amen*, p. 65.
70. Job 38.7.
71. Matt. 2.9.
72. Matt. 2.
73. Revelations 1.9.
74. 'At It', *Frequencies*, p. 15.
75. Cf. Louis Macneice, 'Reflections', *The Collected Poems of Louis Macneice*, ed. E.R. Dodds (Faber and Faber, London, 1966), p. 503.
76. A.S. Eddington. *The Nature of the Physical World* (Cambridge University Press, Cambridge, 1928), pp. xi–xii.
77. Author's interview, see 62 above.
78. Eddington, *The Nature of the Physical World*, pp. xvi–xvii.
79. 'Gradual', *Later Poems*, p. 178.
80. Ibid.
81. 'Suddenly', *Later Poems*, p. 201.
82. See *H'm*: 'Postscript', p. 22 and 'Other', p. 36.
83. 'The Lesson', *Poetry Wales*, Vol. 30, No. 3 (1995), p. 24.

Chapter 5 The *Via Negativa*

1. *Song at the Year's Turning*, p. 114.
2. Simon Tugwell OP, *Ways of Imperfection: An Exploration of Christian Spirituality* (Darton Longman and Todd, London, 1984).

3.   *Later Poems 1972–1982* (Macmillan, London, 1983), p. 201.
4.   *Between Here and Now* (Macmillan, London, 1981), p. 95.
5.   There may be shades of the *felix culpa* here. The 'love blazing' is reminiscent of the burning bush, which is a type of the Virgin. A further image which might be associated with the figure in the tree is that of the Virgin and child, often depicted in the branches of a tree in sacred art.
6.   This makes an interesting contrast to the images of women as fruit in chapter 1. Here the context validates the language. Here the notion of the body as fruit which may be consumed can be accommodated because of its elevation into the religious frame. The reaching out and taking of this body is institutionalised in the celebration of the Eucharist.
7.   John 1.1.
8.   Ruysbrock *'Samuel' De Vera Contemplatione cap xii.* Quoted by Evelyn Underhill in *Mysticism: A Study in the Nature and Development of Man's Spiritual Consciousness* (Methuen, London, 1911).
9.   *Pietà*, p. 44.
10. 'I wake and feel the fell of dark, not day.' Gerard Manley Hopkins, *Poems and Prose* ed. W.H. Gardner (Penguin, Harmondsworth, 1953), p. 62.
11. Cf. this silence with the silence of 'Sea Watching', *Laboratories of the Spirit*, (Macmillan, London, 1975), p. 64.
12. *Not That He Brought Flowers* (Rupert Hart-Davis, London, 1968), p. 32.
13. 'In the midst of silence a hidden word was spoken to me.' 'Where is this Silence, and where is the place in which this word is spoken? It is in the purest that the soul can produce, in her noblest part, in the Ground, even the being of the soul.' Eckhart, Pred i, *Mysticism*, p. 35. Cf. also T.S. Eliot, 'Ash Wednesday' V.
14. *The Cloud Of Unknowing*, p. 130.
15. Underhill, *Mysticism*, p. 35.
16. Author's interview; see chapter 3, note 62.
17. St Augustine, *Confessions*, book vii, cap xvii (quoted in Underhill, p. 331).
18. See 2 above.
19. Brian Wren, p. 101.
20. *Laboratories of the Spirit*, p. 43.
21. Wren, *What Language Shall I Borrow?* (SCM, London, 1989), p. 124.
22. Caroline Walker Bynum, *Studies in the Spirituality of the High Middle Ages* (University of California Press, London, 1982). Brant Pelphrey, *Christ Our Mother: Julian of Norwich* (Darton, Longman and Todd, London, 1989).
23. Mary Daly, *Beyond God the Father: Towards a Philosophy of Women's Liberation* (The Women's Press, London, 1986). Sallie McFague, *Models of God: Theology for an Ecological Nuclear Age* (SCM Press, London, 1987).
24. Wren, p. 137. In his hymn 'Bring Many Names', Wren begins two stanzas as follows:

> Strong mother God, working night and day,
> planning all the wonders of creation.

And:

> Warm father God, hugging every child,
> feeling all the strains of human living.

25. Addressing God as 'You' in prayer also avoids gender problems.
26. The Latin 'est' did not have gender (without other helps like adjectival endings).
27. *Dionysius the Areopagite on the Divine Names and the Mystical Theology*, ch. IV, ed. C.E. Rolt (SPCK, London, 1920), p. 199.
28. *Between Here and Now*, p. 107.
29. We can see Herbert's 'Justice (1)' as the negative of this. *The English Poems of George Herbert*, ed. C.A. Patrides (Dent, London, 1974).
30. *Laboratories of the Spirit* (Macmillan, London, 1975), p. 25.
31. See J.P. Ward, *The Poetry of R.S. Thomas* (Poetry Wales Press, Bridgend, 1987), p. 90.
32. George Herbert, 'The Pulley', p. 166.
33. *Dionysius the Areopagite*, ch. II, p. 194; also see *The Cloud of Unknowing*, ed. James Walsh, S.J. (Paulist Press, New York, 1981):

> Do not hang back then, but labour in it until you experience the desire. For when you first begin to undertake it, all that you find is a darkness, a sort of cloud of unknowing; you cannot tell what it is, except that you experience in your will a simple reaching out to God. This darkness and cloud is always between you and your God, no matter what you do, and it prevents you from seeing him clearly by the light of understanding in your reason, and from experiencing him in sweetness of love in your affection. So set yourself to rest in this darkness as long as you can, always crying out after him whom you love (ch. 3, p. 120).

> When I say 'darkness' I mean a privation of knowing, just as whatever you do not know or have forgotten is dark to you, because you do not see it with your spiritual eyes. For this reason, that which is between you and your God is termed, not a cloud of the air, but a cloud of unknowing (ch. 4, p. 128).

> See also Meister Eckhart, *The Rhineland Mystics: An Anthology*, introduced, edited and translated by Oliver Davies (SPCK, London, 1989), p. 49.

> If the soul is to see God, then it must see no temporal thing, for as long as the soul is conscious of time or space or of an idea, it cannot know God. (Sermon 68)

34. *The Cloud of Unknowing*, ch. iv, p. 127.
35. *Four Quartets*, 'East Coker' iii, p. 200 (my italics).

36. See 'A Nocturnall upon S. Lucies Day, Being the shortest day'. *John Donne: A Selection of his Poetry*, ed. John Hayward (Penguin, Harmondsworth, 1950).

37. *Paul Ricoeur. A Ricoeur Reader: Reflection and Imagination*, ed. Mario J. Valdes (Harvester Wheatsheaf, Hemel Hempstead 1991), p. 452.

38. See discussion of 'The Annunciation Veneziano', ch. 1.

39. 'Yeats used to compose aloud, whereas I compose on the page' (R.S. Thomas). See *R.S. Thomas Selected Prose*, ed. Sandra Anstey (Poetry Wales Press, Bridgend, 1986), p. 111.

40. Ward p. 90.

41. Cf. 'Eternity', *The Poems of William Blake*, ed. W.H. Stevenson (Longman Group, Harlow, 1971), p. 162.

42. Underhill, p. 331.

43. Epiphany. In the Church Calendar, the Feast of the Wise Men is celebrated on the first Sunday after Christmas.

44. T.S. Eliot, 'Marina'.
    G. Herbert: 'A true Hymne'

My joy, my life, my crown!

B. Pascal:

> From about half past ten in the evening to
> about half an hour after midnight.
>   Fire.
> God of Abraham, God of Isaac, God of Jacob,
> Absolute certainty: Beyond reason. Joy. Peace.
> Forgetfulness of the world and everything but God.
> The world has not known thee, but I have known thee.
> Joy! joy! tears of joy!

45. Meister Eckhart, Oliver Davies, *The Rhineland Mystics*, p. 56.

46. Jean-Paul Sartre, *Being and Nothingness*, trans. Barnes (Methnen, London, 1969), pp. 23, 24.

47. *H'm*, p. 17.

48. Charles Coulson, *Science and Christian Belief* (Oxford University Press, London, 1955).

49. 'The Gap', *Frequencies*, p. 7.

50. Job 26. 14 (Jerusalem Bible). Also Nicholas of Cusa says: 'And step by step we come close even to certain incorruptible footprints of Him in which . . . we come . . . to perceive Him more clearly' (Book III, chapter XI, in F.C. Happold, *Mysticism*, p. 341.

51. Author's interview; see chapter 3, note 62.

Chapter 6   *Counterpoint*

1. See James Davies, 'Participating Readers: Three Poems by R.S. Thomas', *Poetry Wales*, Vol. 18, No. 4 (1983), pp. 72–83.

2. R.S. Thomas, *Counterpoint* (Bloodaxe Books, Newcastle upon Tyne, 1990), p. 9.

3. *H'm*, p. 2.

4. Author's interview, see chapter 3, note 62.
5. David Jasper, *The Study of Literature and Religion: An Introduction* (Macmillan, London, 1989), p. 69.
6. In the philosophy of Kant, a 'schema' is 'a rule or principle that enables the understanding to unify experience' (*Collins Dictionary*).
7. We might note that the page is conceived in the tree in the way that, ironically, the machine is conceived in the mind.
8. John 1. 1.
9. 'Bored with it', p. 22.
10. 2 Corinthians 18.
11. See Eliot *Four Quartets*, 'Burnt Norton' 1: 'to what purpose/ Disturbing the dust on a bowl of rose-leaves'.
12. *Mass for Hard Times*, 'R.I.P. 1588–1988', p. 35.
13. Rosemary Woolf, *English Religious Lyric in the Middle Ages* (Clarendon Press, Oxford, 1968), p. 167.
14. Gerardus Van Der Leeuw, *Sacred and Profane Beauty: The Holy in Art* (Weidenfeld and Nicolson, London, 1963).
15. *Hymns and Songs* (Methodist Publishing House, London, 1969).
16. In referring to revelation as 'life as the Scripture shows it to be', I mean to suggest God's omniscient view of human life in so far as it is revealed through Scripture. I do not mean to suggest that the Holy Bible presents a simplistic alternative to the complexities of life.
17. *Counterpoint*, p. 58.
18. Luke 10. 27.
19. *Experimenting With An Amen*, p. 65.
20. Matt. 12. 39; Mark 8. 12.
21. Author's interview, see chapter 3, note 62.
22. John 18. 36.
23. In *Peter Pan and Wendy* (Pavilion Books, London, 1989) p. 119, the fairy, Tinkerbell, will die unless children believe in fairies.
24. Matt. 4. 8.
25. Thomas animates the cross in *Pietà* (p. 14):

> The tall Cross
> Sombre, untenanted,
> Aches for the Body
> That is back in the cradle
> Of a maid's arms.

26. This reading is supported and elaborated by the poem on p. 30:

> You know – the changeling
> in the manger. Those limbs –
> pistons. That smile
> that had the polish
> of the machine . . .

27. *Counterpoint*, p. 26.
28. 'Bored with it', *Counterpoint*, p. 22.
29. 'Ihesu, swete sone dere'. Mary's lament for the poverty of her son's birth 'passes from description of present to that of future suffering,

partly by the image "For pi credel is als a bere", a simile recalling the common representation in art of the manger as an altar': Woolfe, *English Religious Lyric in the Middle Ages.*
30. We should bear this in mind when we come to *A.D.*
31. We have already noted Donne's *Hymne* as an example of this medieval belief. See also *Legenda Aurea* – tree of cross/tree of life.
32. 'Was there a resurrection?', *Counterpoint*, p. 25.
33. 'Rough', *Laboratories of the Spirit*, p. 36; 'God's Fool', *Counterpoint*, p. 36; 'R.I.P. 1588–1988', *Mass For Hard Times*, p. 36.
34. *Counterpoint*, p. 25.
35. B.C., *Counterpoint*, p. 12.
36. Nicaea refers to the declaration of faith, known as the Nicene Creed, which attempts to define the nature of the Incarnation.
37. *Counterpoint*, p. 22.
38. See 'Kneeling', *Not That He Brought Flowers*, p. 32.
39. *Counterpoint*, p. 40.
40. *Counterpoint*, p. 42.
41. See 'Synopsis', *Frequencies*, p. 44:

> the beast that rages
> through history; that presides smiling
> at the councils of the positivists.

See also 'Dau Gapel', *Y Fflam* (1948), reproduced in *R.S. Thomas Selected Prose*, ed. Sandra Anstey, p. 41: 'Why, I wonder, when we think of the past, do we tend to see it as if at the end of a corridor with the result that we get an impression of darkness?'
42. 'Pre-Cambrian', *Frequencies*, p. 23; 'Perspectives', *Later Poems*, p. 166; 'Inside', *Later Poems*, p. 199.
43. *Between Here and Now*, p. 108.
44. *Counterpoint*, p. 26.
45. See Thomas's Introduction to his selection of Edward Thomas's poetry.
46. The image of the telescope has been used before by Thomas and will reappear in *Mass For Hard Times*, p. 84.
47. *Adversus Jovinianum*; see Roger Ellis, *Patterns of Religious Narrative in the Canterbury Tales* (Croom Helm, London and Sydney, 1986), p. 235.
48. 'The Gap', *Laboratories of the Spirit*, p. 37. (Another poem with the same title appears in *Frequencies*, p. 7. This is not an unusual practice with Thomas.)
49. D.Z. Phillips recognises this in *R.S. Thomas: Poet of the Hidden God* (Macmillan, London, 1986): 'It is as if the poet-priest has to relearn the most primitive religious responses' (p. 146).
50. *Mass for Hard Times*, p. 59.
51. Gerald Hammond, *Fleeting Things: English Poets and Poems 1616–1660* (Harvard University Press, Cambridge, MA, and London, 1990), p. 271.
52. Psalm 8.5.
53. See 'The New Mariner', *Between Here and Now*, p. 99.
54. Cf. William Carlos Williams, *Paterson*: 'Signs everywhere of birds nesting', p. 246.

55. See George Herbert, 'A Wreath', p. 188.
56. Genesis 22. For a fuller account of this, see Sabine Volk-Birke, 'World History from BC to AD: R. S. Thomas' *Counterpoint*', *Literature and Theology*, Vol. 9, No. 2 (1995), pp. 199–226.
57. W.B. Yeats, 'Among School Children', p. 242.
58. John 1.14.
59. Interestingly, the notion of 'fallen language' preoccupies many modern critical theorists. See, for example, Elaine Tuttle Hansen, *Chaucer and the Fictions of Gender* (Berkeley, Los Angeles and Oxford, 1992), p. 168. Gerhard Joseph, *The Chaucer Review*, Vol. 17, No. 4 (1983), p. 350.
60. 'The New Mariner', *Between Here and Now*, p. 99.
61. *Counterpoint*, p. 44.
62. 'The withholding', *Counterpoint*, p. 45.
63. See chapter 2, note 54.
64. Derek Walcott interview, BBC Radio 4, 17 January 1993.
65. See Exodus 33. 18–23; also 1 Kings 19. 11.
66. *Counterpoint*, p. 44.
67. 'Sonata in X', *Mass For Hard Times*, p. 82.
68. This poem has the added interest of being one of two poems which reappear in *Mass for Hard Times*. There it is named 'Migrants', and has a slightly different organisation, in that it consists of only two stanzas, the second being a sestet rather than divided into the two tercets of its first appearance.
69. John 3. 8.
70. William Wordsworth, 'Ode: Intimations Of Immortality', p. 297.
71. St Paul: 2 Corinthians 12. 10; Exodus 3. 2; Revelation 3. 20; George Herbert, 'Love 111', p. 192.

Chapter 7 Conclusion

1. Meister Eckhart, Sermon 42; Oliver Davies, *The Rhineland Mystics* (SPCK, London, 1989), p. 48.
2. *The Cloud of Unknowing*, ch. 6, p. 130.
3. *A Ricoeur Reader: Reflection and Imagination*, ed. Mario Valdés (Harvester Wheatsheaf, Hemel Hempstead, 1991), p. 452.
4. *The Cloud of Unknowing*, ch. 6, p. 130.
5. *Laboratories of the Spirit*, p. 44.

Bibliography

Primary Texts: Volumes of poetry by R.S. Thomas

Song At The Year's Turning 1942–54 (Rupert Hart-Davies, London, 1955).
Poetry For Supper (Rupert Hart-Davis, London, 1958).
Tares (Rupert Hart-Davis, London, 1961).
The Bread Of Truth (Rupert Hart-Davis, London, 1963).
Pietà (Rupert Hart-Davis, London, 1966).
Not That He Brought Flowers (Rupert Hart-Davis, London, 1968).
Young And Old (Chatto and Windus, London, 1972).
H'm (Macmillan, London, 1972).
Selected Poems, 1946–1968 (Bloodaxe, Newcastle upon Tyne, 1986; first published by MacGibbon/Hart-Davis, London, 1973).
What is a Welshman? (Christopher Davies, Llandybie, 1974).
Laboratories Of The Spirit (Macmillan, London, 1975).
The Way Of It (Coelfrith Press, 1977).
Frequencies (Macmillan, London, 1975).
Between Here And Now (Macmillan, London, 1981).
Later Poems 1972–1982 (Macmillan, London, 1983).
Ingrowing Thoughts (Poetry Wales Press, Bridgend, 1985).
Destinations (Celandine Press, Shipston-on-Stour, 1985).
Neb: golygwyd ganGwenno Hywyn (Caernarvon, Gwaesg Gwynedd, 1985).
Experimenting With An Amen (Macmillan, London, 1986).
Welsh Airs (Poetry Wales Press, Bridgend, 1987).
The Echoes Return Slow (Macmillan, London, 1988).
Counterpoint (Bloodaxe Books, Newcastle upon Tyne, 1990).
Cymru or Wales (Gwasg Gomer, Llandysul, 1992).
Mass For Hard Times (Bloodaxe Books, Newcastle upon Tyne, 1992).
Collected Poems 1945–1990 (Dent, London, 1993).

Secondary texts

Allchin, A.M., Ann Griffiths: *The Furnace and the Fountain* (University of Wales Press, Cardiff, 1987).
Anstey, Sandra, ed., *Critical Writings on R. S. Thomas* (Poetry Wales Press, Bridgend, 1982).
Arnott, Peter D., *An Introduction to the Greek Theatre* (Macmillan, London, 1961).
Barrett, William, *Irrational Man: A Study in Existential Philosophy* (Greenwood Press, Westport, CT, 1977).
Barrie, J.M., *Peter Pan and Wendy* (Pavillion Books, London, 1989).
Bazin, Germain, *Impressionist Paintings in the Louvre* (Thames and Hudson, London, 1958).

Bell, Idris H., *Welsh Poetry* (Clarendon Press, Oxford, 1936).

Berger, John, *Ways of Seeing* (BBC and Penguin, London, 1972).

Bertram, Anthony, *Botticelli* (The Studio Publications, London & New York, 1948).

Beauvoir, Simone de, *The Second Sex* (Penguin Books, Harmondsworth, 1972; first published Gallimard, Paris, 1949).

Blake, William, *The Complete Poems*, ed. W.H. Stevenson (Longman Norton, New York, 1971).

Brown, Roger L., *The Welsh Evangelicals* (Tair Eglwys Press, Tongwynlais, Cardiff, 1986).

Burrow, J., 'Essays on Medieval Literature: Fantasy and Language', in *The Cloud of Unknowing* (Clarendon Press, Oxford, 1984).

Bynum, Caroline Walker, *Jesus as Mother: Studies in the Spirituality of the High Middle Ages* (University of California Press, London, 1982).

Capra, Fritjof, *The Turning Point: Science, Society and the Rising Culture* (Fontana, London, 1983).

Carli, Gudiol and Mme Souchal, *Gothic Painting: The Contact History of Art* (Weidenfeld and Nicolson, London, 1965).

Chaucer, Geoffrey, *Complete Works*, ed., F.N. Robinson (Oxford University Press, London, 1957).

Clark, Kenneth, *The Nude: A Study of Ideal Art* (John Murray, London, 1956).

——*Landscape into Art* (John Murray, London, 1949).

Coleridge, S.T., *Biographia Literaria* (Dent Everyman, London, 1956).

——*The Poems of Coleridge*, ed. John Lane (The Bodley Head, London, 1909).

The Concise Mythological Dictionary (G.P. Putnam's Sons, London, 1963, reprinted 1989).

Coulson, Charles, *Science and Christian Belief* (Oxford University Press, London, 1955).

Daly, Mary, *Beyond God the Father: Towards a Philosophy of Women's Liberation* (The Women's Press, London, 1986).

Davies, James, 'Attempts to Evade: R.S. Thomas's *Impressions*', *Anglo-Welsh Review*, No. 79 (1985), pp. 70–83.

——'Participating Readers: Three Poems by R.S. Thomas', *Poetry Wales*, Vol. 18, No. 4 (1983), pp. 72–83.

Davies, Oliver, *The Rhineland Mystics: An Anthology* (SPCK, London, 1989).

Davies, R.T., *Medieval English Lyrics: A Critical Anthology* (Faber and Faber, London, 1963).

Eddington, A.S., *The Nature of the Physical World* (Cambridge University Press, Cambridge, 1928).

Eliot, T.S., *Collected Poems 1909–1962* (Faber and Faber, London, 1963).

Ellis, Roger, *Patterns of Religious Narrative in the Canterbury Tales* (Croom Helm, London and Sydney, 1986).

Gardner, Helen, *Religion and Literature* (Faber and Faber, London, 1971).

——*The Art of T. S. Eliot* (Cresset Press, London, 1949).

Gaunt, William (notes by Kathleen Adler) *Renoir* (Phaidon Press, London, 1962).

Gill, Stephen, ed., *Wordsworth* (Oxford University Press, Oxford, 1984).

Glasscoe, Marion, ed., *Julian of Norwich: A Revelation of Love* (University of Exeter, Exeter, 1976).

Gold, Penny Schine, *The Lady and the Virgin: Image, Attitude, and Experience in Twelfth-Century France* (The University of Chicago Press, Chicago, 1985).

Goldberg, David J. and Rayner, John D., *The Jewish People: Their History and Their Religion* (Penguin, Harmondsworth, 1989).

Hammond, Gerald, *Fleeting Things: English Poets and Poems 1616–1660* (Harvard University Press, Cambridge, MA. and London, 1990).

Happold, F.C., *Mysticism: A Study and an Anthology* (Penguin, Harmondsworth, 1990).

Hayward, John, ed., *John Donne: A Selection of his Poetry* (Penguin, Harmondsworth, 1950).

Herbert, George, *The English Poems of George Herbert* (Dent, London, 1974).

Herrick, Robert, *The Poetical Works of Robert Herrick*, ed. F.W. Moorman Humphrey Milford (Oxford University Press, London, 1921).

Hirn, Yrjo, *The Sacred Shrine* (Macmillan, London, 1912).

Hodgson, Phyllis, ed., 'Epistle of Discretion of Stirrings', *The Cloud of Unknowing and Related Treatises* (Catholic Records Press, Exeter, 1982).

Holdsworth, Angela, *Out of the Doll's House. The Story of Women in the Twentieth Century* (BBC Books, London, 1988).

Hughes, Glyn Tegai, *Williams Pantecelyn* (University of Wales Press, Cardiff, 1983).

Hughes, Ted, *The Iron Man* (Faber and Faber, London, 1968).

Hymns and Songs: A Supplement to the Methodist Hymn Book (Methodist Publishing House, London, 1969).

Inge, W.R., *Personal Religion and The Life of Devotion* (Longmans, London, 1924).

Jasper, David, *The Study of Literature and Religion: An Introduction* (Macmillan, London, 1992).

Jung, Carl Gustav, *Man and his Symbols* (Aldus in association with W.H. Allan, London, 1964).

Joseph, Gerhard, 'Chaucer's Coinage: Foreign Exchange and the Puns of *The Shipman's Tale*', *The Chaucer Review*, Vol. 17, No. 4 (1983), p. 351.

Knox, R. Buick ed., *Reformation Conformity and Dissent: Essays in Honour of Geoffrey Nuttall* (Epworth Press, London, 1977).

Lethbridge, J.B., 'R.S. Thomas talks to J.B. Lethbridge', *Anglo-Welsh Review*, No. 74 (1983), pp. 36–56.

Levey, Michael, *From Giotto to Cézanne: A Concise History of Painting* (Thames and Hudson, London, 1962).

The Mabinogion, trans. Gwyn Jones and Thomas Jones (Dent, London, 1949).

MacDonald, Hugh, ed., *The Poems of Andrew Marvell* (Routledge and Kegan Paul, London, 1952).

Macneice, Louis, *The Collected Poems of Louis Macneice*, ed. E.R. Dodds (Faber and Faber, London, 1966).

Mcfague, Sallie, *Metaphorical Theology* (SCM, London, 1983).

—— *Models of God Theology for an Ecological, Nuclear Age* (SCM, London, 1987).

McClatchy, J.D., ed., *Poets on Painters: Essays on the Art of Painting by Twentieth Century Poets* (University of California Press, Berkeley, 1988).

Morris, Meredith W., *The Renaissance and Welsh Literature: Being a Review of*

Some of the Welsh Classics in the Light of the Humanistic Movement (James James, Maesteg, 1908).

Mullins, Edwin, *The Painted Witch: FEMALE BODY: MALE ART* (Secker & Warburg, London, 1985).

Partridge, Eric, *Name this Child: A Dictionary of Modern British and American Given or Christian Names* (Hamish Hamilton, London, 1986).

Pater, Walter, *The Renaissance: Studies in Art and Poetry*, ed. Donald Hill (University of California Press, Berkeley, 1980).

New Pelican Guide To English Literature, ed. Boris Ford: 8. *The Present* (Penguin, Harmondsworth, 1983).

Pelphrey, Brant, *Christ our Mother: Julian of Norwich* (Darton, Longman and Todd, London, 1989).

Phillips, D.Z., *Through A Darkening Glass: Philosophy, Literature and Cultural Change* (Blackwell, Oxford, 1982).

—— *R.S. Thomas: Poet of the Hidden God* (Macmillan Press, London, 1986).

Pissarro, J., *Monet's Cathedral* (Pavilion Books, London, 1990).

'Probings: an Interview with R.S. Thomas', *Planet*', Vol. 80 (1990), pp. 28–52.

Pound, Ezra, *Selected Poems* (Faber and Faber, London, 1975).

Pugh, Sheena, 'Counterpoint: R.S. Thomas' Review', *Poetry Wales*, vol. 91.

Powell, Anthony, *A Question of Upbringing* (Collins Fontana, London and Glasgow, 1967).

Rewald, John, *The History of Impressionism* (Secker and Warburg, London, 1973).

Ricoeur, Paul, *Essays on Biblical Interpretation*, ed. Lewis S. Mudge (Fortress Press, USA, 1980).

Rilke, Rainer Maria, *Selected Poems*, trans. by J.B. Leishman (Penguin, Harmondsworth, 1964).

Rivers, Isobel, *Classical and Christian Ideas in English Renaissance Poetry* (George Allen and Unwin, London, 1979).

Rolt, C.E., *Dionysius the Areopagite on the Divine Names and the Mystical Theology* (SPCK, London, 1920).

Russoli, Franco, *Renaissance Painting: The Contact History of Art* (Weidenfeld and Nicolson, London, 1962).

Ryan, John, ed., *The Hymns of Ann Griffiths* (Ty Ar Y Graig, 1980).

Sartre, Jean-Paul, *Being and Nothingness: An Essay on Phenomenological Ontology* trans. Hazel E. Barnes (Methuen, London, 1969).

Schiller, G., *Iconography of Christian Art*, Vol. I, trans. Janet Seligman (Lund Humphries, London, 1971).

Strelka, J.P., ed., *Literary Criticism and Myth* (Pennsylvania State University Press, University Park, 1980).

The Poems of Alfred Lord Tennyson (Collins, London and Glasgow, 1954).

Thomas, Edward, *Selected Poems: Selected and Introduced by R.S. Thomas* (Faber and Faber, London, 1964).

Thomas, R.G., '*Humanus Sum*: A Second Look at R.S. Thomas', *The Anglo-Welsh Review*, vol. XVIII, No. 42 (1970), pp. 55–62.

Tilby, Angela, *Soul* (BBC, London, 1992).

Tugwell, OP Simon, *Ways of Imperfection* (Darton Longman and Todd, London, 1984).

—— *The Way of the Preacher* (Darton Longman and Todd, London, 1979).

Tuttle, Elaine Hanson, *Chaucer and the Fictions of Gender* (Berkeley, Los Angeles and Oxford, 1992).

Underhill, Evelyn, *Mysticism: A Study in the Nature and Development of Man's Spiritual Consciousness* (Methuen, London, 1911; University Paperbacks, 1960).

Valdés, Mario J., *Reflection and Imagination: A Ricoeur Reader* (Harvester Wheatsheaf, Hemel Hempstead, 1991).

Van Der Leeuw, Gerardus, *Sacred and Profane Beauty: The Holy in Art* (Weidenfeld and Nicolson, London, 1963).

Volk-Birke, Sabine, 'World History from BC to AD: R.S. Thomas' *Counterpoint*', *Literature and Theology*, Vol. 9, No. 2 (1995), pp. 195–226.

Walsh, S.J., James, ed., *The Cloud of Unknowing* (Paulist Press, New York, 1981).

Ward, J.P., *The Poetry of R.S. Thomas* (Poetry Wales Press, Bridgend, 1978).

Warner, Marina, *Alone Of All Her Sex: The Myth and the Cult of the Virgin* (Weidenfeld and Nicolson, London, 1976).

Whitman, Walt, *A Choice of Whitman's Verse*, sel. Donald Hall (Faber and Faber, London, 1968).

Williams, William Carlos, ed., *Selected Poems* (Penguin, Harmondsworth, 1976).

—— *Pictures From Breughel and Other Poems* (New Directions, New York, 1967).

Woolf, Rosemary, *Religious Lyric in the Middle Ages* (Clarendon Press, Oxford, 1968).

Wren, Brian, *What Language Shall I Borrow? God-talk in Worship: A Male Response to Feminist Theology* (SCM, London, 1989).

Index

213